"If you read one book on autism, this should be the one! There is no other account of psychological theories that is as clear, as engaging and as succinct. The authors not only explain what research has revealed about the nature of this complex condition, they critically analyse the impact of the research on the life of people with autism and their families. They break new ground by exploring the consequences of the still new concept of neurodiversity for a future research agenda and, true to their principles, constructively incorporate comments by autistic people from all walks of life."
—**Professor Dame Uta Frith**, Emeritus Professor of Cognitive Development, University College London, UK

"This book gives an accessible overview of psychological theory in regard to autism, including recent developments and controversies. The highlight however is the commentary remarks at the end of each chapter by autistic people. A must read for all those studying autism and those working with autistic people."
—**Dr. Damian Milton**, Lecturer in Intellectual and Developmental Disability, Tizard Centre, University of Kent, UK

"For more than two decades, Francesca Happé has led the way in explaining the psychology of autistic people to students and experts alike. Now joining forces with Sue Fletcher-Watson, this new introduction brings the voices of autistic people themselves, their families and communities to the forefront of their analysis. The result is a magnificent book that will cause us all to think anew about autistic psychology and experience."
—**Professor Liz Pellicano**, Macquarie University, Australia

"This book is a must-read for everyone interested in understanding the current landscape of autism. It includes everything you will want to know from history to biology; from theory to practice; presented in a balanced and lucid style that will engage all readers. The book is remarkable achievement that will, like the first edition, become an instant classic."
—**Professor Helen Tager-Flusberg**, PhD, Boston University, USA

"For many people, myself included, Francesca Happé's 1995 book was their gateway to autism research. This update, written with Sue Fletcher-Watson is much-needed and long overdue. Like the first edition, it provides a wonderfully lucid yet concise introduction to psychological accounts of autism. But it also serves as an historical document, reflecting the seismic changes in our understanding of and attitudes towards autism over the past quarter century and the growing voice of autistic people in challenging preconceptions about their own condition and influencing the priorities and goals of autism science."
—**Dr. Jon Brock**, Macquarie University, Australia

Autism

Based on Francesca Happé's best-selling textbook, *Autism: An Introduction to Psychological Theory*, this completely new edition provides a concise overview of contemporary psychological theories about autism. Fletcher-Watson and Happé explore the relationship between theories of autism at psychological (cognitive), biological and behavioural levels, and consider their clinical and educational impact.

The authors summarise what is known about the biology and behavioural features of autism, and provide concise but comprehensive accounts of all influential psychological models including 'Theory of Mind' (ToM) models, early social development models and alternative information processing models such as 'weak central coherence' theory. The book also discusses more recent attempts to understand autism, including the 'Double Empathy Problem' and Bayesian theories. In each case, the authors describe the theory, review the evidence and provide critical analysis of its value and impact. Recognising the multiplicity of theoretical views, and rapidly changing nature of autism research, each chapter considers current debates and major questions that remain for the future.

Importantly, the book includes the voices of autistic people, including parents and practitioners, who were asked to provide commentaries on each chapter, helping to contextualise theory and research evidence with accounts of real-life experience. The book embraces neurodiversity whilst recognising the real needs of autistic people and their families. Thus *Autism: A New Introduction to Psychological Theory and Current Debate* provides the reader with a critical overview of psychological theory but also embeds this within community perspectives, making it a relevant and progressive contribution to understanding autism, and essential reading for students and practitioners across educational, clinical and social settings.

Sue Fletcher-Watson is Senior Research Fellow at the Patrick Wild Centre, University of Edinburgh, and leads the Development/Autism/Research/Technology, or DART, lab group. She has been awarded the British Psychological Society Margaret Donaldson Prize and a certificate of excellence from *Autism Rights Group Highland* for "amplification and inclusion of autistic voices".

Francesca Happé (FBA FMedSci) is Professor of Cognitive Neuroscience and Director of the Social, Genetic and Developmental Psychiatry Centre at the Institute of Psychiatry, Psychology and Neuroscience, King's College London. She has worked in autism research for over 30 years, was President of the International Society for Autism Research and has been awarded the British Psychological Society Spearman Medal, the Experimental Psychology Society Prize and the Royal Society Rosalind Franklin Award.

Autism

*A New Introduction
to Psychological Theory
and Current Debate*

Sue Fletcher-Watson and
Francesca Happé

Routledge
Taylor & Francis Group

LONDON AND NEW YORK

Published 2019
by Routledge
2 Park Square, Milton Park, Abingdon, Oxon OX14 4RN

and by Routledge
52 Vanderbilt Avenue, New York, NY 10017

Routledge is an imprint of the Taylor & Francis Group, an informa business

British Library Cataloguing-in-Publication Data
A catalogue record for this book is available from the British Library

Library of Congress Cataloging-in-Publication Data
Names: Fletcher-Watson, Sue, author. | Happé, Francesca, author.
Title: Autism : a new introduction to psychological theory and current debates /
    Sue Fletcher-Watson & Francesca Happé.
Description: 2nd edition. | Milton Park, Abingdon, Oxon ; New York, NY :
    Routledge, 2019. | Revison of: Autism / Francesca Happé. 1995. | Includes
    bibliographical references.
Identifiers: LCCN 2018053243 (print) | LCCN 2018054196 (ebook) |
    ISBN 9781315101699 (Ebook) | ISBN 9781138106116 (hardback) | ISBN
    9781138106123 (pbk) | ISBN 9781315101699 (ebk) Subjects: LCSH: Autism.
Classification: LCC RC553.A88 (ebook) | LCC RC553.A88 H36 2019 (print) |
    DDC 616.85/882—dc23
LC record available at https://lccn.loc.gov/2018053243

ISBN: 978-1-138-10611-6 (hbk)
ISBN: 978-1-138-10612-3 (pbk)
ISBN: 978-1-315-10169-9 (ebk)

Typeset in Minion Pro
by Apex CoVantage, LLC

Contents

Preface and Acknowledgements

Preface

This book is intended mostly for undergraduate and post-graduate students studying psychology, or related subjects. Our primary goal has been to provide a comprehensive and critical overview of the available psychological theories of autism, and to enable students to understand something about this fascinating way of being. The text acts as an introduction to a range of concepts, which can be explored further, and we signpost recommended reading, flagging work by autistic writers wherever possible. The book is enhanced by the inclusion of beautiful sketch-note summaries by Marisa Montaldi at the start of every chapter, which illustrate and highlight the key content presented.

A note on language

The language used to describe autism is currently the subject of intense and passionate debate. Our primary goals in this work have been to:

- Use language that is respectful to people on the autism spectrum and to those who support them.
- Recognise the very real challenges experienced by autistic people and their families, without portraying autism as a problem to be fixed.
- Ensure that the language we use recognises autism as a lifespan condition experienced by people of all genders and ages, from all walks of life and all around the globe.

For this reason we have not used any functioning labels in the text, and minimised any use of medical and deficit-focused terminology. However, we have included some person-first language (e.g. person with autism), although we know this will not be the preference of many autistic people. Our reasons for doing so include the fact that, historically, person-first language was part of the early disability rights agenda – this was not a language construction imposed by the neurotypical/non-disabled community. Gernsbacher[1]

---

1 Gernsbacher, M. A. (2017). Editorial Perspective: The use of person-first language in scholarly writing may accentuate stigma. *Journal of Child Psychology and Psychiatry*, 58(7), 859–861.

recently pointed out that language can be stigmatising when different constructions are used to describe people with and without a disability – as in the phrase "*typically developing children and children with autism*" – and we have tried to avoid this throughout by using matched constructions as far as possible.

An oft-cited online survey[2] shows that about 60% of autistic respondents approved the use of the identity-first construction "autistic" to communicate about autism, and just under 40% endorsed "autistic person" specifically. Thus identity-first language receives strong support in the community, and many have written eloquently about the importance of this kind of language for their well-being and identity.[3] We have no desire to over-ride this wide-spread and well-articulated preference, and the majority of language here is identity first. However, in the same survey, more than 30% of the autistic group surveyed approved the use of the person-first phrase "has autism" to communicate about autism. Moreover, about 25% of respondents on the autism spectrum selected either "has autism/Asperger's syndrome" or "person with autism/Asperger's syndrome" when asked to pick only *one* preferred language option. It is very clear from the data that, even within an autistic group, there is diversity in opinion, and we have chosen to reflect that diversity in our choice of language in this book. To readers of the future, we can only apologise if this choice seems to have been retrograde.

Community contributors

We would like to thank ten members of the autistic community for providing insightful and fascinating reflections to each chapter, and for giving feedback on the content and tone of the book. They are as follows:

Jon Adams	Claire Evans-Williams
Harriet Axbey	Ann Memmott
Kabie Brook	Fergus Murray
James Cusack	Anya Ustaszewski
Martijn Dekker	Daniel Wechsler

Community contribution: Marisa Montaldi – *user experience designer, illustrator and autist*

It has been an indescribable privilege to illustrate the concepts and messages in this book, and I hope this work has done them some measure of justice. I'd like

---

2 Kenny, L., Hattersley, C., Molins, B., Buckley, C., Povey, C., & Pellicano, E. (2016). Which terms should be used to describe autism? *Perspectives from the UK autism community. Autism*, 20(4), 442–462.

3 www.identityfirstautistic.org/

to note that I am neither an academic nor, despite being autistic, am I in touch with the latest research – so had it not been for this work, my understanding of my own condition would have easily continued to be decades out of date.

I received my diagnosis at age 13, in 2002, and like for many autists, my school life mostly comprised an environment and teachers lacking faith in my ability or prospects, and I had little reason to think otherwise. It wasn't until, with open-minded family, I was given the option to leave school and pursue my own education in whatever form it took that I began to see more. I eventually chose to continue studying, on my own, and self-taught my GCSEs.

Fast-forwarding to after post-graduate study, I now work in software, designing user experiences: a discipline requiring empathy, imagination, a marriage of holistic and detailed perspective and an unbiased approach to human behaviour and data – traits that deeply resonate with me but contradicted the consensus on autism. My journey here forced my understanding of my own condition to evolve, as well as how "broken" I should consider myself to be. Now witnessing a similar evolution reflected in the research is both astounding and painfully validating.

Most striking to me are the psychological theories around information processing in Chapter 8. There's this one account of a boy 'mistaking' a pillow in a model bed for a piece of ravioli. I can see how that might appear charmingly peculiar from some perspectives, yet there's little evidence suggesting he is confused at all. He might simply be thinking in a different order, and I suspect we may be surprised by how large an effect that simple difference can have.

This world we share is beautifully complex (the social universe especially), and we humans often leverage assumptions and bias in order to navigate, infer and interpret it effectively. What if this boy is simply *assuming* less and *noticing* more? Observed by someone who assumes *more* and notices *less*, he may well appear confused or even deficient. But to perceive something so impartially might just mean growing up in a world that makes *that little bit less sense* and learning to revel in it with open arms. It may only be a slightly different way of being, but in situations more significant than ravioli bedding, it is easy to imagine how that can create large ripples in everyday lives.

For me, being diagnosed was an unstated, seismic reassurance that I was indeed different, but that *it is* OK and that I'm not alone. And I wouldn't change it for a second.

Living diagnosed, however, is different. Being labelled with a 'deficiency in understanding' that is both poorly understood and, by definition, disqualifies you from understanding your deficiency, can gradually undermine your confidence in your own perception and reality (and therefore an entire population's). Yet it may not be until reading a book like this that the realisation confronts you. Witnessing research grow more towards what I've sensed to be true, but felt too "diagnosed" to argue for, is both retroactively heartbreaking and dramatically empowering.

I can't certify whether I'm the way I *am* because I *can* and therefore *choose* to be, or because I can't be any other way. But I do enjoy this way. And likewise, does the neurotypical mind choose to be its way, or can it not be anything else?

Acknowledgements: Sue

My first thank you has to go to Franky for not just allowing me to help her update her masterful 1994 text, but for giving me the benefit of her experience, knowledge, hard work and support during the process. The original book is a beautiful piece of writing that shaped my thinking about autism as a student, and it was a delight to be able to draw on that framework and style for this new text. It's been a huge honour to have this opportunity to work with Franky, who has had a tremendous impact on the field and richly deserves her exceptional reputation. She's also *very* good at correcting "which" to "that" whenever I get it wrong (frequently).

I must also thank some key people for getting me to the place where I feel like writing a book is something I can do – Sue Leekam and Helen McConachie shaped my identity as a psychologist and continue to provide me with sage advice and regular ego boosts. My colleagues at University of Edinburgh and beyond have been patient while I spent days ignoring their emails in an effort to write: thank you Catherine, Rachael, Lorna, Maggi, Bérengére, Shereen, Sinéad, Bethan, Mihaela and Ruth; thank you to all the endless Andrews; thank you to my DivComp collaborators (so FET) and the *Shaping Autism Research* team. Thank you also to Greta Todorova, Andrew McKechanie, Andy Stanfield and Jon Spiers, as well as three anonymous reviewers, for reading and giving helpful comments on a first draft.

I'd never have kept my head above water over the past year without the love and support of my friends: KCO, Robin, Fi, Duncan, Rebecca and the Wyatt girls – special mention to Ed for providing writing soundtracks. Thank you a million times over to my family – Mum and Dad, you gave me every advantage in life; Minny and Hedda, you inspire me; Ben, your intelligence, patience and generosity know no bounds.

Finally, thank you to the hundreds of autistic people – friends and tweeters, colleagues and advisers – who have challenged and inspired me. Kabie, this book, and all my work, would be vastly inferior without you. Damian, you're a true pioneer and an inspiration. Working in this field is endlessly fascinating and a great privilege.

Acknowledgements: Francesca

When Sue approached me about the idea of writing a new version of my very old book, I was delighted. Over the years, I have refused a few suggestions from publishers that I should write an updated edition, but the idea of writing a new version with Sue at the helm was instantly appealing. I knew she was a researcher of enormous energy, insight and warmth, but the process of writing together has shown me what an amazing person and scientist she is! So my first thanks go to her, for her hard work, endless positivity, patience and humour!

As I write, it is coming up to 30 years since I started my PhD, and I can't help but reflect on how tremendously lucky I was, so many years ago, to be accepted as a student by Uta Frith at the Medical Research Council's Cognitive Development Unit. Uta has been the best mentor, colleague and friend anyone could have, and I am enormously grateful for her wisdom, support and kindness over almost 30 years. I also owe a great debt to Neil O'Connor and Ati Hermelin, Uta's own PhD supervisors, who gave me my first experience of autism as a volunteer research assistant one university vacation. I am very proud to consider myself amongst their academic grandchildren! I have also benefitted from the generosity and wisdom of many other great autism researchers including the much-missed Lorna Wing and Sula Wolff, both of whom kindly gave me time and advice when I was setting out as a PhD student, and Marian Sigman who was so encouraging to me when a post-doc. More recently, I am lucky to have as my office neighbour the indomitable Michael Rutter, still working very hard at 85. My many wonderful colleagues at the Social, Genetic and Developmental Psychiatry Centre and the Institute of Psychiatry, Psychology and Neuroscience make my job an absolute pleasure.

Over the last 30 years, I have been very fortunate to collaborate with and supervise many brilliant scientists at the early stages of their now-illustrious careers, including Rhonda Booth, Essi Viding, Rebecca Charlton, Greg Wallace, Liz O'Nions, Eva Loth, Coralie Chevallier, Catherine Molesworth, Pam Heaton, Geli Ronald, Dave Williams, Naomi Fisher, Fran Davies, Eamon McCrory, Janice Rigby, Kim Murray, Tori Hallett, Yulia Kovas, Alice Jones, Pedro Vital, Fiona McEwen, Claire Harworth, Steph Lietz, Antonia San José Cáceres, Anna Cattrell, Beata Tick, Vicky Brunsdon, Nic Shakeshaft, Esra Yarar, Bosiljka Milosavljevic, Vinnie Carter Leno, Sophie Sowden, Lucy Livingston, Hannah Pickard, Debbie Spain and many more. Emma Colvert, who has led our autism twin study for more than a decade, and the many research assistants (notably Vicky Milner), placement students (notably Simone Capp) and project students on that team, deserve special mention. I have learnt more than I can say from all these lovely people, and I am grateful for their inspiration and friendship.

Autistic friends, scientists and self-advocates have, of course, taught me a huge amount, and I would like to thank in particular Ros Blackburn, Richard Exley, Dinah Murray, Wenn Lawson and James Cusack. Autism family members, especially the late Robin Murphy, and Saskia and Michael Baron, have also been fundamental to my discovering how little I really know about autism.

Friends (autistic and not) and family have supported me, put up with my 'narrow special interest' in autism, encouraged me and made possible the difficult juggling act of work and family life. The fathomless kindness of my parents, which I appreciate even more as a parent myself, and their huge help with our three children, has been fundamental to my ability to pursue a career I love. Finally, and most importantly, I must thank Daniel for more than 25 years of love and friendship (and counting), and our children Poppy, Joe and Sam, who are such delightful, surprising, enchanting and impressive people. Pushka, our cat, does not get thanked, as she mainly walked over the keyboard as I attempted to write. AMDG.

1 Introduction

ORIGINALLY PUBLISHED IN 1994, this book has now been rewritten and updated dramatically to reflect the significant strides that have been made, not just in psychological research and theory but in socio-political theorising about autism, and in public awareness and acceptance. Nevertheless, the aim of this book remains the same – to acquaint you with current research and thinking about autism in a concise yet comprehensive way. We focus particularly on the cognitive level of explanation, which is the purview of psychological research. At the end of each chapter, recognising the fast pace of thinking about autism, we highlight current "big questions" for the field. In each chapter, we have also invited autistic people to provide their personal perspectives. These sections will, we hope, contextualise the content by providing relevant insights into the lived experience of autism. Our goal is to ensure that this academic text is firmly embedded in real-world, community priorities.

Further reading is suggested in two ways – references in the text will allow you to find out more about specific issues raised, while suggested reading (usually in the form of books or review articles) appears at the end of each chapter, allowing you to deepen your knowledge of those aspects of autism that particularly interest you. Throughout the book, discussion has been kept as brief as possible in the hope that the book will provide a manageable overview of autism, tying together a number of quite different areas. It should whet your appetite for the more detailed consideration of specific aspects of autism provided by the suggested readings.

1. Levels of explanation

If a Martian asked you what an apple is, you might reply that it is a fruit or that it is something you eat, you might describe it as roundish and red, or you might try to give its composition in terms of vitamins, water, sugars and so on. The way you answer the question will probably depend on why you think the Martian wants to know – are they hungry, do they want to be able to recognise an apple or are they simply curious? None of these answers is *the* answer, since each answer is appropriate for a different sense of the question. Similarly, different types of answer can be given to the question, "What is autism?" In order to find the right answer for the question in any one context, we need to think about our reasons for asking. One can think about this distinction between the different senses of a question in terms of different levels of explanation.

In the academic study of autism, three levels in particular are useful; the biological, the cognitive and the behavioural. It is important to keep these levels distinct, because each of the three levels does a different job in our understanding of autism. So, for example, to inform the search for possible causes of autism, it may be appropriate to look at biological features, while to address family priorities, it may be more important to consider the behavioural description.

Morton and Frith (1995) introduced a specific diagrammatic tool for thinking about levels of explanation in developmental conditions such as autism. Figure 1.1, taken from Morton and Frith (1995), shows their causal models of the three levels and the possible relations between these levels in different diagnostic categories. Pattern (a) is the case of a condition defined by its unitary biological origin, which may have diverse effects at the cognitive and behavioural levels. An example of this type of condition might be Fragile X syndrome, as currently conceptualised; Fragile X syndrome is diagnosed in the presence of a specific gene mutation on the X chromosome. However, not all individuals so defined have the same cognitive or behavioural features; while many will have severe learning difficulties and social anxiety, others may have an IQ score in the average range and appear socially confident.

Pattern (b) shows a condition with multiple biological causes, and several different behavioural manifestations, but a single defining cognitive feature. Dyslexia, according to some cognitive theories (e.g. Hulme & Snowling, 2016), may be an example of such a condition. A number of biological causes may converge in causing a cognitive difference in the phonological system, leading in turn to multiple behavioural difficulties (e.g. with reading, spelling, auditory memory, rhyme and sound segmentation). Many attempts have been made to characterise autism in this way (see Chapter 6).

Pattern (c) is the case of a condition defined by its behavioural features alone, with multiple biological causes and cognitive natures. Conduct disorder,

FIGURE 1.1   Causal models of three types of disorder

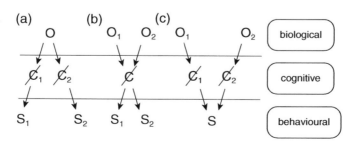

as currently diagnosed, may be such a condition; children who show antisocial behaviours, for whatever reason, may be grouped together under this label for the purposes of understanding and support.

Throughout this book, we will be using the notion of levels of explanation, to keep separate different issues and questions. In Chapter 3, the diagnosis of autism is discussed, and the focus is on the behavioural level – since autism is currently recognised on the basis of behavioural features rather than, for example, biological etiology. In Chapter 4, the biological level is addressed, since research suggests that ultimately autism is rooted in genetic factors. In subsequent chapters the remaining of the three levels is discussed – the cognitive level.

Cognitive theories aim to span the gulf between biology and behaviour – between the brain and action – through hypotheses about the mind. This level, the level of cognition, is the primary focus for this book. The term cognitive is used here not in contrast to affective; we do not promote a dichotomy of 'rational' versus 'emotional' states. Rather, it is intended to cover all aspects of the working of the mind, including thoughts and feelings. This level of analysis might also be called the "psychological" level, except that psychology also includes the study of behaviour.

Keeping the three levels of explanation (biology, cognition, behaviour) distinct, helps in thinking about a number of issues to do with autism. So, for example, people often ask whether autism is part of the ordinary continuum of social behaviour – are we all "a little bit autistic"? The answer to this question is likely to be different at the different levels of explanation. At the behavioural level the answer may appear to be "yes", at least in some respects. For example, an autistic person may behave much like a very shy, but non-autistic, person in some situations. Nearly everyone – autistic or not – has some motor stereotypies (e.g. finger tapping). Here, the uniquely autistic experience may be to do with quality and how such behaviours co-occur. For example, the difference between one person's sensory sensitivity to artificial lighting and another person's autism is not simply a matter of intensity of reaction, but of patterning and complexity.

At the biological level, the answer is also complicated. In some cases, autism is linked to rare genetic mutations, not present in neurotypical individuals. However, in most cases, the genetics of autism is more like the genetics of height; lots of common genetic variants contribute to the outcome for an individual. It appears that these common variants, each of tiny effect, contribute both to diagnosed autism and to subclinical traits. At the cognitive level, too (depending on the theory you endorse), autistic people may be quite distinct from the neurotypical range. So, for example, very different cognitive reasons may underlie apparently similar behaviour by individuals with and without autism – think of an autistic person and a "normal" rebellious teenager, both of whom may dress unconventionally for a job interview. Likewise, an autistic child's social difficulties might have a quite different cause (at the cognitive level) from a non-autistic shy person's – although the behaviours produced (avoiding large groups, social anxiety, limited eye contact) may be very similar. We'll return to this interesting question in Chapters 8 and 9.

At the cognitive level of explanation, in Chapter 5, we will first provide an overview of how the cognitive level may be used to link behavioural and biological features. We will review criteria for a good psychological theory, considering quality and quantity of evidence and practical impact. Subsequently, Chapters 6–8 will describe and evaluate the available cognitive models of autism in three distinct groups. Primary deficit models attempt to identify a single difference (nearly always characterised as a deficit), which has a root, causal role in determining autism. Developmental progress models tend to frame autism as the result of multiple interacting processes across early development. Cognitive difference models are concerned with the complex ways in which people with autism relate to their environments and attempt to characterise autism on that basis.

In the final two chapters of the book, we will review the contribution that psychological theory has made to our understanding of autism and to practice in schools, clinics and beyond. This will include a discussion of alternative approaches to understanding autism – e.g. sociological models – and the possibility that our biological-cognitive-behavioural framework would benefit from the addition of a fourth level of explanation. In Chapter 10, we wrap up with a discussion of the key issues for the future of autism research.

2. Timescales of explanation

As well as trying to answer the question, "What is autism?", this book explores why or how autism occurs. In other words, this book is concerned with *causal* theories of autism. In thinking about causal explanations, it is useful to keep distinct not only three *levels* of description but also three *timescales*. Causes can be examined in terms of evolutionary time, taking as the unit for discussion the gene and considering pressures acting in the process of natural selection. A second timescale of cause is development, where the individual (or the biological, behavioural or cognitive mechanism within the individual) is considered. Developmental time includes key features like the existence of sensitive periods in some systems, where a specific window of time may exist for specific causes to have specific effects (e.g. imprinting in the chick) – the same causal agent acting on the organism after this time will not have the same consequences. Lastly, there is the time span of "online" mechanisms – that is moment-to-moment or processing time.

In considering autism, the latter two timescales are particularly important (see, for example, Chapters 6 and 7). An example may help to clarify the distinction and to illustrate that the same influence may have rather different effects in terms of disruptions to development and disruptions to processing.

Think of the effects of large quantities of alcohol acting as a cause on the three timescales. In evolutionary time, imagine that the existence of alcohol in foodstuffs leads to the selection of individuals with the ability to taste this substance and avoid consuming large quantities of foods containing alcohol – since being drunk does not increase reproductive success! In developmental time, alcohol has different effects – in large quantities, it may hamper the physical and mental development of the foetus. Later in the life course, but still in developmental terms, intake of large quantities of alcohol may have long-term effects on adults, for example, cirrhosis of the liver. In terms of processing time, however, the effects of alcohol are usually pleasant – that's why we drink it! In large amounts, though, it has effects on our behaviour, for example, causing slurring of speech and loss of balance. These are "online" effects in the sense that they persist only for so long as the maintaining cause is there – the high blood alcohol level. The developmental effects, however, will persist, even after the individual has sobered up. This example may seem a long way from autism but, as will emerge in Chapters 7 and 8, psychological theories of autism can be very different depending on whether they focus on developmental or processing causes.

In the context of autism research, we might also 'zoom in' on the developmental timescale a little more closely. Autism is characterised as a 'neurodevelopmental' condition, meaning that it emerges from differences in brain development. Two key lessons emerge from this characterisation of autism. One is that any research needs to take into account the chronological age of the participants and, if different, their developmental level too. Without this context, it is impossible to determine whether a behaviour is typical or atypical, delayed or divergent, concerning or not. Take as an example the typical child's learning of irregular past tenses, which follows a u-shaped curve. In early development, children learn and imitate the correct irregular forms of verbs and plurals (e.g. "we went to the park"; "I saw two sheep"). Later, as children, from about 2 years, start to recognise and apply grammatical rules, they tend to overgeneralise these, making charming over-regularisation errors ("we goed to the park"; "I seed two sheeps"). And later still, children competently apply grammatical rules and have learnt the cases where an irregular form is correct.

We can see from this example how important it is to understand the developmental stage reached by an individual before passing judgement on their competence. Developmental processes do not necessarily follow simple upward trajectories from less to more skilled. Moreover, the same pattern of behaviour (in this case, correct use of irregular word forms) may be apparent at different stages for different reasons (in this case, mimicry versus mastery). One relevant example more specific to autism relates to the prevalence of restricted and repetitive behaviours in children: a large survey of typically developing toddlers showed that behaviours like lining up toys, hand-flapping and specific narrow interests are very common in 2-year-olds (Leekam et al., 2007). This kind of information is essential when, among other things, attempting to identify markers of autism in early development. Understanding how and why children engage in such patterns of behaviour can also play a role in understanding the possible function of these repetitive movements and activities in the life of someone with autism.

Developmentally sensitive research is vital for at least three reasons. First, longitudinal studies help untangle cause and effect, and move us beyond inspecting correlation to inferring causation. We'll see this in Chapter 7, where we look at studies of infants genetically predisposed to autism. Second, developmental trajectories can uncover importantly different sub-groups and help distinguish 'phenocopies'. For example, although many of the young children adopted from terrible deprivation in Romanian orphanages showed autistic-like behaviours, most grew out of these in a way not typical of autism. Third, cross-sectional research that takes a 'snapshot' at one age is subject to confounds, including cohort effects. This is very relevant to the study of ageing in autism, discussed in Chapters 3 and 10, because diagnostic criteria were much narrower in the 1960s and '70s than today, the picture we see in autistic 60-year-olds diagnosed in childhood is likely to be quite different from that for a newly diagnosed 60-year-old, or for today's autistic children when they reach 60.

3. Some facts and fiction

At this point in the original version of this book, published in 1994, an attempt was made to clear up a series of myths and misunderstandings about autism. Rather than replace these with a new list, we replicate the original here and provide some commentary on each item. It is fascinating and instructive to consider how much the field has moved on, but also how some of these myths have stuck around for so long.

1   *Autism is* **not** *caused by "refrigerator parenting"*.

The 'refrigerator mother' is a mythical creature – described in more detail in Chapter 2 – whose cold parenting was supposed to cause autism. Thankfully, the belief that parenting styles cause autism is largely dispelled, and we might not need to flag this nowadays. However, a high-pressure focus on the parent remains. The current practical guidance on autism is often focused on 'early intervention' as a way to prevent what are seen as negative outcomes for autistic children. Following diagnosis, parents are often under pressure to find 'solutions' and to do so quickly – there is a sense of time running out. Instead, parents of newly diagnosed children would benefit from more encouragement to find things their child loves and do them often; advice on creating a safe, predictable environment in the home; and support for their whole family's adjustment and well-being. So, although this myth is now less influential, there remains a wider problem in supporting parents raising children with autism. Autistic parents are more likely to have autistic children (since autism is highly heritable) but recognition of this group's existence, let alone support for their particular needs, remains very poor.

2   *Autism* is *a biologically based disorder.*

This one is also certainly true, but it is striking that little progress has been made in determining precisely what this biological basis is. As we will see in Chapter 4, genetic, neurological and any other biological markers of autism remain elusive.

3   *Autism is* not *confined to childhood.*
4   *Autism* is *a developmental disorder which lasts throughout life.*

These two are also still accurate, though now we would use 'difference', 'condition' or perhaps 'neurotype' rather than disorder. It remains a consistent criticism of research that lifespan issues are rarely taken into account and a disproportionate amount of research focuses on children. This is partly due to challenges recruiting autistic adults (see Chapter 3) and the scientific priority given to understanding causal factors and mechanisms, which often means studying childhood.

5   *Autism is* not *always characterised by special, or "savant", skills.*
6   *Autism* is *found at all IQ levels, but is commonly accompanied by general learning difficulties.*
7   *Autism is* not *just a "shell" within which a "normal" child is waiting to get out.*

These characterisations of autism are not inaccurate but the details and language have shifted, as have the issues one might choose to flag up today. In particular, estimated rates of learning disability in the autistic population vary widely, but are often around 50% – a much lower proportion than was thought in 1994 (Elsabbagh et al., 2012). Savant skills have been reported in a third of adults with autism (Howlin et al., 2009), and more generally, an uneven profile across standard ability tests is very common. While many autistic people might perform poorly in specific domains of standardised testing, in tests of visuo-spatial reasoning or pattern recognition, their strengths may come to the fore (Courchesne et al., 2015). It is true that autism is not covering up a "normal" child, and the neurodiversity movement that has developed since the original edition of this book celebrates that difference, rather than seeing autism as a failure to match the 'typical'.

It is also important to note that while autism is lifelong, it is not a life sentence – autistic people (both with and without a learning disability) have, and do, and can, achieve great and beautiful things. An autistic person's personal satisfaction with their life depends not so much on their being autistic, as on the capacity and willingness of those around them to understand, accept and support them. Throughout this book, we hope to employ psychological theory and evidence to promote such understanding, recognising differences, without labelling autistic people as deficient or inferior.

8   *Autism* **is** *a severe disorder of communication, socialisation and imagination.*

The more researchers have learnt about autism, the harder it gets to sum up the condition in a single sentence – and that's just drawing on research evidence, let alone the multiplicity of lived experiences. We can say categorically how autism is diagnosed, but that's not the same as what it is. In each of these listed domains, evidence for differences is mixed. That isn't to say that differences don't exist – they do, and sometimes they are disadvantageous – but the precise nature of the difference is hard to pin down.

What about severity? As you will see in Chapter 3, we believe that attempting to use 'severity' estimates to describe autism is futile. When invoking a concept of severity, what we are usually trying to capture is the level of support an individual requires – in which case reporting the support need itself is both more accurate and more helpful. While this book characterises autism in terms of difference rather than deficit, there is no doubt that some of the experiences that typically accompany autism – poor sleep, restricted diet, epilepsy, language delay, learning disability and poor mental health, not to mention encountering prejudice, bullying and discrimination – can be severely upsetting and disabling.

What new facts might we add to counter more recent myths? An obvious one would be '*vaccines do not cause autism*'. This scare is entirely traceable to flawed and sometimes actively fraudulent science. There is now a vast and conclusive body of evidence disproving the link between vaccines and autism. We might also emphasise that '*not all autistic people are male*', given that research has often overlooked or even systematically excluded women, girls and non-binary people from autism studies.

4. Current debates

Summary

This book will be structured around two descriptive frameworks. First, we will consider autism at different levels of explanation: biological, cognitive and behavioural. In our pursuit of accurate models of the causes and nature of autism, we will also consider different timescales of influence: evolutionary, developmental and online. Since autism is now characterised as a developmental condition – with a manifestation that changes in important ways across different life stages – the developmental timescale will be particularly important in considering psychological models. We have seen how radically the understanding of autism has changed since the last version of this book was published. In this new text, we attempt to address the ever-changing understanding of autism by highlighting topical issues and big questions for the future at the end of every chapter.

Big questions

One question we grappled with while writing this book is, what right do we have as neurotypical researchers, without lived experience of autism, to write an authoritative text on autism? We couldn't possibly write a book about the experience of autism, of course – but we are psychologists, and so we can try to write about psychological theories of autism. We hope it is legitimate for us to have a platform to present and discuss those theories, but we are very aware that there are many other ways to view autism. These include other disciplinary perspectives, but also – very importantly – autistic voices and experiences. We wanted to give space in our book for stakeholders to comment and reflect, providing a contrasting, critical perspective or enriching our academic content with personal experiences.

This leads to another big question – how to incorporate autistic voices without tokenism? In the context of this book, we have invited people to contribute by identifying a core theme within each chapter and asking an interested person to comment on that theme. Our goal is to include autistic contributors whose personal experience actively resonates with the topic of each chapter.

A final point to raise is that these written accounts from autistic people are not accessible to the very large proportion of the autistic community who aren't able to read or write with confidence – young children and people with learning disabilities or limited language. In an attempt to represent these people, some of our contributors are autistic parents of autistic children, or autistic professionals who have day-to-day contact with autistic people who are less able to speak for themselves. Others had a profile in childhood which might then have been designated 'severe autism', but have acquired a lot of communication skills since that time.

COMMUNITY CONTRIBUTION: DANIEL WECHSLER – PHD STUDENT RESEARCHING HOW FAMILY AND SOCIAL ENVIRONMENTS AFFECT MENTAL HEALTH OUTCOMES IN PEOPLE WITH NEURODEVELOPMENTAL CONDITIONS

In reading this broad chapter, I think an important thing to remember is that scientific theories of autism focus on differences between people with and without autism, or differences associated with certain autistic traits in the population. They do not describe autistic people themselves, nor their lived experience. It is easy to read about autism and picture an 'autistic person' (usually a child or someone we know), whose personality and experience of the world are almost built around the differences or autistic traits described. Scientific theories focus on differences because these can help us understand what the condition of autism is. However, people are more than just bundles of measurable traits, and each autistic person is first and foremost a human, with a lived experience that is often closer to what we would think of when we imagine any human life. For instance, I have quite typical long-term goals, ambitions and challenges for someone of my age and in my career. However, as a result of autism-related sound sensitivity, I also experience a lot of stress from excessive noise in my household and neighbourhood. This has affected my mental health and my ability to study and has made it difficult to find a suitable place to move out. However, rather than having defined my life, this feature of autism has made it more difficult for me to focus on my otherwise 'normal' goals.

More generally, each autistic person has his or her own personality, priorities and preferences, goals and struggles. I have met quite a few people with autism, all with very different personalities to me. Some I liked and others I very much disliked! Perhaps surprisingly, I consider most of my 'neurotypical' friends more similar to me than any autistic person I've met so far. Similarly, while some autistic people embrace an autistic identity, others do not consider it a central part of their life or personality. By adulthood, many autistic people will also have one or more comorbid conditions, and these might feature more prominently in their everyday life than features of autism. Crucially, each individual with autism has their own unique strengths, difficulties and needs, and these should be the central concern for anyone who wants to work with autistic people. Understanding autism can make it easier to help autistic people, but I would urge the reader not to think of autism as a personality, or a different 'type' of person. Instead, think of it as a set of changes to an otherwise very human life. These changes can be extreme or not so extreme, positive or negative, and can make for a meaningful but often tumultuous experience.

Recommended reading

Karmiloff-Smith, A. (1998). Development itself is the key to understanding developmental disorders. *Trends in Cognitive Sciences, 2*(10), 389–398.

Kenny, L., Hattersley, C., Molins, B., Buckley, C., Povey, C., & Pellicano, E. (2016). Which terms should be used to describe autism? Perspectives from the UK autism community. *Autism, 20*(4), 442–462.

Milton, D. E. (2014). Autistic expertise: A critical reflection on the production of knowledge in autism studies. *Autism, 18*(7), 794–802.

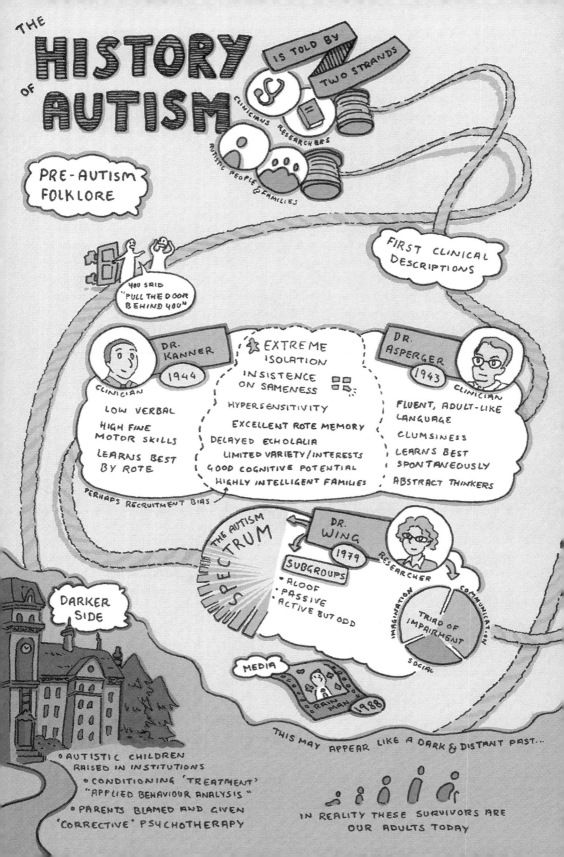

2 The history of autism

THERE ARE TWO strands to the history of autism – the history according to professionals, mostly clinicians and latterly researchers, and the history according to autistic people and their families. Here we provide a brief overview of key influential figures from both strands, who have helped to shape how autism is viewed today.

1. Kanner's autism

He wandered about smiling, making stereotyped movements with his fingers, crossing them about in the air. He shook his head from side to side, whispering or humming the same three-note tune. He spun with great pleasure anything he could seize upon to spin. . . . When taken into a room, he completely disregarded the people and instantly went for objects, preferably those that could be spun. . . . He angrily shoved away the hand that was in his way or the foot that stepped on one of his blocks.

(Kanner, 1943; reprinted in Kanner, 1973)

This description of a 5-year-old boy called Donald was written over 70 years ago in Kanner's landmark paper *Autistic Disturbances of Affective Contact*. The term "autistic" comes from Bleuler (1908), who used the word (from the Greek "autos" meaning self) to describe the social withdrawal seen in adults with schizophrenia. Despite radical changes in our conceptualisations of autism, clinicians and teachers today still remark on similar features to those described by Kanner so many years ago. Moreover, autism has almost certainly always existed. Folktales can be found in nearly every culture that tell stories of individuals with unusual behaviour and a literal interpretation of the world. The following stories come from two very different cultures, but each centre on a character who we might now describe as autistic. The first tale comes from India:

One time Sheikh Chilli was hotly in love with a girl, and he said to his mother: "What is the best way of making a girl fond of one?" Said his mother: "The best plan is to sit by the well, and when she comes to draw water, just throw a pebble at her and smile". The Sheikh went to the well, and when the girl appeared, he flung a big stone at her and broke her head. All the people turned out and were going to murder him, but when he explained matters, they agreed that he was the biggest fool in the world.

(From *151 Folktales of India*, Kang & Kang, 1988)

The second folktale comes from Malta:

In a village, there lived a boy called Gahan. It was Sunday and Gahan's mother wanted to go to church early. But Gahan didn't like getting up in the mornings, so he said he would stay in bed. When his mother was ready to go, she came into Gahan's room. "I'm off to church now", she said. "When you get up, if you decide to come to the church, be sure and pull the door behind you". "Don't worry, mother", said Gahan, "I won't forget". After a while Gahan climbed out of bed, washed and dressed and was just about to leave when he remembered what his mother had said. He opened the front door, pulled it down, held it by the knocker and began to pull it along behind him. You can imagine how all the people laughed when they saw Gahan walking along the street dragging the door behind him. When he arrived at the church he walked straight in. But he made such a banging and clattering noise that everyone turned to see what was happening. They, too, thought that it was very funny, but Gahan's poor mother was very embarrassed. "What on earth are you doing?" she asked. "Well, mother", answered Gahan, "you asked me to pull the door behind me if I left the house, didn't you?"

(From *Folktales from Australia's Children of the World*, Smith, 1979)

These tales suggest that the unexpected behaviours of people with autism have been recognised in many different cultures over the centuries. But it was not until Kanner wrote about a group of 11 children with a puzzling but similar constellation of features that autism was clinically recognised. These features, as described by Kanner, included the following:

Extreme autistic aloneness: the children did not relate to people as expected and appeared to be happiest when left alone.
Anxiously obsessive desire for the preservation of sameness: the children were extremely upset by changes of routine or surroundings, such as a different route to school, or a rearrangement of furniture.
Excellent rote memory: the children Kanner saw showed an ability to memorise large amounts of material (e.g. an encyclopaedia index page), which was out of line with their apparent learning difficulties.
Delayed echolalia: the children repeated language they heard, but did not appear to use words to communicate beyond their immediate

needs. They would also use "you" when referring to themselves and "I" for the other person (termed "pronoun reversal"), following from a direct repetition of the other speaker's remark. In the same way, children with autism may use the whole of a question instead of a typical request (e.g. "Do you want a sweet?" meaning "I want a sweet").

Hyper-sensitivity to stimuli: Kanner noticed that many of the children he saw reacted strongly to certain noises and to objects, such as vacuum cleaners, elevators and even the wind. Some also had feeding problems or would eat only a very restricted diet.

Limitation in the variety of spontaneous activity: shown in the children's repetitive movements, verbalisations and interests. However, Kanner felt that the children showed a good relation to objects, such as dexterity in spinning things or completing jigsaw puzzles.

Good cognitive potentialities: Kanner believed that the outstanding memory and dexterity shown by some of his cases reflected a superior intelligence, despite the fact that many of the children had been considered to have severe learning difficulties.

Highly intelligent families: Kanner remarked that all his cases had intellectual parents. However, this is probably due simply to a referral bias – Kanner's sample is unlikely to have been representative; only the well-connected managed to see the famous child psychiatrist at Johns Hopkins Hospital.

In his later writing (Kanner & Eisenberg, 1957), Kanner isolated just two of these many features as the key elements of autism: "*Extreme isolation and the obsessive insistence on the preservation of sameness*". The other aspects he considered to be either secondary to and caused by these two elements (e.g. communicative impairments), or nonspecific to autism (e.g. stereotypies). In Chapter 3, we will reassess Kanner's description of autism and consider changing diagnostic criteria in relation to that original set of case studies.

2. Asperger's autism

While Kanner is often considered the first person to have characterised autism, Hans Asperger was working at the same time in Austria with a group of children he also identified as having a shared set of features (Asperger, 1944). Recent examinations of the history of autism research and clinical practice have raised the question of whether Asperger 'got there first' and Kanner partly drew on his original work (Silberman, 2016). This possibility may have been hidden by the fact that it took many decades for Asperger's work to be translated from the original German (Asperger, *trans.* Frith, 1991). Questions have also been raised, just as we were finalising this book, about Asperger's work under the prevailing Nazi regime, with a new paper revealing a disturbing level of complicity from the physician (Czech, 2018). Asperger's writings have shaped our understanding of the condition and cannot be ignored in the history of autism. As we write, the autism community is adjusting to the shocking new information about Asperger's role in the evil treatment of disabled children by the Nazi death machine and discussing whether the term 'Asperger's syndrome' (no longer in the diagnostic manuals) is still appropriate and acceptable.

Kanner and Asperger were both foundational to our understanding of autism and their descriptions are similar in many ways. Both men believed the social differences in autism to be innate (in Kanner's words) or constitutional (as Asperger put it) and to persist through life into adulthood. In addition, Kanner and Asperger both noted the children's lack of eye contact, their stereotypies of word and movement, and their marked resistance to change. The two authors report the common finding of isolated special interests, often in idiosyncratic objects or topics. Both seem to have been struck by the attractive appearance of the children they saw. Kanner and Asperger make a point of distinguishing the disorder they describe from schizophrenia, on the basis of three features; the improvement rather than deterioration in their patients, the absence of hallucinations and the fact that these children presented as autistic from their earliest years. Lastly, both Kanner and Asperger believed that they had observed similar traits – of social withdrawal or atypicality, intense delight in routine and the pursuit of special interests to the exclusion of all else – in the parents of many of their patients.

There are three main areas in which Asperger's and Kanner's reports disagree, if we believe that they were describing the same sort of child. The first and most striking of these is the child's language abilities. Kanner reported that 3 of his 11 patients never spoke at all and that the other children did not use what language they had to communicate. Asperger, by contrast, reported that each of his four case study patients (and, by implication, most of the unspecified number of such children he met) spoke fluently – even "like little adults". Asperger notes their "freedom" and "originality" in language use, and reports that two of his four cases had a tendency to tell "fantastic stories".

Asperger's description also conflicts with Kanner's on the subject of motor abilities and coordination. Kanner (1943) reported that *several of the children were somewhat clumsy in gait and gross motor performance, but all were very skillful in terms of finer muscle coordination*. Asperger, by contrast, described all four of his patients as clumsy and recounted their problems not only with school sports (gross coordination) but also with fine motor skills such as writing.

The last area of disagreement in the clinical pictures painted by Asperger and Kanner is that of the child's learning abilities. Kanner believed that his patients were best at learning rote fashion, but Asperger felt that his patients performed "best when the child can produce spontaneously" and suggests that they are "abstract thinkers". The same dichotomy can be observed in different approaches to autistic support and education today.

How are we to understand and resolve these contradictions? One possibility is to separate what we refer to as autism into sub-categories: autism vs. Asperger's syndrome. Indeed, these sub-types were introduced into previous iterations of the diagnostic manuals (more on this in Chapter 3). Another is to consider autism in terms of a spectrum that varies not only between people but also across the lifespan and in different contexts. This was the main contribution made by our next foundational clinician-researcher in the history of autism, Lorna Wing.

3. Wing's autism

For a long time, autism research moved slowly – although researchers such as Michael Rutter and Eric Schopler were publishing new ideas and results, attention to this 'very rare' condition was limited and major developments did not take place until some decades later. At that point, Lorna Wing – an exceptional clinician, researcher and the parent of an autistic daughter – began to pioneer a new understanding. Next, we provide a few more examples of how parents of children with autism have shaped understanding, awareness and especially service provision. However, a more in-depth history of autism research and practice can be found elsewhere (Feinstein, 2011; Donvan & Zucker, 2017), revealing the massive contribution made by people – such as Bernard Rimland in the USA – who had both family and professional knowledge of autism.

In 1979, Wing and her colleague Judith Gould published a seminal paper, which first introduced what came to be called the "triad of impairments" (Wing & Gould, 1979). The paper reported on a large epidemiological survey, raising the methodological bar relative to the groups of case studies which had been used to define autism up to that point. Drawing on a screened sample of 914 children, and detailed data from 132, Wing and Gould grouped the features of autism into three categories: social interaction, communication and imagination. Social interaction and communication difficulties aligned closely with the original observations by Kanner (and Asperger, though at that time, his work was not yet known in England). Wing and Gould noted atypicalities in the interaction styles of children and absence, or unusual use, of speech. The 'imagination' domain was a novel way to conceptualise the presence of repetitive and stereotyped behaviours, as well as unusual styles of play, especially an absence of pretending, or "symbolic play". Later, this work was re-capitulated in adults (Shah et al., 1982), detecting the same clusters of features in a large clinical sample. This last observation, of reduced pretend play, was also foundational to the 'Theory of Mind' (ToM) account of autism (see Chapter 5).

Wing and Gould's paper also introduced a new way to sub-categorise children based on their social approach style (at any one point in time) into one of three groups (see Figure 2.1 and also Castelloe & Dawson, 1993):

Aloof: these children were described as being either "aloof and indifferent in all situations" or as making social contact in order to satisfy a need, but then retreating immediately.

Passive: this group accepted social contact, but did not seek it out. In the playground, for example, they might be given a role in a play scenario, but require direction from their non-autistic peers to sustain it.

Active but odd: these children did approach others to engage in social interaction, but did so in an atypical way. A consequence of their peculiar behaviour was that they "were sometimes rejected by their peers" – an early flag for the fact, now increasingly recognised, that the responses of non-autistic people play a key role in the experience and adaptation of autistic children (Grossman, 2015).

Attempts at sub-grouping have continued using more data-driven approaches (e.g. Grzadzinski et al., 2013; Prior et al., 1998; Stevens et al., 2000) though to date, none of these has proven definitive. Meanwhile, Wing took a different tack with the publication of her book *The Autistic Spectrum* (1996), which gave prominence to this term, highlighting variability between individuals who share the same broad diagnosis. In particular, Wing emphasised that difficulties and strengths present themselves differently across the lifespan, and in different environmental contexts. Her work, published over a period in which diagnoses of autism were dramatically on the increase, had a particular impact on educational practice as teachers, more than clinicians, began to take responsibility for the progress of children on the autism spectrum.

FIGURE 2.1   An illustration of Lorna Wing's "aloof, passive, odd" sub-types

the aloof   the passive   the odd

Reproduced from Uta Frith, 1989, with kind permission of the author and of the artist, Axel Scheffler.

4. Myths and controversies

So far, we have emphasised the contributions made by some of the early pioneers to the clinical characterisation of autism. This history of course includes
many other key figures, and there is further reading by and about some of
these at the end of the chapter. However, the clinical and academic history of
autism is also sadly laden with tragic examples of negative characterisations
of autism, leading to misguided and sometimes abusive treatments. While
we do not have space to explore these in detail, it would be remiss of us to
ignore them.

One of the most pervasively damaging theoretical accounts was the
so-called refrigerator mother model, a psychogenic theory that attributed the
presence of autism in children to a lack of caring and responsive parenting,
rather than to a biological cause (see Donvan & Zucker, 2017 for a full history). Blame was laid wholly at the feet of the mother, in line with the heavily
gendered parenting roles of the time. Many autistic children were taken from
their families and raised in institutions, and mothers were given psychother-
apy to try to correct their parenting. One early approach to educating autistic
children was Applied Behaviour Analysis (ABA), developed by Ivar Lovaas
using the principles of conditioning first established in animals. Children
were taught basic skills in discrete steps, using both reward and punishment to
encourage 'correct' behaviour. While ABA has evolved considerably from this
time, and now covers a wide array of approaches, it remains controversial to
many for its apparent pursuit of a highly normative 'ideal' child, focusing on
behaviour alone and reliance on evidence of efficacy that has been considered
weak (Dawson et al., 2008).

The often-upsetting history of autism research and practice is essential
reading for anyone choosing to specialise in the field. While we designate it as
'history', many autistic adults today were raised in this context, and psychogenic theories still have a harmful influence in some parts of the world. For
further reading we point our readers to *Neurotribes* (Silberman, 2016) and *In a
Different Key* (Donvan & Zucker, 2017).

5. Baron's autism

Thankfully, many parents survived the damage done by psychogenic theories
and have been prominent in shaping research, and especially practice. Michael
Baron, whose son was one of the earliest children diagnosed with autism in the
UK, founded a school for autistic learners, together with other parents. This
group went on to evolve into today's *National Autistic Society* (NAS) which
provides information and support to autistic people and their families across
the UK. Founded in 1962, the NAS was the first autism association in the world
and inspired and fostered similar parent-led groups internationally. In 2003,
the *National Autistic Society* appointed Dr Larry Arnold as their first autistic

trustee – a landmark moment in the autistic rights movement. *Scottish Autism* was similarly founded by parents, with five families mortgaging their houses to set up what was then *The Scottish Society for Autism* in 1968 and creating the first autism-specific school in Scotland. Baron continues to be a prominent spokesperson on behalf of autistic people, especially those with a learning disability, and their families.

Parents have also been prominent in shaping public perceptions of autism and have inspired researchers. Browsing in a second-hand bookshop as a student, Francesca chanced upon Clara Claibourne Park's account (1968) of raising her autistic daughter, which sparked her enduring interest in autism. Almost two decades later, Sue was captivated as a PhD student by Charlotte Moore's frank and affectionate book (2004) about her autistic sons. Parents have also founded some excellent online resources for learning more about autism, building communities of expertise and shared support – the *Thinking Person's Guide to Autism* is an excellent place to start.

The pioneering efforts of parents have left a legacy of charitable autism support organisations and schools from which the community continues to benefit. However, there are also tensions between parts of the autism community (largely driven by non-autistic parents of autistic children) that emphasise a need for cure or rehabilitation versus parts of the community (largely driven by autistic adults) that are focused on acceptance and rights. When the co-founders of *Autism Speaks* (a USA parent-led charity) visited the UK and spoke about their mission 'to fight and cure autism' (making an analogy with fighting cancer), the *Something About Us* campaign, led by Dinah Murray, was developed to "*establish a creative autistic presence; give autistic people a chance to say what people most need to hear about autism; have the widest possible exposure; rebalance a specific event to diminish Autism Speaks' impact; create alliances and generate obligations*" (Murray, personal communication). Similarly, the title of the book *Loud Hands: Autistic People Speaking* was selected specifically to counter the notion of "quiet hands" – i.e. no 'stimming' or flapping – which is a part of many early intervention programmes. For psychologists working in practice or research, these tensions between different perspectives within the broad community of stakeholders can be challenging to navigate and interpret. Being informed about the differing perspectives, and the personal experiences which underlie them, is crucial for anyone in the field.

6. Sinclair's autism

A history of autism cannot be complete without considering the accounts of autistic people. Women have been particularly prominent in this literature – Temple Grandin's *Emergence: Labelled Autistic* was the first autistic autobiography and, along with Donna Williams' *Nobody, Nowhere*, became a classic in the growing canon of first-person accounts of autism.

There are also academic writers on the subject, one of the most prominent of whom is Jim Sinclair. Sinclair was an early leader for the autistic community, co-founding *Autism Network International* in 1992. Xe[1] has subsequently shaped scholarly argument in support of neurodiversity, writing in 1993 that:

> *autism is a way of being. It is pervasive; it colors every experience, every sensation, perception, thought, emotion, and encounter, every aspect of existence. It is not possible to separate the autism from the person – and if it were possible, the person you'd have left would not be the same person you started with.*

(Sinclair, 1993)

Later, in *Being Autistic Together* Sinclair describes how *Autism Network International* was set-up and the founders discovered that "*the time autistic people got to spend together was precious to many of us. People enjoyed it and wanted more of it*" (Sinclair, 2010). As a consequence, the first autistic-led event for autistic people and their allies, *Autreat*, was launched in 1996, inspiring similar events around the world.

Simultaneously in Europe, Martijn Dekker launched *Independent Living on the Autism Spectrum*, or InLv, an online network with the slogan "*where those who are different, find that they're not alone*". Autistic-led organisations are now proliferating and include the *Autistic Self-Advocacy Network* (founded 2006), *Autism Rights Group Highland* (founded 2005) and the *Autism Women's Network* (founded 2009). In 2005, *Aspies for Freedom* celebrated the first Autistic Pride Day, now celebrated internationally on June 18 every year. More recently, the journal *Autonomy* was launched by autistic academics to publish disability rights and sociological autism research, often by neurodivergent scholars (Arnold, 2013).

Led by autistic advocates, community leaders and scholars, we now find ourselves at a turning point in the conceptualisation of autism. Autistic people have become pioneers of the larger disability rights agenda, emphasising a social model of disability (Shapiro, 1994; Solomon, 2008) and demanding a role in shaping the policies and services that affect their lives (Ne'eman, 2010). This characterises the disabling consequences of autism, like all disabilities, as being the result of an environment that fails to enable individuals who do not operate in the same way as the mainstream majority. A more nuanced account, the post-social model, shifts the focus subtly from the environment as the culprit to the interaction between the individual and their environment (see Chapter 9 for more on this). To take a simple example, someone who doesn't walk requires both a personal aid (e.g. a wheelchair) and an enabling environment (e.g. ramps, wide doorways) to get around. Disability rights campaigners

---

1   We believe this is Dr Sinclair's preferred pronoun.

are beginning to have success in placing ableism (prejudice against disabled people) alongside racism, sexism and homophobia as a major source of disadvantage in our society.

7. Neurodiversity

Within the disability rights movement, autism is often characterised as a 'hidden disability' – meaning that it is not marked out by obvious physical features. Other hidden disabilities include many of what psychologists term "neurodevelopmental disorders" – e.g. attention deficit hyperactivity disorder, dyslexia, dyspraxia, epilepsy and Tourette's syndrome. Moving away from the negative terminology of 'disorder', the term neurodiversity was coined by InLv member Judy Singer, who wrote, "*We are beginning to divide ourselves . . . according to something new: differences in 'kinds of minds' . . . swinging the 'Nature-Nurture' pendulum back towards 'Nature'*" (Singer, 1998). Neurodiversity thus describes variability in brain structure and function, and resulting cognitive processes, accounting for differences between all individuals and, in cases of neurodivergence, also giving rise to diagnostic categories. Neurodivergent people may find that their experiences of the world and of other people do not align with the norm, and this is attributed to basic, underlying neurological differences. Crucially, neurodiversity dictates that neurodivergent people are *different, not less.*

It is important to emphasise that adopting a neurodiversity stance does not preclude providing support to people in need, nor does it deny the very real challenges experienced by many autistic people and their families. Autism is often accompanied by mental health difficulties (e.g. anxiety, depression), medical conditions (e.g. epilepsy) and behavioural features (e.g. self-harm, poor sleep, limited diet) which have significant negative impact on the individual and those around them. Autism is also associated with intellectual disability in many cases (though see Dawson et al., 2007, for thoughts about intelligence testing and autism). Limited verbal communication and/or additional language impairment presents a significant barrier for many. Even where autism is accompanied by high IQ and fluent speech, it might be categorised as a learning difficulty as it offers barriers to learning, where learning is expected to occur in a typical classroom. All of these issues are worthy of research attention and targeted support. The essence of neurodiversity tells us that, in identifying such areas for support and measuring suitable outcomes, our goal should be to provide relief in areas of need but not to eliminate an individual's neurodivergent status.

The motto "*nothing about us without us*" foregrounds the need for disabled people to be involved in all aspects of decision-making about disability. In the context of autism practice and research, we must work closely with autistic people and their allies to deliver research that matters to them (Milton, 2014). This does not mean abandoning psychological theory nor scientific rigour. It does mean developing participatory research practices

(Fletcher-Watson et al., 2018; Scott-Barrett et al., 2018) and framing our questions, designing our methods and disseminating our findings in a way that is respectful and embracing of autistic differences.

8. Current debates

Summary

The history of autism has moved through phases, largely influenced by English-speaking clinicians drawing on a series of case studies and then bigger data sets. Increasingly, our conceptualisations of autism are being influenced by autistic scholars and the autistic community. The clinical model of autism at each phase since the condition entered the diagnostic books has influenced the focus of research at that time. Today's neurodiversity framework is just beginning to have an impact on research, and some of the latest findings in this area are covered in Chapter 9. Much has been learnt about autism, but much still remains to be understood. In the next chapters, the current state of knowledge concerning the behavioural, biological and cognitive nature of autism will be reviewed, and some continuing debates and future research questions are discussed.

Big questions

What is next for our understanding of autism? The autism field has moved through many phases, and we can expect dramatic shifts to come. Can we envisage a future in which autism leaves the diagnostic manuals all together and becomes a self-determined personal identity? If so, what will this mean for the provision of evidence-based supports for the difficulties experienced by autistic people?

How can we cater to diversity within the autistic community? At the moment, the majority of autistic people who are playing a role in shaping research and practice are those without intellectual disability. It remains challenging to engage directly with autistic people who are minimally verbal or learning disabled. The viewpoint of parents can be very valuable here, but these may not easily reconcile with the perspectives of autistic people. Certainly, respect for, and acceptance of, autism must encompass the whole community.

Does "neurotypicality" necessarily exist and what does that mean for neurodivergence? Neurodivergence is used to describe everyone who is categorically distinct from a neurotypical standard. All autistic people are neurodivergent, but not all neurodivergent people are autistic – other neurodivergent people might have ADHD or Tourette's syndrome, for example. Meanwhile, the term neurodiversity encompasses individual differences between all people. Neurodiversity, like biodiversity or ethnicity, doesn't automatically imply that there is a norm from which all others diverge. Instead, we are all different and diverse. Taken this way, how can we use the concept of neurodiversity to encourage greater acceptance, without undermining neurodivergent people's need for support and understanding?

COMMUNITY CONTRIBUTION: MARTIJN DEKKER – *AUTISTIC ADVOCATE AND FOUNDER OF AUTISTIC ONLINE COMMUNITY, INLV*

The history of autism is one of competing and opposing narratives. As described in this chapter, in the 1940s, Leo Kanner and Hans Asperger described autism in terms of case studies with interpretations: one form of narrative.

In the 1960s and 1970s, parents started organising to counter the pernicious narrative that they were responsible for causing their children's autism. Understandably, then, these parents became the centre of their own narrative. Applied Behaviour Analysis (ABA) and Intensive Behavioural Intervention came along, offering the promise of normalisation to parents whose autistic children had been written off as hopeless. But if a child failed to be rendered 'indistinguishable from their peers', parents were blamed once again: for not trying hard enough, for not following the method to its painful and harmful extremes, etc. The result was an entrenched attitude of distrust and defensiveness among 'tragic hero' parents.

Meanwhile, autistics were increasingly seen as non-persons. As ABA pioneer Lovaas said in an interview, "*You have a person in the physical sense – they have hair, a nose and a mouth – but they are not people in the psychological sense*" (Chance, 1974). As a result of such attitudes, autistic people were, and in many of the world's places still are, 'disappeared' to institutions, tortured, abused, ignored, etc. Through all the changes and new paradigms, one factor remained constant: the perspective of autistic people was consistently erased from the narrative.

Then, in the early 1990s, the Internet ceased to be a network for the academically privileged and was made available to mere mortals. Autistic people, who previously had no way of communicating with each other, quickly started finding each other online. In 1992, Autism Network International started the ANI-L mailing list, the first online community run for and by autistics. Hosted by Syracuse University, ANI-L quickly started developing its own autistic subculture and political paradigm (Sinclair, 2005).

In 1996, only just diagnosed after a childhood and young adulthood spent being different without knowing why, I entered the scene as the need was felt for an alternative to ANI-L. Long before social media, creating a new online group was difficult, but I already had experience with programming and online communication. Using my home dial-up line and specialist software, I started my own entirely self-hosted set of email groups for and by autistics, emphasising inclusion and diversity instead of one shared culture and one shared set of political beliefs. The group was called InLv, an abbreviation of 'Independent Living on the autistic spectrum'.

Spread over many parts of the world, participants discovered their autistic identity through a shared, yet deeply personal, exploration of a different way of being. For all our cultural, political and neurological diversity, we found plenty in common, not only in the shared experience of trauma and marginalisation but, for many of us, also in a certain fundamental autistic way of being (Dekker, 1999). Text-only communication proved a gateway to understanding, not a barrier. 'Autism' became my key for belonging, for the first time in my life, to a community of some description. The idea of being autistic became embedded in my sense of identity.

Early on, the notion emerged from discussions on InLv that human neurology is innately diverse, an aspect of biodiversity, and that this neurodiversity (Singer, 1998) is as valuable to the human ecosystem as any other form of diversity. We conceived neurodiversity as an inherently inclusive notion. Far from 'dictating' that neurodivergent people are 'different, not less', we were very much including those of us who felt less or broken, accepting them as human beings on par with those who felt non-disabled or even superior. Neurological diversity does not prescribe anything, such as how one should consider one's own condition. It simply exists; it's a fact. What we were advocating was the political recognition of the logical and ethical consequences of that fact – that is, equal rights for all neurodivergent people, including our right to exist, live, love, work, procreate, etc., like anyone else.

These days, neurodiversity activism has, in large part, moved beyond that original idea. Many now promote a specific and prescriptive 'paradigm' that, by claiming there is no such thing as a suboptimal neurological configuration (Grace, 2015; Walker, 2014), excludes autistic people who find themselves disabled or broken. Too often, I hear of autistic people joining a group of neurodiversity advocates hoping to meet kindred spirits, only to find themselves being told precisely what to believe, how to identify and how to communicate, with any perceived transgression resulting in a swift ban (e.g. O'Leary, 2018). An ironic situation for a movement founded on the idea of embracing diversity.

Like those 1960s–1970s parents trying to prove they didn't cause their children's autism, autistic activists these days are ever more distrustful and defensive. In trying to defend our right to exist, we are falling into the trap of taking our own narrative too seriously. The challenge neurodiversity activists face as we approach the 2020s, then, is basically one of growing up and learning once again to accept those who are different from ourselves.

Section references

Chance, Paul. (1974). 'After you hit a child, you can't just get up and leave him; you are hooked to that kid': O. Ivar Lovaas interview with Paul Chance. *Psychology Today*, January 1974, http://neurodiversity.com/library_chance_1974.html

Dekker, Martijn. (1999). *On our own terms: Emerging autistic culture.* Autism99 online conference. Republished 2015, www.autscape.org/2015/programme/handouts/Autistic-Culture-07-Oct-1999.pdf

Grace, Ally. (2015). Ten things you reject by embracing neurodiversity. *Respectfully Connected (blog)*, http://respectfullyconnected.com/2015/02/ten-things-you-reject-by-embracing/

O'Leary, Fiona. (2018). The Asperger's/autistic divide. *Personal blog*, 19 February 2018, https://fionaolearyblog.wordpress.com/2018/02/19/the-aspergers-autistic-divide/

Sinclair, Jim. (2005). Autism network international: The development of a community and its culture. *Self-published*, www.autreat.com/History_of_ANI.html

Singer, Judy. (1998). Odd people in: The birth of community amongst people on the autistic spectrum: A personal exploration of a new social movement based on neurological diversity. Thesis, Faculty of Humanities and Social Science, University of Technology, Sydney, 1998. Republished in "Neurodiversity: The birth of an idea" (2016). www.amazon.com/dp/B01HYOQTEE

Walker, Nick. (2014). Neurodiversity: Some basic terms & definitions. *Neurocosmopolitanism (blog)*, 27 September 2014, http://neurocosmopolitanism.com/neurodiversity-some-basic-terms-definitions/

Recommended reading

Bascom, J. (2012). *Loud hands: Autistic people, speaking*. Washington: Autistic Self-Advocacy Network.

Donvan, J. J., & Zucker, C. B. (2017). *In a different key: The story of autism*. London, UK: Allen Lane.

Feinstein, A. (2011). *A history of autism: Conversations with the pioneers*. Hoboken, NJ: John Wiley & Sons.

Grandin, T. (1986). *Emergence, labeled autistic*. Novato, CA: Academic Therapy Publications.

Silberman, S. (2016). *Neurotribes: The legacy of autism and how to think smarter about people who think differently*. Sydney: Allen & Unwin.

Williams, D. (1992). *Nobody nowhere: The extraordinary autobiography of an autistic girl*. New York: Jessica Kingsley.

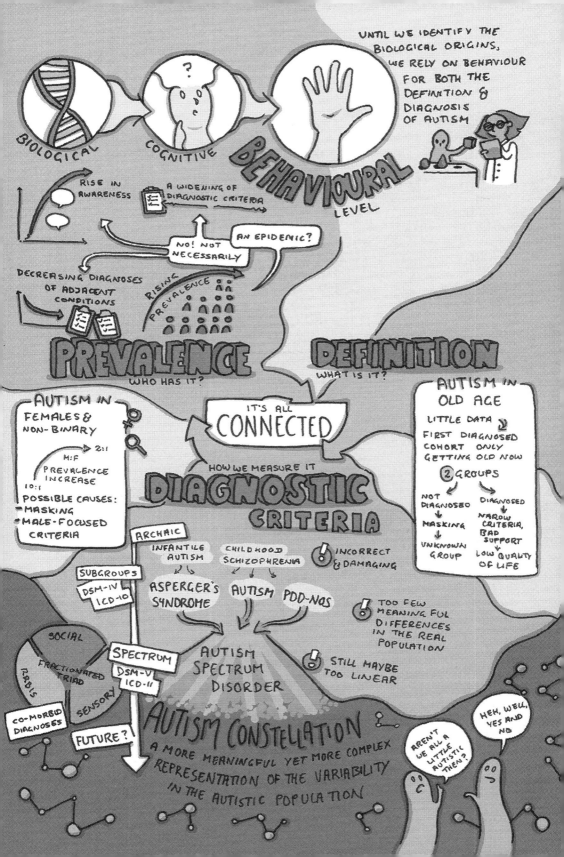

3 Autism at the behavioural level

ALTHOUGH WE KNOW autism has a genetic foundation, leading to neurobiological differences (see Chapter 4), it is diagnosed on the basis of a set of behaviours. The key reason for this is that, despite attempts, no reliable biological marker has been found. A reliable marker must show adequate sensitivity and specificity: meaning that it must be found in virtually all members of a group, and it must be exclusive to that group. At the moment, the best biomarker candidates we have for autism resemble attempts to identify which UK region you are from based on hair colour. Yes, there are group differences in prevalence of red hair between Scotland and other UK nations, but red hair is not found in a large enough percentage of the Scottish population to be sensitive and is found too widely elsewhere to be specific.

Our reliance on behaviour to identify autism leads to challenges for the field, as we will see in this chapter and beyond. Interpreting changing prevalence estimates or identifying meaningful sub-groups is extremely hard given the variability in how behavioural diagnostic features have been defined over time, and the potential differences in how they are applied in different settings.

1. Current and changing diagnostic criteria

The current diagnostic criteria, in both the 5th edition of the *Diagnostic and Statistical Manual of Mental Disorders* (*DSM-5*; APA, 2013 – see Table 3.1) and the forthcoming 11th edition of the *International Classification of Diseases* (*ICD-11*; WHO, 2018) specify only one category for autism. This is termed "Autism Spectrum Disorder" (ASD) in recognition of the variability of presentation. The use of the word 'disorder' as part of the diagnostic terminology is rejected by many autistic people, who emphasise that autism is a natural part of variation in the human population. For this reason, we refer to autism, rather than ASD, in this book. Nonetheless, for a diagnosis, the current pattern of traits or symptoms must be significantly impairing for the individual in at least some important aspects of life. It is important to recognise that when we say a trait is "impairing", we mean that in the context of a world largely designed by and for neurotypical people (for more on this, see Chapters 9 and 10).

TABLE 3.1 *DSM-5* criteria for Autism Spectrum Disorder

Autism Spectrum Disorder 299.00 (F84.0)

Diagnostic Criteria

A. Persistent deficits in social communication and social interaction across multiple contexts, as manifested by the following, currently or by history (examples are illustrative, not exhaustive, see text):

1. Deficits in social-emotional reciprocity, ranging, for example, from abnormal social approach and failure of normal back-and-forth conversation; to reduced sharing of interests, emotions or affect; to failure to initiate or respond to social interactions.

2. Deficits in non-verbal communicative behaviours used for social interaction, ranging, for example, from poorly integrated verbal and non-verbal communication; to abnormalities in eye contact and body language or deficits in understanding and use of gestures; to a total lack of facial expressions and non-verbal communication.

3. Deficits in developing, maintaining and understanding relationships, ranging, for example, from difficulties adjusting behaviour to suit various social contexts; to difficulties in sharing imaginative play or in making friends; to absence of interest in peers.

B. Restricted, repetitive patterns of behaviour, interests, or activities, as manifested by at least two of the following, currently or by history (examples are illustrative, not exhaustive; see text):

1. Stereotyped or repetitive motor movements, use of objects, or speech (e.g. simple motor stereotypies, lining up toys or flipping objects, echolalia, idiosyncratic phrases).

2. Insistence on sameness, inflexible adherence to routines, or ritualised patterns or verbal non-verbal behaviour (e.g. extreme distress at small changes, difficulties with transitions, rigid thinking patterns, greeting rituals, need to take same route or eat food every day).

3. Highly restricted, fixated interests that are abnormal in intensity or focus (e.g. strong attachment to or preoccupation with unusual objects, excessively circumscribed or perseverative interest).

4. Hyper- or hyporeactivity to sensory input or unusual interests in sensory aspects of the environment (e.g. apparent indifference to pain/temperature, adverse response to specific sounds or textures, excessive smelling or touching of objects, visual fascination with lights or movement).

C. Symptoms must be present in the early developmental period (but may not become fully manifest until social demands exceed limited capacities, or may be masked by learnt strategies in later life).

D. Symptoms cause clinically significant impairment in social, occupational or other important areas of current functioning.

E. These disturbances are not better explained by intellectual disability (intellectual developmental disorder) or global developmental delay. Intellectual disability and Autism Spectrum Disorder frequently co-occur; to make comorbid diagnoses of Autism Spectrum Disorder and intellectual disability, social communication should be below that expected for general developmental level.

Continued

TABLE 3.1 Continued

Specify if:

With or without accompanying intellectual impairment
With or without accompanying language impairment
Associated with a known medical or genetic condition or environmental factor
Associated with another neurodevelopmental, mental or behavioural disorder
With catatonia

Diagnosis, according to both the *DSM-5* and *ICD-11*, requires evidence of features in two domains: atypicalities in social and communication behaviours, and the presence of restricted and repetitive behaviours. Features should be present from the early years, though diagnosis can happen much later, and frequently does. Both manuals highlight sensory sensitivities – both hypo and hyper – and potential for concurrent intellectual and/or language disability. *ICD-11* provides more detail on the differentiation of autism with and without intellectual disability and also explicitly mentions the fact that some autistic people may mask their symptoms to fit in. Finally, both systems also allow autism to be diagnosed in the presence of other conditions – such as Attention Deficit Hyperactivity Disorder (ADHD) or anxiety – when previously clinicians were instructed to select only a single diagnosis, denying the possibility of co-occurrence.

Previous versions of both diagnostic manuals (*DSM-IV* and *ICD-10* – APA, 1994; WHO, 1992) specified a series of sub-classifications of autism, such as autistic disorder, Asperger's syndrome, atypical autism or pervasive developmental disorder – not otherwise specified (PDD-NOS). The current and former diagnostic classification systems represent different approaches to handling the variability between people who share underlying features of the same condition. We can identify the condition as a spectrum, with inherent variability, or attempt to sub-divide based on intensity of features or specific markers (e.g. Asperger's syndrome was distinct because it was not associated with a delayed onset of language).

Why do we see these changes in diagnostic criteria and concepts? Each iteration of the diagnostic manuals attempts to respond to the growing body of research, as well as trying to improve diagnostic processes. An example of the former is the decision to collapse the distinction between Asperger's disorder and autistic disorder. A large body of work suggested few meaningful differences between these groups when current intellectual ability was equivalent (e.g. Eisenmajer et al., 1996; Macintosh & Dissanayake, 2004). Indeed, an influential study of diagnoses given across a range of expert clinics in America showed that the best predictor of which diagnosis was given (Asperger's, Autism, PDD-NOS) was not any characteristic of the individual being diagnosed, but which clinic they went to! (Lord et al., 2012a). An example of a change in criteria reflecting ease of clinical use is the collapsing of social and communication criteria; it is hard to think of any piece of social behaviour a clinician might look for/ask about that does not involve communication, and vice versa. The overall aim of the changes in *DSM-5* was to move to a system where a broad category diagnosis was accompanied by a detailed description of the individual's strengths and needs, rather than trying to squeeze people into specific categories they didn't necessarily fit.

Because the *DSM* tends to be more influential in research and therefore on psychological theory, which is our focus in this book, we will use this as the framework for subsequent discussions.

2. Diagnostic criteria in practice

The variability in diagnostic manuals is nothing compared to the variability of presentation in the autistic population. When identifying autism, clinicians must be alert to the fact that the same feature may be manifest in dramatically different forms between individuals. For example, communication difficulties could mean that an individual is entirely non-speaking, speaking a great deal but mainly by echoing, or speaking fluently but with an atypical approach to conversational rules or understanding of non-literal language (e.g. irony, metaphor). Socially, a young autistic child may seem oblivious to others, while another individual on the spectrum may be keen to make friends but be unsure how to do so, making approaches that seem odd to neurotypical peers. Likewise, restricted and repetitive behaviours could mean lining up toys, spinning and flapping, a very 'black and white' thinking style, or might be evident as an immersive and impressively detailed interest in organic chemistry. One relevant dimension is clearly the presence or absence of intellectual disability (technically defined as an IQ less than 70 on a standardised assessment, accompanied by difficulties with daily living skills), but it is simplistic to suggest that IQ level alone determines how features are manifest.

As an example, let us consider the communication delays which are so prevalent in autism (Tager-Flusberg et al., 2005). A non-speaking autistic child may present with a significant intellectual disability which has contributed to their difficulties acquiring speech. Another non-speaking child may have no such intellectual barrier, but instead, their communication could be associated with anxiety-related mutism. Another factor which plays into this characterisation is the extent to which a feature presents obstacles in daily life. If either child can learn to communicate, for example via independent use of a text-to-speech device using visual symbols or Makaton signs, then this apparently profound difference might be minimally disabling (at least in environments where those communication modes are understood). Likewise, a specialist and all-consuming interest in geology could be something of a hindrance when trying to chat up a potential romantic partner (unless they are also a geologist!), but a boon when seeking employment in the mining industry.

FIGURE 3.1   The autistic constellation

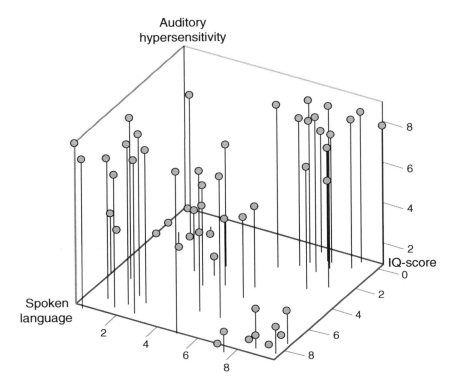

In this three-dimensional space, we illustrate IQ scores, spoken language and a sensory feature often experienced by autistic people, as orthogonal dimensions. All data are hypothetical only. Autistic people may be located in every available point in the resulting three-dimensional space, but there is the potential, if we measure the right things, to identify clusters where features often overlap.

One attempt to visualise this complexity is shown above, where we try to illustrate autism as a constellation, rather than a spectrum.[1] Here we show how a specific feature of autism (in this case, sensory hyper-sensitivity) might be plotted with intellectual ability and language profile. Autistic people, with a diagnosis, may locate themselves anywhere in the resulting three-dimensional space. Their exact location would further vary with context and across the lifespan. This space can be reproduced with different measures on each axis, using features which have relevance to theory, features more important for everyday life, or both in combination. For example, we might plot satisfaction with social relationships and against the number of social relationships and

---

1   Thanks to Caroline Hearst who inspired our use of this term: www.autangel.org.uk/autism-constellation.html.

level of anxiety. Importantly, in this case, having few social relationships might cluster together with high relationship satisfaction and low anxiety. This group of people might be characterised as happy with a small number of friends, reflected in low anxiety scores. Another group might have few friends, but high anxiety and low satisfaction with their relationships. Could helping them achieve more social contact lower their anxiety? A third group might have high satisfaction, large amounts of social contact and high anxiety. Perhaps having a big social circle is both rewarding and stressful – could a better balance be achieved between the two?

These examples illustrate that it is important to contextualise any such measurement within an individual's own priorities – working with allies to identify these where the person themselves may find it hard to self-advocate. In the previous example, provided an individual is not at risk as a result of their relative isolation, a small amount of social contact should not be characterised as a sign of impairment, as in the first cluster described. The key take home message is that autism, both conceptually and in terms of lived experience, is manifest in complex interacting domains. To discuss the 'autistic spectrum' in a linear fashion, or to attempt to measure 'severity' vastly over-simplifies and misrepresents the reality. Where a measure of support need is relevant we propose using exactly that terminology – as it is in the *DSM-5*: e.g. *Level 3: requiring very substantial support.*

3. Making a diagnosis

Reliance on loosely defined diagnostic criteria presents challenges to differential diagnosis, risks of mis-diagnosis and difficulty matching a diagnosis with a relevant support package. Measures have been put in place to limit these problems. In the UK, the National Institute of Clinical Excellence (NICE) and the Scottish Intercollegiate Guidelines Network (SIGN) have both published criteria for a robust diagnostic process for autism. This should include multidisciplinary assessment, direct observation of the individual across settings (e.g. clinic, home, school) and the use of standardised assessment tools. The widely used Autism Diagnostic Observation Schedule (now ADOS-2, Lord et al., 2012b) and Autism Diagnostic Interview (ADI-R, LeCouteur et al., 2003) are two such standardised diagnostic measures using direct observation and clinical history, respectively. Nevertheless, concerns remain about diagnostic practices. These tools are lengthy and costly to obtain and train in, making them impractical for low resource settings. Open-access diagnostic tools that are brief and can be administered by a range of people, are urgently needed, especially when one remembers that the vast majority of autistic people live in low- and middle-income countries. The utility of existing diagnostic tools for diagnosis in adulthood has also been questioned, as has the influence of such measures on the gender balance of diagnosed individuals (more on this later in the chapter). Despite flaws in the process, it should be emphasised that one function of the clinical diagnostic process is not only to offer an autism diagnosis when appropriate but also to take the opportunity to get to know the individual and their family. An in-depth diagnostic process has advantages, placing the clinician in a strong and informed position to make a diagnosis and, ideally, signpost relevant information and access to services for the future. Although we note that this is an ideal, rather than a reality, for many people, at the same time preliminary evidence indicates that having a diagnosis may yield benefits in terms of improved quality of life and reduced stress for the families of autistic people (McKechanie et al., 2017).

At present, a reliable, clinical diagnosis of autism is rare before the age of 3 years, though some argue it is possible as young as 18 months. This is primarily because the types of social behaviours that are characteristically different in autism (according to the diagnostic criteria noted earlier) do not emerge reliably in typical children until around three years. Moreover, restricted and repetitive behaviours are common in all children at about two years old (Leekam et al., 2007a). However, there is substantial interest in the possibility of pinpointing earlier indicators of autism. The search for very early signs that would allow one to predict which children would turn out to have autism, has been prompted by two different concerns. Practical considerations have pressed for earlier diagnosis in the hope that very early intervention might produce benefits on early stage outcomes like onset of language. Theoretical considerations urge the early identification of autism in order to explore the causal direction in development – for example, do differences in processing of faces lead to or result from difficulties in social interaction? The emergent findings on early signs will be reviewed in Chapters 4 and 7.

A relatively recent phenomenon is that people have begun to self-identify as autistic, often later in life and sometimes prompted by the diagnosis of a child in the family. There is little or no research evidence so far on the validity or consequences of this choice. However, it is certainly easy to understand why many people might recognise autism in themselves but either not feel the need for an external confirmation by a medical professional, or actively refuse to undergo a formal diagnostic evaluation that ends in being labelled with a 'disorder' (Kapp et al., 2013). At the same time, self-identification does raise concerns. Are there individuals who would not be independently identified as autistic, merely seeking to align themselves with a group that seems to be getting a certain amount of public attention? Are people who would benefit from mental health support mis-identifying the causes of their feelings? These cases are hopefully in a small minority. Nevertheless, the phenomenon of self-identification presents challenges to academic research, not least in efforts to estimate prevalence.

4. Prevalence estimates

How common is autism? Understanding this is crucial for service provision planning, including budgeting for the economic impact of autism, which is estimated to be very high in the UK (Knapp et al., 2009) and USA (Buescher et al., 2014; Lavelle et al., 2014). Kanner and Asperger both described the condition as rare. However, current prevalence estimates in Western countries tend to hover around 1% of the population. There is considerable global variation – a meta-analysis cited rates from 0.3% to 1.2% with a median rate of 0.6% (Elsabbagh et al., 2012) and called for more epidemiological work in low and middle-income countries. It is virtually impossible to trace the precise roots of this variability, but it is likely that differences in diagnostic procedures account for much of the range. In particular, we can see that those countries with less developed healthcare systems consistently produce the lowest prevalence estimates. Cultural differences likewise impact decisions post-diagnosis (Mandell & Novak, 2005) and should be taken into account within, as well as between, countries.

Accounting for the dramatic changes in autism prevalence estimates over time has been the focus of considerable media attention and academic effort (Fombonne, 2005). A range of headline-grabbing accounts have been put forward including the effects of pollution, changes to diet and, famously and tragically, vaccines. While it is known that there are environmental factors that contribute to autism – the condition is not 100% heritable – there is no robust evidence to support any of these accounts. In the case of the role of vaccines, this hypothetical causal factor has been thoroughly, rigorously and conclusively disproven (Jain et al., 2015; Taylor et al., 1999, 2014). Instead, variation in prevalence estimates of autism can probably be attributed to a combination of the following factors.

First, the diagnostic criteria for autism have changed dramatically since autism was first enshrined in diagnostic manuals (as 'infantile autism' in *ICD-8*, 1967; 'childhood schizophrenia' in *DSM-I* and *II*, and then 'infantile autism in *DSM-III* in 1980). Specifically, they have broadened to admit a much wider variety of individuals under the diagnostic umbrella. Alongside this change, there has been a dramatic rise in awareness of autism, not just in the public but among medical professionals. If you visit your family doctor now to discuss concerns about your child's development, autism will be a potential explanation on everyone's radar (at least if your child is a boy!) in a way that was not the case 30 or even 20 years ago. This growing awareness, combined with broadened diagnostic criteria, may have given rise to a degree of diagnostic substitution as well. As autism diagnoses have increased, diagnoses of global developmental delay or intellectual impairment, have declined. This would imply that there is no absolute increase in the numbers of affected individuals, merely in the way they are being categorised. A fourth facet of this general process of raising awareness and widening categories, has been an increase in identification of autism in populations where that diagnosis was previously not considered. Diagnostic rates in adults are rising sharply, as adults with intellectual disability are re-assessed for autism as well, and as others start to recognise autism in themselves. Anecdotally, there seems to be a specific phenomenon of parents, and sometimes grandparents, seeking a professional opinion for themselves, following their child's diagnosis.

Finally, in some cases differences in prevalence may result from differences in methodology. The Centers for Disease Control and Prevention in the USA recently published an estimate of 1 in 68, far exceeding any previous figure. However, the methods employed in this study have been criticised. There was no direct assessment involved – instead the estimate was based on prevalence of what appeared to be autism-linked features in the case notes of children and young people referred for evaluation by education or clinical service providers.

Is autism prevalence still increasing? There are a couple of UK studies that suggest that prevalence has reached something of a plateau over the last two decades, stabilising after the introduction of new diagnostic criteria in the early 1990s (Baxter et al., 2015; Taylor et al., 2013). Whether the recent changes in *DSM-5* and *ICD-11* will affect prevalence again remains to be seen. In addition, adult diagnosis and diagnosis among women and girls seem to be undergoing a recent sharp increase, which may not yet be represented in the latest epidemiological data.

5. Sensory symptoms and associated features

As we have seen, diagnosis is based on the presence of features in both of two, 'core' domains: social and communication behaviours, and restricted and repetitive behaviours. However, a range of other features are mentioned in diagnostic manuals and are certainly 'core' to the autistic experience, if not strictly required for diagnosis.

Chief among these is an array of sensory symptoms, normally in the form of marked hyper- or hypo-sensitivity to sensory input that non-autistic people would take in their stride (Ben-Sasson et al., 2009; Leekam et al., 2007b). These sensitivities can occur in every sensory domain, including disruptions to 'internal' senses, such as interoception, proprioception and kinaesthesia (Schauder et al., 2015) – though these may be related to conditions commonly associated with autism (e.g. alexithymia – difficulty identifying one's own emotions) rather than to autism itself (Shah et al., 2016). The same person may experience both hyper-sensitivity – such as an aversion to the sound of a vacuum cleaner – and hypo-sensitivity – such as a preference for strong, immersive squeezing sensations or apparent insensitivity to cold. This mix of over and under sensitivity can also be apparent within a single sensory domain, and of course experiences and responses may change with context and across the lifespan.

Sensory sensitivities present significant obstacles to daily life for many autistic people. A need to avoid aversive sensory input can result in autistic people becoming reluctant to leave their homes. Sensory-seeking behaviour can also cause problems, as in the case of a young man who would pinch strangers in the supermarket in order to hear the high-pitched squeal that inevitably followed. Sensory sensitivities can be beneficial as well, and many autistic people describe the intense beauty and pleasure of their heightened responses. Enhanced discrimination of pitch, smell or touch sensations are useful in some careers or hobbies. Synaesthesia appears to be prevalent above usual rates among autistic people, and some have used this to inspire visual art, create music or support memory and learning (e.g. Tammet, 2007).

Autistic people also receive other diagnoses at higher rates than the general population. Of particular note are high rates of anxiety, depression and epilepsy. These conditions are in turn linked to early mortality in autism; in addition to deaths related to seizures, suicide is more common than previously realised (Hirvikoski et al., 2016). Research is only just beginning to get to grips with the general and mental health of autistic people, in order to address this tragic pattern (Cassidy & Rodgers, 2017). The work is challenging. One example comes from investigations into anxiety in autism. Meta-analysis indicates that up to 40% of autistic children meet criteria for multiple anxiety disorders (van Steensel & Bogels, 2011). However, disentangling these data is a challenge – to what extent is the apparent co-occurrence a superficial consequence of overlap in self-report measures used both to capture autistic traits and features of anxiety? On the other hand, experiencing anxiety or depression should not be considered merely a component of autism, dismissed without proper investigation or treatment. One promising route to developing our understanding in this area has been the identification of an underlying psychology construct, *intolerance of uncertainty*, which is hypothesised to underpin both certain features of autism and aspects of anxiety (Wigham et al., 2015) – we will consider this in more detail in Chapter 5.

One thing is certain however: for many people, it's not autism that is a problem, but all the baggage that goes with it. One of the major challenges for a psychological approach to the condition is to account for and address these difficulties. Treatments for co-occurring problems like anxiety are available, some of which already have autism-specific evidence showing potential for benefit (e.g. Guénolé et al., 2011). In other cases, further work is needed to explore whether and how 'mainstream' psychiatric and psychological interventions should be adapted to autism (Spain et al., 2015).

6. The constellation and the autisms

The Autistic Spectrum was a term coined by Lorna Wing to describe autistic heterogeneity, but as we have seen, it now seems too linear to adequately capture the complex dimensions of variability between autistic people. When people write about some being "at one end of the spectrum", it seems to suggest that we might theoretically be able to line up all the autistic people in the world in order of how autistic they are! Rather, variability between autistic people is more like variability between feminine people. Asked to sort a group of people according to "most to least feminine" you might consider a range of factors – body shape, clothing, hairstyle, career choice, personality and manner. But the chances you'd come to the same order as another person are surely very low. You might simply reject the notion that one person can be more or less feminine than another, but even if you didn't, you'd probably give up trying. Autistic writers have sometimes referred to the autism constellation, which seems better: "*It is more like a constellation than a spectrum. It does not move along one line going from low to high, it circles in many spheres*" (Hearst, 2015). Whatever terms we choose to capture variability in the autistic population, there's no doubt that it exists. Consequently, desire to parse autism into meaningful sub-groups is strong.

A good reason to identify sub-groups is to provide the right supports to the right people. For example, we might identify in childhood those who would be most likely to experience anxiety or depression in adolescence and put in place efforts to increase their resilience and coping strategies. However behavioural sub-types haven't proved very successful, beyond a simple characterisation of autism plus or minus intellectual disability and/or language impairment. One reason is that the same individual may pass through different presentations as they age. For example, Asperger's syndrome became problematic as a separate category as it was realised that often a 'classically' autistic child grows into an 'Asperger-type' adult. Another difficulty in the quest to identify sub-groups is that the sample sizes required are so huge. Capturing detailed genetic and phenotypic information, let alone relating this to developmental trajectories and adult outcomes, would require huge investments and sometimes international protocols. One such study is underway – the EU-AIMS (European Autism Interventions – A Multicentre Study for Developing new Medications) consortium is funded by the largest single grant for autism research worldwide and seeks to develop the knowledge and infrastructure to underpin new treatments for autism. Identifying biomarkers for personalised or precision medicine approaches is a key goal for this huge and ambitious project (Loth et al., 2017). The project also provides a salutary lesson in the importance of engagement from the outset; subsequent consultations with the autism community revealed significant gaps between community priorities and the original consortium goals (Russell et al., 2018).

As well as attempts to identify meaningful sub-groups within the spectrum, the notion of the broader autism phenotype (BAP) has also been extensively studied. This term is used to capture the pattern of autistic-like traits found in the general population. The BAP is generally measured via self-report of a range of behaviours such as, *I would rather go to a library than a party*, or *I find it easy to "read between the lines" when someone is talking to me* (Baron-Cohen et al., 2001). BAP traits are normally distributed in the general population and found in higher rates among the biological relatives of people with autism (e.g. Bishop et al., 2004). BAP traits have been correlated with diverse features, including sensory sensitivity (Robertson & Simmons, 2013), studying science and technology subjects (Stewart & Austin, 2009) and ability to read non-verbal communication cues (Ingersoll, 2010). However, it remains somewhat debated how much can be said about autism from studies exploring autistic-like traits in non-autistic people. This literature risks trivialising the autistic experience in the same way that relating a feeling of sadness to clinical depression (however well-intentioned) risks trivialising that diagnosis. Nonetheless, the evidence to date does suggest that similar genetic influences operate on autistic traits and at the subclinical and diagnosed levels (Constantino & Todd, 2003; Robinson et al., 2011).

7. The fractionated triad

While the notion of 'the autisms' reflects our current belief that autism has different etiologies (reflected perhaps in different featural patterns) in different individuals on the spectrum, heterogeneity can also be understood in terms of the 'fractionated triad' idea (Happé et al., 2006). This suggests that, even within one individual, different behavioural features of autism – whether we split those into a triad, dyad or any other number of clusters – may have multiple, distinct causes. This notion came from studies that showed that, in the general population, atypicalities in social skills or communication are often found without rigid and repetitive behaviour or interests. Furthermore, correlations between ratings of the three aspects of the traditional diagnostic triad are low or moderate (Happé & Ronald, 2008). In addition, twin studies of traits in the general population, or clinical-level features of autism, suggest distinct genetic influences on the three aspects of the triad (Robinson et al., 2012). These findings fit with evidence from family studies of the BAP in relatives of autistic people, where a great-aunt may be described as a loner who shunned company, while granddad is socially able but very rigid, eating the same food for lunch every day and working as a proofreader with a fantastic eye for detail. According to this account, autism is the result of a 'recipe' of genetic and environmental 'ingredients', with differences in social communication style and preference for routine deriving from different sources. In just the same way, we might recognise that we are each an amalgam of different aspects, with, for example, our mother's curly hair and our father's sticky-out ears!

Another contribution to this concept comes from the idea of resilience factors. Resilience is the capacity to recover from, or avoid the negative effects of something. For example, having good friends at school might provide resilience to the negative effects of parental divorce. In the case of autism, good executive functions are one candidate resilience factor that don't make a person any less autistic, but might make them more resilient to some of the negative consequences of being autistic. An autistic person with good working memory and planning abilities might be able to learn rules to operate in the neurotypical world, monitoring and tracking social behaviours and working out how they are expected to respond. While we do not advocate for such an exhausting approach, but such phenomena may relate to compensation (Livingston & Happé, 2017) or 'camouflaging' and the under-identification of autism outside the male gender. There is more on this next, and we'll revisit the fractionated triad idea in Chapter 6 in relation to cognitive aspects of autism. The key point about this putative account is that it suggests autism is a composite of different and somewhat independent behavioural aspects, that have different origins at the biological and/or cognitive levels.

8. Autism and gender

All the epidemiological studies of autism show a significantly greater number of boys than girls in the population. Historically, a ratio of c.5:1 males to females was accepted, and the sex ratio was thought to vary with ability, reaching perhaps 10:1 among cognitively able individuals, and falling to 2:1 amongst those with intellectual disability. Thus, most girls diagnosed with autism also had an intellectual disability (Lord & Schopler, 1987), and it was thought that females required a "higher etiological load" to manifest autism. However, this picture is now changing. In the last five years, interest in the female profile of autism has risen sharply, accompanied by rising awareness that autism may manifest differently in women and girls. Recent meta-analysis suggests that when thorough epidemiological work is done, versus relying on known diagnosed cases in clinics or registries, the male preponderance falls to 3:1, with little difference across the ability range (Loomes et al., 2017). These figures still reflect the numbers meeting current diagnostic criteria; if our criteria or processes are male biased, we may be missing large numbers of females on the spectrum. Certainly, research has traditionally overlooked and even excluded females from autism research, leading to a vicious cycle of ignorance about possible gender differences.

A great deal of research investigating the female profile of autism has focused on qualitative descriptions of their experience, often revealing significant difficulties prior to receiving a diagnosis. Studies have highlighted that many autistic girls, lacking a diagnosis, experience significant mental health difficulties in adolescence and beyond (e.g. Duvekot et al., 2017). These findings are supported by data on high rates of previously undiagnosed autism in women presenting to eating disorders services (Mandy & Tchanturia, 2015). Why are these girls not picked up by clinical services? One likely explanation is that some autistic girls spend time and effort masking or camouflaging their autism (Dean et al., 2017; Lai et al., 2017). This in turn can lead to exhaustion and mental health difficulties. Another possible cause for this pattern is that, through long years of reiteration that autism is more prevalent in males, clinical services have become conditioned to diagnose boys and also more finely tuned to detecting their autistic features. For example, most clinicians would probably confidently identify the point at which an interest in trains starts to meet the definition of a 'restricted interest'. Would the decision be made so confidently if the interest was something more 'appropriate' to female gender stereotypes (Sutherland et al., 2017) like a fascination with make-up or horses? Perhaps not. And if clinicians don't think 'autism' when they meet a girl with social difficulties, they may think social anxiety, eating disorder or depression: diagnostic overshadowing occurs when clinicians stop at one presenting problem and don't go on to consider, for example, eating disorder *and* autism.

Many questions about the female presentation of autism remain to be answered, and there are some fundamental challenges for the field. For example, one concern is that the instruments used to standardise elements of the diagnostic process for autism may be skewed towards the expected male presentation. Do new assessments need to be constructed in order to capture the female profile? And if so, how do we go about creating such instruments at a time when every diagnosed female has been identified using the old ones?

A further challenge comes from the fact that a large proportion of autistic people identify outside the male/female gender binary (Cooper et al., 2018). The increasing focus on diagnosing and understanding autism in females risks overlooking the complex interplay of gender expectations and autistic features in those who don't fall neatly into a binary gender category. For example, how might autism be manifest in natal males who later identify as non-binary, female or another gender identity? What modifications need to be made to diagnostic instruments to capture their autism accurately? And, conversely, how can we improve the process of transition for autistic transgender people? As yet, research on autism and gender identity is in its infancy but readers would do well to take this crucial consideration into account when considering research that invokes simplistic gender differences in autism.

9. What does autism look like in old age?

The short answer to this question is that nobody really knows. Of course, there are older autistic adults with personal experiences to share, but in terms of being able to make generalised, robust statements about ageing and autism, the data just aren't in yet (Howlin & Magiati, 2017). Since the first children were described by Kanner and Asperger in the 1940s, and the diagnosis did not enter more general use until the 1960s and '70s, the first cohort with recognised autism are only now growing old. Autism was considered rare and was diagnosed by far narrower criteria than today, so attempts to follow these children through to old age are tricky and won't necessarily tell us about the future ageing of people diagnosed by today's wider criteria. There are increasing numbers of people receiving a first diagnosis of autism in adulthood, but these may be unrepresentative by virtue of having managed so long without a correct or complete diagnosis.

As a result, knowledge about the links between autism and the typical ageing processes – cognitive decline, changing social support networks, physical illness – is in its infancy. Also important, and under-researched, are questions about the best way to provide care to an ageing autistic individual. While much remains to be done, awareness of autism in mainstream classrooms is now fairly good, and teachers are increasing in confidence about how to support autistic pupils. To our knowledge, there is no wide-spread effort in progress to similarly inform people working in elder care settings. Another obstacle to understanding ageing in autism is that the kind of support offered to autistic children five, six or seven decades ago was radically different from the kind of support being offered today. This impedes our understanding of the potential lifespan impact of intervention in childhood.

Is there *anything* we can say about ageing and autism? Pat Howlin has followed up one longitudinal cohort of autistic people diagnosed and recruited as children in the 1960s and '70s at the Maudsely Hospital in London. In their 40s and 50s, their outcomes were generally poor in terms of independence, employment and quality of life (Howlin et al., 2014). A large-scale study of health records from more than 1,500 autistic adults found higher rates of almost every mental and physical health condition compared to non-autistic adults (Croen et al., 2015). Less than 10% of the sample were aged 50 plus, but the elevated rates of heart disease, diabetes and conditions associated with ageing (e.g. dementia, Parkinson's) suggests that research on physical health in elderly autistic adults is urgently needed. Autistic adults also generally report lower quality of life than non-autistic people (van Heijst & Geurts, 2015) but a new autism-specific, validated measure for quality of life may provide more optimistic data in the future (McConachie et al., 2017). Anecdotal impressions suggest that many autistic adults find a niche for themselves as they grow older, with like-minded companions, professional fulfilment and passionate hobbies. What is unclear is how to accelerate this process and extend it to reach as many potential beneficiaries as possible.

10. Autistic behaviour and societal norms

Neurotypical syndrome is a neurobiological disorder characterized by preoccupation with social concerns, delusions of superiority, and obsession with conformity.[2]

It is essential when attempting to describe the behavioural profile associated with autism to recognise that autism is largely characterised against a back-drop of presumed normative standards. Probing this context reveals a number of assumptions which, while they may be constructive in permitting scientific investigation to move forward, deserve to be acknowledged at the very least, and possibly challenged.

One assumption, especially when discussing heterogeneity between autistic people, is that non-autistic people all fit neatly into an easily described, "neurotypical" box. This is clearly not the case, but it is easy to see why this

2   https://angryautie.wordpress.com/2013/06/24/the-institute-for-the-study-of-the-neurologically-typical/

notion took hold. First, many studies used standardised measures, such as IQ tests. These have usually been developed with data from very large samples. Such samples tend more and more towards a normal distribution, emphasising average performance and causing variability to be downplayed. The data are used to provide age-norms and it is easy to jump to the, clearly false, conclusion that any non-autistic individual would score right on the nose for their age.

Second, many studies that provide the foundation for our understanding of 'typical' development and behaviour rely on very narrowly defined samples. Published data disproportionately draw on university undergraduates, or the children of university staff and their friends, often in the UK or USA, or other developed nations. These samples are often largely white and in middle to high socio-economic brackets. Control groups are often screened for any kind of mental health problem, resulting in 'super controls', who are not at all population representative. In contrast, when recruiting an autistic group to a research project, because of the relative rarity of autism, researchers cast their net far and wide, often ending up with a more variable group than in the comparison data. That said, we should also note that white, middle-class participants are over-represented in research generally. Furthermore, in some kinds of studies – especially randomised controlled trials (RCTs) – inclusion criteria may be extremely strict, limiting external validity and clinical relevance (Jonsson et al., 2016).

Another way in which societal norms infiltrate supposedly objective autism research is by application of a normative lens to the study questions, design and especially interpretation of data. When the average performance of an autistic group differs from that of a comparison group, all too often, the immediate conclusion is that the autistic response pattern is inferior. This is particularly unjustified in the case when the developmental function or outcome of the behaviour is not well understood. For example, one recent study observed a reduced 'ownership effect' in the toy choices of autistic relative to non-autistic children. Children with autism judged toys purely on their merits, showing no bias contingent on randomly assigned ownership (i.e. having been given the toy by an experimenter). Despite the autistic group showing more rational behaviour, the authors concluded that *"deficits in self-understanding may diminish ownership effects in ASD"* (Hartley & Fisher, 2018, p. 26).

In neuroimaging research, differences in blood flow during a task are interpreted to show problems in the autistic group, regardless of the direction of difference from control data. If the autism group shows greater brain activity they are 'having to work harder to solve the task', but if they show reduced activation, they lack the expected neural specialisation of dedicated brain regions for the key computations! Researchers would do well to reflect on the normative perceptions they bring to their work and consider whether it is appropriate to take a more neutral stance when differences between autistic and non-autistic groups are uncovered. In both examples, of course, differences might truly be disadvantageous, even outside our laboratory settings. If so, it behoves the research team to demonstrate the process by which a disadvantage might arise from the original experimental difference. This has the additional benefit of identifying ways in which disadvantages could be eliminated, without automatically putting the onus on the autistic person to change.

11. Current debates

Summary

Autism is diagnosed on the basis of a pattern of behaviours, including essential criteria (social communication, restricted and repetitive behaviours) and additional common features (possible intellectual or language disability). These manifest in multiple ways, differing widely between individuals and also depending on their life stage and context. Reliance on behavioural markers presents challenges to interpreting changing prevalence estimates and to parsing heterogeneity within the autism constellation, and raises questions about recognition of autism in historically under-researched groups, such as women and the elderly.

Big questions

Investigating so-called core domains is the main focus of psychological research, but these may not present the biggest challenges for the autistic person. Psychologists focus on these, partly because of our beliefs about the causal pathways from a 'core' challenge to a 'surface' behaviour. Do these beliefs hold up under scrutiny, and are they data-driven? Is a focus on 'underlying' features (e.g. executive functions) preventing us from investigating questions that are priorities for the community (e.g. potty training, seizure management, how to get a good night's sleep)?

What is the role of diagnosis in the life of an autistic person? The experience of diagnosis can be positive for the individual and their family members – but why does it have this effect? Are positive experiences related to becoming part of a community, or simply increased self-knowledge? Are there cases where a diagnosis has a negative impact, and how should we respond to this?

Given the rise in self-identification by autistic people, will the clinical diagnosis of autism continue to be of value to the community in the future? After all, the diagnostic category of autism is ultimately no more than a social construct, used to try to describe a pattern of phenomena that may be very different when externally observed versus internally lived. If the diagnostic category were to disappear altogether, what would be the implications for research and service provision?

How can we understand heterogeneity within autism? Is autism a single thing, manifest differently depending on factors such as socialisation, environment, lived experience, and personal resilience? Or are there separate and different 'autisms'? How can we discover the answer while we are reliant on behavioural diagnosis?

How are our conceptualisations of autism shaped by cultural expectations? Is autism the same across cultures? What about in the technology-mediated social world – do autistic people behave in an identifiably 'autistic' manner online and in other digital communication contexts?

COMMUNITY CONTRIBUTION: KABIE BROOK – *AUTISTIC ACTIVIST, SPEAKER AND ADVOCATE*

The change to specify only one category for autism in the most recent revision of diagnostic criteria was widely welcomed by many autistic people. From the point of view of autistic activists, those fighting for autistic people's rights, we had always referred to autistic people in an inclusive way, fighting for the rights of all autistic people rather than just certain kinds of autistic people with the firm belief that we are all equal and that no-one should be left behind in the fight for equality.

Most autistic people recognise that the divisions were artificial, in practical terms of little use to us and quite often damaging. A person's diagnostic label often had little to do with who they were and could often become a source of disablement.

For example, my own son was diagnosed at a young age; he went to a mainstream school where he was described as 'unteachable'. Teachers said that they had 'taught him all that they could'; they made predictions that he would leave school with no qualifications, that we should feel grateful that he was good at sports but give up on him ever learning to read. I found out that he was sitting at the back of the class, mostly ignored and given colouring sheets to pass time. At this point, as parents, we decided to shift our priorities; we decided that learning to read and be happy were the most important goals for our son. We wanted him to get through education with as little damage to his mental health as possible. As autistic parents, we had a deep understanding of living life as a minority group within a mostly neurotypical world. We knew that learning can be lifelong, but damage done by others can also last a lifetime.

My son now is at university studying a degree that suits his interests and getting good marks. His journey involved finding teachers who believed in him and understood him, including an autistic teacher who understood how to teach him, how to harness his ability and accept that his way of learning and speed of learning may differ from a neurotypical child.

I have heard similar stories to this from many autistic people, people who struggled to master basic self-care skills but went on to be successful academics or hold important positions within their chosen field of work but were still seen as failing neurotypicals rather than as fully rounded successful autistic people. Grading people, ignoring spiky profiles (including variability day to day, week to week, etc.), predicting what the future holds for people is extremely unreliable. Myself, my family and friends' trajectories as well as those of autistic people in general aren't based on 'off the peg' stereotypes; we often don't turn out as non-autistic people expect. Yet there seems to be an increasing drive, a need almost, to the extent of being obsessional to classify us, put us into neat categories, to view us in a similar way as bugs under a microscope and all of this is measured by the overwhelmingly neurotypical practitioner who will never fully understand what it is to be autistic but still wields so much power over our community: the autistic community.

As autistic people when we talk to the non-autistic practitioner it often feels as though we need an interpreter. We are easily misunderstood by people who do not share our disposition. Watching clinicians talking to my autistic children is always interesting and frustrating; what's said, what's meant and what meaning is attached by the listener is often very different. Even so, it is always the autistic person who is said to have the deficit, when of course in reality all communication is an active two-way process requiring shared understanding to guarantee success (see Damian Milton's *Double Empathy Problem*, mentioned in Chapter 9, for more on this). Likewise with sociality: we need the others to be social, therefore deficits in social communication are subjective with the majority being labelled correct and the minority deviant: wrong, broken. 'Deficits' in social communication are lessened when we are more alike to those we mix with. Many autistic people have said that they gain great benefit from meeting up with other autistic people. Indeed, Autscape, a retreat style conference run by and for autistic people (www.autscape.org) has been life changing for many, myself included. Being in autistic space, immersion in autistic community and culture is nurturing, self-affirming and a reminder of our unbrokenness rather than the day-to-day struggle that most experience in an almost alien non-autistic society.

The autistic population is a very varied one – just as the non-autistic population is. It often feels though that this is somehow forgotten by clinicians. Our individuality, our personalities don't fit textbook definitions which lean heavily to very one-dimensional white males. This expectation of almost 'blandness' and 'very male' works against autistic people: women, transpeople, non-binary people, people of colour or from low-income backgrounds, even white quiet males are missed or passed over. I have heard more than once from autistic women about their fight to even get a GP referral for diagnosis because of the belief that autism is a male 'condition'. For me the current diagnostic problem needs to be solved for all autistic people and the conversations don't seem to be going there – yet.

It feels as though where we are now is merely a 'tinkering' when what we need is a revolution. Clinicians rarely truly understand autistic people; they don't see us as friends, as a community, as equals. The deficit model often leads to a lack of access to services – for example health and education because the 'problem' is always seen to be centred within the autistic person. This needs to be looked at differently, clearly seeing that autistic people, even if we are a minority group, we are full citizens and society should no longer accept our exclusion.

Recommended reading

Baird, G., Douglas, H. R., & Murphy, M. S. (2011). Recognising and diagnosing autism in children and young people: Summary of NICE guidance. *British Medical Journal, 343*(d6360), 10–1136.

Howlin, P., & Magiati, I. (2017). Autism spectrum disorder: Outcomes in adulthood. *Current Opinion in Psychiatry, 30*(2), 69–76.

James, L. (2017). *Odd girl out: An autistic woman in a neurotypical world.* London: Pan Macmillan.

Lawson, W. B. (2015). *Older adults and autism spectrum conditions: An introduction and guide.* London, UK: Jessica Kingsley Publishers.

Smith, P. A., Wadsworth, A. M., McMahon, W., Cottle, K., Farley, M., Coon, H., Gregg, C., Bakian, A., Grandin, T., Endow, J., & Baron, M. (2016). *Autism spectrum disorder in mid and later life.* London, UK: Jessica Kingsley Publishers.

Tammet, D. (2007). *Born on a blue day: Inside the extraordinary mind of an autistic savant.* New York, NY: Simon & Schuster.

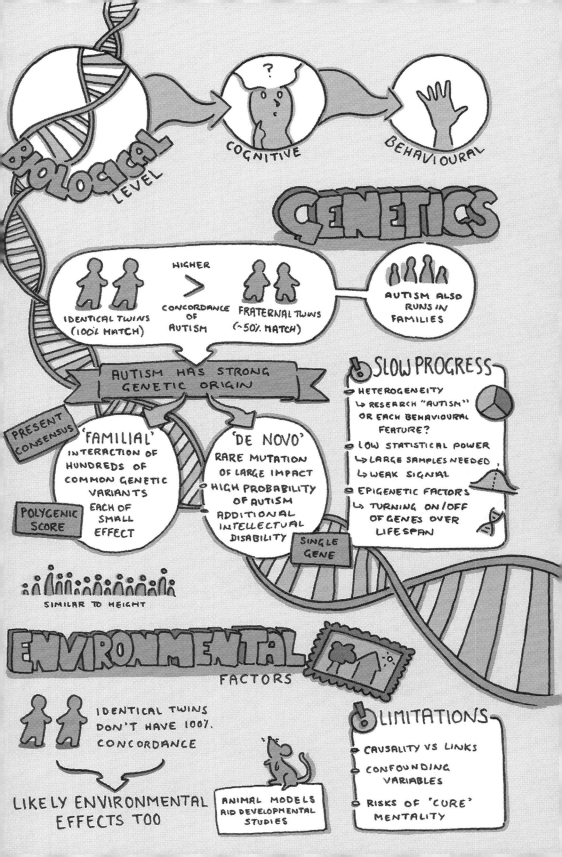

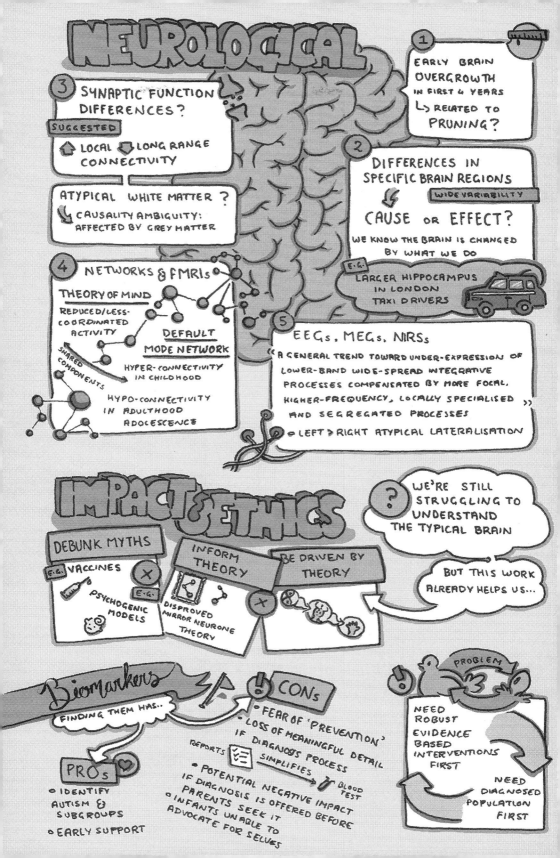

4 Autism at the biological level

WHEN THE ORIGINAL version of this book was written, it was still necessary to say that autism is not caused by psychogenic factors and to directly refute the 'refrigerator mother' myth by giving evidence (then still limited) of the biological basis of autism – e.g. high rates of epilepsy. Thankfully, this no longer needs to be argued for. There is now good awareness, in most places, that autism is a strongly genetic condition arising from a complex interaction of genetic and environmental factors. Nonetheless, huge efforts have gone into finding the genetic and neural bases of autism, with what some might consider a disappointing lack of major breakthroughs. Research *has* identified plenty of biological features that differ between people with and without autism, and also features that vary dimensionally with a specific behaviour. But at the time of writing there are no biological features that provide a distinctive marker, or specific cause, of autism (Muhle et al., 2018).

Heterogeneity of etiology may be one reason why progress has been slow; many people now talk of 'the autisms' to reflect the belief that different individuals have different biological paths to autism. The research funds spent on finding the etiology of autism are also a matter of controversy and debate, with many stakeholders concerned that biological research is focused on finding a 'cure' and arguing for greater funding towards more immediately improving the lives of people on the spectrum. We recognise the strength of feeling among the community and reject the notion that autism might be something to be cured. But it is wrong to suppose that biological research, even that focused on 'causes', cannot align with community priorities. Through a better understanding of biology, we can develop meaningful opportunities for intervention for difficulties that commonly co-occur with autism and that autistic individuals might choose to address. An example might be developing drugs to modulate how the brain responds to sensory input, to allow an individual to choose to dampen down sensory experiences which they find overwhelming. We will return to these debates at the end of this chapter, after briefly reviewing the current state of understanding of the genetics and neural bases of autism, and how cognitive theory can inform studies of the biology of autism.

1. The contribution of genetics

The first evidence that autism had a strong genetic origin came from seminal twin studies that showed that identical twins, who share 100% of their genes, showed a much higher concordance (i.e. probability that, if one has autism, the other twin will too) than fraternal twins, who share on average 50% of their genetic material (Bailey et al., 1995; Folstein & Rutter, 1977). This finding, and the resulting high heritability estimates, have been replicated many times in subsequent and much larger studies (Tick et al., 2016). Autism also runs in families, with an increased likelihood of autism occurring in the younger brother or sister of an autistic child.

The field of genetics moves very fast, and specific information about candidate genes would soon date and be unhelpful here. However, it is important to note that the present consensus is that in the majority of cases autism is the result of the action of hundreds of common genetic variants, each of very small effect. In this respect, autism would not be different from other quantitatively distributed traits, such as height. Research is therefore moving away from looking for 'autism genes' and towards constructing 'polygenic scores', where an individual can be given a score according to how many of the autism-associated genetic variants they have. Such a score would, once we have data from sufficiently large autistic and non-autistic samples, give a probabilistic (not deterministic) estimate of the likelihood someone will show autistic traits or meet diagnostic criteria for autism.

By contrast, for a minority of those with autism – usually those who have additional intellectual disability – a rare genetic mutation can be found that is believed to cause their autism, because most or all people with that mutation are autistic. Discovering such rare mutations of large effect can be hard; the causal role of a mutation never seen before is difficult to establish since we all carry many unique mutations. It may also be that even these 'big hits' from rare mutations depend for their ultimate effect on the genetic background of the individual; the other common genetic variants they inherit may intensify or ameliorate their developmental outcome.

Thus, autism is due to a mixture of common inherited genetic variation across many genes each of small effect and rare mutations of large impact. The former would be considered 'familial' and the latter 'de novo' in most cases. How can genetic research on autism move forward given this huge heterogeneity? One approach is to try to map the many different implicated genes onto a smaller number of biologically relevant pathways (Geschwind, 2008). If indeed there is convergence on particular pathways of importance, this approach may give clues to the development of therapeutics that could target particular commonly co-existing symptoms, e.g. anxiety.

Why hasn't more progress been made towards understanding the genetic causes of autism? There are several major challenges, including heterogeneity within the constellation; the 'fractionated triad' idea would suggest, for example, that searching for genes affecting one dimension of autism, such as an individual's social interaction profile, will be more productive than searching for genes predisposing to autism as a whole. Less contentious reasons for slow progress include low statistical power. Compared to many other clinical groups, studies of autism genetics are at an early stage, with relatively small sample sizes. Hundreds of thousands of DNA samples may be needed, especially if each genetic variant has a tiny effect and hence a weak signal. In addition, genes may interact with one another and be turned on or off by genetic or environmental factors throughout development. Research into epigenetic factors that moderate the action of genes is at an early stage, partly because, unlike our DNA – which is the same in every cell of our bodies – epigenetic signatures will differ in different tissues and over the lifespan. Getting DNA samples from saliva or even blood is relatively easy compared to getting brain tissue for epigenetic analysis!

The ultimate aim of all this work is to find biomarkers that would aid in so-called personalised or 'precision medicine' instead of a one-size-fits-all approach, understanding the different possible biological bases of autism should in principle lead to better individualised therapies (Geschwind & Staite, 2015). One example might be a drug to improve synaptic function, ultimately giving a person with a learning disability more capacity to learn new information. Of course, it will be vital that this work is informed by stakeholder views, helping to identify drug targets that are acceptable and important to the autism community, and avoid mere 'normalisation' as an end in itself. One risk is that some biomedical researchers may feel that their work, being relatively far-removed from the everyday experience of autistic people and their allies, doesn't require significant stakeholder input. However, we might also note that basic biomedical research takes many years – sometimes decades – to deliver results with a practical application. In which case, there is a particularly pressing reason to work with stakeholders from the very outset. Basic scientists must stay abreast of the latest thinking about autism to avoid their hard work and scientific innovations producing a treatment that nobody wants.

2. Candidate neurological underpinnings

Just like the search for the genetic basis of autism, the hunt for what might be different in the brains of people in the autism constellation has attracted huge interest but, perhaps, not progressed as far as some might have hoped. Once again, this is probably due, in part, to the biological heterogeneity that has led some authors to talk about 'the autisms' rather than 'autism'. The 'fractionated triad' notion may again relevant; Figure 4.1 shows how different brain regions may relate to different diagnostic features of autism. For example, one of the better replicated neurobiological findings in autism is early brain over-growth in the first four years of life (Zwaigenbaum et al., 2014). However, only a minority of autistic children show this pattern of accelerated early growth of head circumference (Ecker, 2017). There are also important contextual factors to consider: are head circumference norms up to date, applicable to different regions or populations and is overall growth and body size taken into account? Nevertheless, this finding has been interpreted as important and researchers have speculated that perhaps the normal pruning of the brain (by programmed cell death: apoptosis) and the 'use it or lose it' principle of synaptic competition are disrupted in toddlers with autism.

FIGURE 4.1   Brain regions in relation to diagnostic features of autism

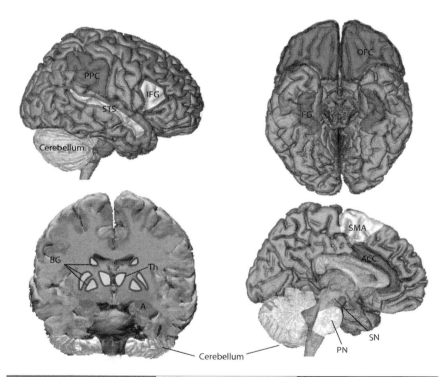

Social Impairment	Communication Deficits	Repetitive Behaviors
OFC - Orbitofrontal Cortex	IFG - Inferior Frontal gyrus (Broca's Area)	OFC - Orbitofrontal Cortex
ACC - Anterior Cingulate Cortex	STS - Superior Temporal Sulcus	ACC - Anterior Cingulate Cortex
FG - Fusiform Gyrus	SMA - Supplementar Motor Area	BG - Basal Ganglia
STS - Superior Temporal Sulcus	BG - Basal Ganglia	Th - Thalamus
A - Amygdala	SN - Substantia Nigra	
Mirror Neuron Regions	Th - Thalamus	
IFG - Inferior Frontal gyrus	PN - Pontine Nuclei	
PPC - Posterior Parietal Cortex	Cerebellum	

Reproduced from Amaral et al., 2008, with kind permission of the author

As well as possible differences in total brain volume, differences in specific brain regions have been reported, and researchers have attempted to link these to the behavioural features of autism (Ecker et al., 2015). The most frequently implicated regions include frontotemporal and frontoparietal regions, the amygdala – hippocampal complex, cerebellum, basal ganglia and anterior and posterior cingulate. However, while structural neuroimaging studies may show group differences between those with autism and without, there is wide variability within groups too, and there are no findings to date that reliably mark autism as different at the individual level. Individual differences in brain and behaviour, as well as what we know of the functions of different brain regions, have led researchers to link specific regions to autism features. For example, the frontotemporal regions and amygdala have been linked to socio-emotional processing, and the frontostriatal system (orbitofrontal cortex and caudate nucleus) have been implicated in repetitive/stereotyped behaviours. Whether these differences are a cause or an effect of autism is open to question; the amygdala is also enlarged in non-autistic children with anxiety disorders, for example. We know the brain is changed by what we do and learn, as in the well-known finding of larger hippocampal volume in London taxi drivers (Maguire et al., 2000). Therefore, it is likely that brain differences reflect, at least in part, differences in the lives (more stressful) and behaviours (more repeated) of autistic people.

Beyond measuring the size of different brain regions, differences in structural and functional connectivity have been reported. At the micro level, many researchers think that autism will prove to be defined by differences in synaptic functioning, maybe having to do with a modification of neural excitation and inhibition in which the neurochemicals GABA (gamma-Aminobutyric acid) and glutamate are key. At a macro level, it has been suggested that local connectivity is increased and long-range connectivity decreased in autism (Ameis & Catani, 2015). Diffusion Tensor Imaging (DTI) allows visualisation of the integrity of white matter, including the major neural highway connecting the right and left hemispheres, the corpus callosum. Abnormalities in white matter have been reported, but since development of white matter is inherently affected by grey matter development, it is unclear if these are primary or secondary in autism. Ideally, information from structural and functional neuroimaging would be combined with histological studies of post mortem tissue, but to date, there are still relatively few donations in international brain banks.

When the previous version of this book was written, it mentioned the promise of functional neuroimaging studies, which had just begun with PET (positron emission tomography). The far less invasive technique of magnetic resonance imaging (MRI) was yet to be applied to autism. Since that time, there has been an explosion of functional imaging research using fMRI. Among other things, this has identified a network of brain regions reliably activated during Theory of Mind (ToM) tasks in neurotypical volunteers, including medial prefrontal cortex, posterior superior temporal sulcus/temporoparietal junction, praecuneus and temporal poles. Studies with autistic volunteers engaging with the same ToM tasks, typically show reduced and/or less coordinated activation across this 'mentalising network'. Interestingly, this network overlaps with the so-called default mode network: the functionally interconnected set of brain regions (posterior cingulate cortex, praecuneus, medial prefrontal cortex, temporoparietal junction and hippocampus) that are *less* active when volunteers engage in any task and most active when volunteers are 'at rest'. Differences in the intrinsic functional connectivity of the default mode network have been reported in autism, with the suggestion of a developmental shift from hyperconnectivity between default mode network nodes in childhood to hypoconnectivity in adolescence and adulthood (Padmanabhan et al., 2017).

Other forms of neuroimaging are also being used to explore brain function in autism, including electroencephalography (EEG), magnetoencephalography (MEG) and near infrared spectroscopy (NIRS). A recent systematic review of autism research using EEG and MEG (O'Reilly et al., 2017) found "*a general trend toward an under-expression of lower-band wide-spread integrative processes compensated by more focal, higher-frequency, locally specialized, and segregated processes*" as well as fairly consistent reports of atypical lateralisation (increased left>right functional connectivity ratio). Beyond imaging the active brain, techniques such as transcranial magnetic stimulation (TMS) and transcranial direct current stimulation (tDCS) can be used to modulate the functioning of specific brain regions. These methods are being used to interrogate brain functions and test cognitive theories in neurotypical volunteers. Experimental therapeutic uses are also being explored in a range of clinical groups, including autism, although too few properly controlled trials exist to draw conclusions at this time.

3. Other biological influences

Although the genetic contribution to autism is large, even identical twins don't show 100% concordance, and gene-environment interactions may be hidden in traditional estimates of heritability. Are there environmental factors that contribute to the etiology of autism? Almost certainly. Although to date the evidence regarding aspects of our environment to which we are widely exposed (e.g. pollution, everyday chemicals or foodstuffs) is weak. There are rare exposures that can be directly linked to increased rates of autism; for example, the anti-epilepsy drug valproate appears to be linked to autism if taken during pregnancy (Christensen et al., 2013).

A review of meta-analyses and systematic reviews, at the time of writing, found no link between autism and vaccination, thiomersal exposure, maternal smoking or assisted reproduction (Modabbernia et al., 2017). Birth complications associated with reduced blood supply/oxygen or trauma to the infant showed strong links to autism, while other aspects of pregnancy, such as birth by caesarean and maternal obesity or diabetes showed weaker connections, with evidence insufficient to date on the role of nutrition. Evidence of a link between autism and older paternal age is strong, and may be due to genetic changes in sperm produced later in life. Modabbernia and colleagues consider a range of mechanisms for the highlighted environmental factors including "*non-causative association (including confounding), gene-related effect, oxidative stress, inflammation, hypoxia/ischemia, endocrine disruption, neurotransmitter alterations, and interference with signalling pathways*". They also highlight the limitations in research in this area and the need for "*prospective design, precise exposure measurement, reliable timing of exposure in relation to critical developmental periods and . . . genetically informed designs*".

Of course, discovering the effects of possible environmental factors is difficult because we can't easily or ethically run RCTs of exposures. For this reason, animal models are important; for example, scientists can control the age of mouse fathers to check that paternal age effects in humans are not just a reflection of autistic traits, making finding a partner and having children happen a bit later in life. Mouse models are used to study the effects of genetic perturbations, as well; 'knock-out' animal models help to uncover what key genes do and what the effects are of specific mutations. Journalists are fond of headlines saying, "Scientists Create Autistic Mouse", but, of course, these are wildly misleading! Animal models are probably most useful in tracing the mechanistic effect of identified genetic changes, through proteins formed and their functions in an organism. Looking for 'autistic behaviour' in an animal is far less likely to be productive; even if repetitive grooming or burrowing can be seen in a mouse, how do we know that has anything in common with repetitive behaviours in autism? One of the reasons some scientists are keen to see a connection is because such animal analogues provide the possibility of trialling interventions, either genetic or pharmacological. For example, studies with mouse models of Rett syndrome, a degenerative disorder caused by mutations in the X-linked gene MECP2, have shown the ability to effect remarkable reversal of impairments closely aligned to the clinical symptoms in humans (e.g. motor and breathing problems), even in mature animals (e.g. Tillotson et al., 2017). However, the idea of treating or preventing autism – as opposed to alleviating the disadvantageous things that often accompany autism, such as intellectual disability, language impairment, epilepsy, anxiety – is not only ethically controversial but deeply problematic.

4. Cross-pollination between neurobiological and cognitive explanations

We still have no clear neurological or broader biological explanatory model of autism, neither to explain onset nor to predict progression across the lifespan. In fact, we are still struggling to understand the typical brain. So how can the neurobiological data we have impact our understanding of autism?

First, they can be used to debunk myths about the causes of autism. Twin studies in the 70's put an end to the, then-dominant, psychogenic models of autism that placed responsibility for autism on parent behaviour. Findings of brain changes that date to the first trimester of pregnancy suggest that later environmental exposures cannot be sole causes of autism.

Second, they can be used to identify treatments with potential to impact epilepsy and possibly intellectual disability. If biomarkers for these could be found, early or even preventative treatment might be possible.

Third, they can potentially inform our psychological theories, since some psychological theories make specific biological predictions. One example is the 'broken mirror' theory of autism, which locates the origin of social and communication difficulties in a faulty 'mirror neuron system' (Williams et al., 2001). Mirror neurons, first discovered in monkeys, are neurons that fire when the animal performs or sees a specific action performed. The broken mirror hypothesis proposed that a 'faulty' mirror neuron system in autism impedes imitation and social cognition. This psychological theory, therefore, makes predictions testable through neuroimaging, as well as through psychological experiments (e.g. reduced interference of observed movements on own movements). However, robust evidence that autistic and neurotypical groups differ in the functioning of the mirror neuron system has not, ultimately, been forthcoming (Hamilton, 2013).

It is also worth highlighting that the link between psychological and biological research is a two-way street: our cognitive theories can also help direct research into the biology of autism. Perhaps the most obvious example is the use of theory and well-designed cognitive tasks in functional neuroimaging (Philip et al., 2012). Psychological theory can also aid in genetic studies, for example helping us rethink who is 'affected' in a family pedigree. Based on the hypothesis that unusual eye for detail may underlie specific talents in autism, overlapping genetic influences were found on parent-reported autistic traits and special skills (in music, maths, art or memory) in 8-year-old twins in the Twins Early Development Study (Vital et al., 2009). If you wanted to explore genetic influences in a family with an autistic child, you might therefore want to note who has talents, as well as who has autism (or both).

Fourthly, animal models need to be informed by psychological theories of the behaviours concerned. For example, if you are interested in whether knocking out a specific gene might contribute to face recognition deficits seen in autism, you need to think about your theory for face processing differences. If your theory is that people with autism do not become face experts, due to looking less at eyes and faces, you might want to test identity recognition in your knock-out mouse; this is best done through olfactory recognition tests, since mice use smell more than sight to identify other mice. However, if your theory is that face processing is different in autism because of detail-focused cognitive style, you wouldn't test your mouse's olfactory skills – you can't separate global and local processing in smell – instead you'd use a visual task where responding to either parts or wholes was rewarded.

5. The quest for biomarkers

One specific manifestation of the application of neuroscience methods to understanding autism is in the quest for early biological markers (Loth et al., 2016). Such biomarkers might be used to identify autism pre-natally or in infancy, or to identify sub-types of autism (one of "the autisms" perhaps). This normally involves recruitment of a sample who are more likely than the general population to get an autism diagnosis and tracking them pre- and post-natally. One such group is the infant siblings of autistic children. We will review the findings and (methodological, statistical) challenges of this technique in Chapter 7, but here we want to draw attention to some conceptual issues for the field.

First, the pursuit of biomarkers raises a series of ethical issues. Most pressing is the question of how to apply the new knowledge, if a pre-natal marker is identified. Autistic activists have noted the accepted practice in some countries of early termination of pregnancy in the event that a chromosomal disorder is identified in the foetus – as often happens in the case of Down syndrome. Autistic people and their allies are understandably deeply concerned that the same practice could become available, even usual, if a pre-natal marker for autism were detected. It is hard for neurotypical people to imagine how distressing it must be to think parents in the future could be offered the option to terminate a pregnancy if their unborn child had the same condition as you. Researchers and clinicians have pointed out that there is scientific value in identifying very early, including pre-natal, markers of autism and that this research quest should not be construed as a 'prevention of autism' agenda. However, it is understandable that the community remain concerned. We should all remain cognisant of these issues and be vigilant in ensuring that new discoveries result in understanding and practical applications that support and enable the autistic community.

Additional ethical issues are raised by the methodology commonly used to probe for early signs of autism: namely, the recruitment of infants in high-likelihood groups, and the collection of detailed data from them and their families over sometimes very long periods of time. Sue recently conducted research into the attitudes of the autism community to this work (Fletcher-Watson et al., 2017a, 2017b). The international survey uncovered overwhelming support for the endeavour in general, and an impressive level of endorsement of scientific priorities (e.g. earlier diagnosis) but also some important details. For example, phrases like "higher chance" or "higher likelihood" were endorsed above the term "at risk", which is commonly used to describe infant siblings recruited for studies. Parents specifically valued transparency from the research team and wanted to be fully informed about their child's scores at each data collection point – something that is rarely permitted by ethical review panels. The results highlight the value of asking people about their attitudes and experiences, and, as far as possible, aligning research protocols and study communications with community values.

A key focus for the pursuit of early biomarkers for autism, agreed upon by researchers and many in the autism community, is earlier diagnosis. This leads to our second issue for the field: can we uncritically accept earlier diagnosis as an important target? On the one hand, families are keen to reduce waiting times from first concerns to confirmed diagnosis. If a biomarker were identified it could streamline the process and produce economic savings if fewer professionals were involved, compared with the multi-disciplinary assessment that is currently considered best practice. However, replacing the current system with a single blood test or brain scan would take away the rich and complex appraisal of strengths and needs that is a key feature of the diagnostic pathway. Diagnosis should be more than just a label, ideally, it's about families working with an expert team to understand the individual and make a plan for their future support needs. So even if a biomarker were identified, we would still want to accompany this with a series of assessments and many aspects of today's, slow, laborious, but thorough, diagnostic pathway should be retained.

What about earlier diagnosis in the sense of "earlier in the child's life", as opposed to "more rapidly after concerns are raised"? Would this be a positive outcome for autistic people and their allies? Again, this might be a mixed blessing at best. One worry is that diagnosis that precedes parents raising their own concerns could have a negative impact on the family, compared with a diagnosis that offers an explanation for a difference that has already been noticed. While we're not aware of research directly addressing this question, it easy to imagine that a diagnosis that provides a helpful explanation of something which is already apparent to the family would be received more positively than a label applied out of the blue.

But wouldn't earlier diagnosis allow earlier intervention? And that would be beneficial for families? Indeed, support during periods of developmental plasticity in infancy and toddlerhood could target the fundamental skills that psychological theory and research say underpin later language, cognitive, social and learning outcomes. This is true, but we should also note that there are no robust evidence-based interventions for very early life. As it stands, parents might receive a diagnosis in infancy but then be left without suitable support for months or years. Although work is being done to develop options for use in infancy (Green et al., 2015, 2017; Rogers et al., 2014), we know from other areas of the autism literature how gradual progress is when creating new interventions and especially translating these into practice (Dingfelder & Mandell, 2011). Huge swathes of the autistic population still do not receive any specialist support even at older ages (Salomone et al., 2016) and non-conventional approaches without supporting evidence are rife (Salomone et al., 2015).

This is a chicken-and-egg problem to some degree: we can't develop the interventions until we have a diagnosed population, and we ought not to diagnose the population until we have the interventions. Furthermore, in any intervention we have a responsibility to look for possible harms, and to seek the involvement and endorsement of the autism community. This is especially challenging and important when intervening in infancy: participants cannot advocate for themselves and the long-term effects of modifying the early environment are not known, and could be profound. Autistic advocates have raised serious concerns about some practices, for example, which they point out systematically train autistic children to comply with adult instructions, and extinguish behaviours (such as hand-flapping) which are part of the child's self-expression and self-calming repertoire (Bascom, 2012). We ought not to recommend interventions for infancy without a deep understanding of the long-term and interactional effects of the change – and this will take many years to describe accurately.

6. Current debates

Summary

Large sums of research funding are currently spent on trying to understand the biological and neurological profiles associated with autism, whereas there has been a relative paucity of funding for studies into service, intervention and societal issues (Pellicano et al., 2013). It would be good to see an equal investment in autism research likely to have a direct and positive impact on people alive today.

While plenty of group differences and trait relationships have been found, there are currently no clear biological markers, nor powerful bio-based explanatory models of autism. The pursuit of a biological explanation can add value, not least by de-bunking some dangerous myths about autism, and may contribute to treatments for things like epilepsy. They may also be important in understanding variability within the autism constellation, or help us make sense of differences between 'the autisms'. However, to make the most of this scientific endeavour, neurobiological studies need to be informed by psychological theory (and, eventually, vice versa). Moreover, it is essential that these discoveries are embedded in a strong ethical framework ensuring that any findings are put to positive use.

Big questions

In pursuit of a model of the many autisms, which are the promising routes to take: genetic? neurological? psychological? behavioural? Which methodologies are more likely to arrive at a place where we can meaningfully and usefully identify sub-groups?

If a biomarker for autism was found, but was (as is likely) not 100% reliable – how would we handle mismatch between people who have the biomarker, and people who show high levels of autistic traits but don't have the biomarker? Would people with real needs be denied help because they don't meet this new biological criterion for autism?

Biology in itself doesn't tell us how to make the world more autism-enabling, or what tack a teacher should take. Taking the example of Down syndrome, knowing the genetic cause hasn't yet resulted in bespoke supports to optimise individuals' development. Similarly, knowing the brain differences in the case of rare conditions such as agenesis (failure to form) of the corpus callosum doesn't in itself tell a teacher how to teach to a child's strengths.

How can we test and develop the translational endeavour? There is a requirement for better communication between scientific disciplines, and experts who combine a deep understanding of both molecular biology, clinical medicine and beyond.

COMMUNITY CONTRIBUTION: ANYA UTASZEWSKI – *AUTISTIC, COMPOSER AND DATABASE ADMIN*

In 2008, a local charity forwarded a letter from Brighton and Sussex Medical Schools, inviting people with a diagnosis of Asperger's to take part in a study looking at why some people showed differences in social behaviour. I was curious to find out more and to have the experience of being a participant in a study whose topic interested me, and that I hoped would also be a learning opportunity.

I strongly oppose a coercive 'cure' for autism and am deeply perturbed by the idea that one day a pre-natal test for autism could exist. My first email to one of the researchers was to enquire as to whether their research would in any way be used to contribute to these. I was assured that this would not be the case and that the researcher himself was supportive of autism rights.

Having completed some psychological questionnaires, I was ready for the MRI scan. A friendly assistant gave me a gown to change into and reminded me to remove anything of metal from my person. I lay down on the flat 'bed' that would slide me into the scanner and was given four buttons to press with my dominant hand, correlating to available answers to questions I would be asked once in position.

The 'bed' moved into the MRI 'tunnel'. To begin with, I was to lie still and then shortly afterwards, look up towards a mirror on which was reflected a screen displaying images accompanied by multiple choice questions.

The only thing I had known about having an MRI was that it was a very noisy process. I was quite anxious about this as I've always had very sensitive hearing. Once the scanner started making its noises, I was pleasantly surprised. The rhythmic repetition, the deep bass pitch and textural density, accompanied by occasional gentle juddering sensations, were beautiful. Then suddenly the sounds changed to something reminiscent of a '60s science fiction weapon, or firing a spaceship's guns on an old DOS game! I felt sonically immersed; this was 'surround sound' in the most literal sense I could imagine.

After over an hour in the scanner, the researchers had the data they needed and the process was complete. I asked if I could have a picture of my brain (shown in Figure 4.2) and if I could be emailed a copy of the study's find-ings once they were ready. Both requests were kindly granted.

Since this experience, I have taken part in many other studies, two of which involved MRI scans. I continue to enjoy both the scans and the opportu-nity to learn from these opportunities and hope that I might, in some small way, be contributing to helping others.

FIGURE 4.2   Images of Anya's brain from the MRI this writing describes

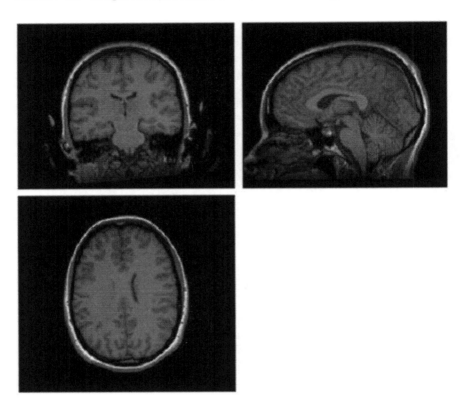

Recommended reading

Ecker, C. (2017). The neuroanatomy of autism spectrum disorder: An overview of structural neuroimaging findings and their translatability to the clinical setting. *Autism, 21*(1), 18–28.

Geschwind, D. H. (2015). Gene hunting in autism spectrum disorder: On the path to precision medicine. *The Lancet Neurology, 14*(11), 1109–1120.

Pellicano, L., Dinsmore, A., & Charman, T. (2013). *A future made together: Shaping autism research in the UK*. London: Centre for Research in Autism and Education, University College London.

Vorstman, J. A., Parr, J. R., Moreno-De-Luca, D., Anney, R. J., Nurnberger Jr, J. I., & Hallmayer, J. F. (2017). Autism genetics: Opportunities and challenges for clinical translation. *Nature Reviews Genetics, 18*(6), 362.

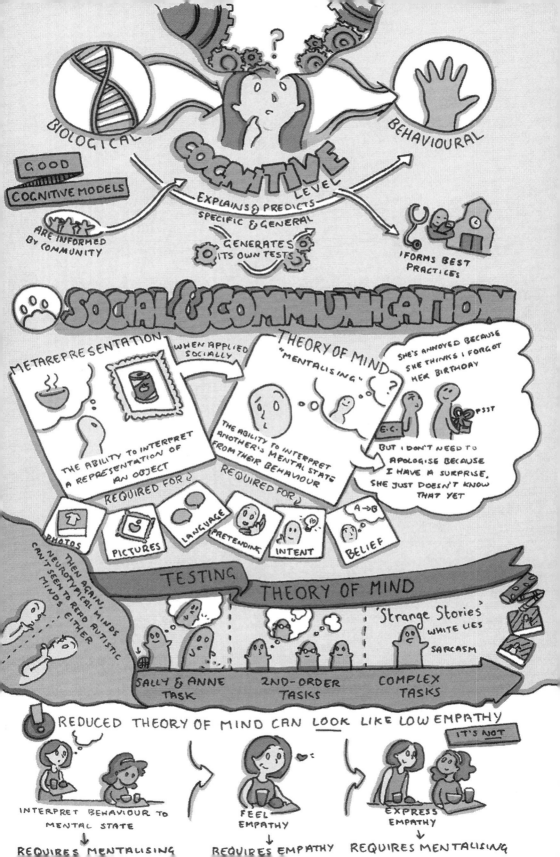

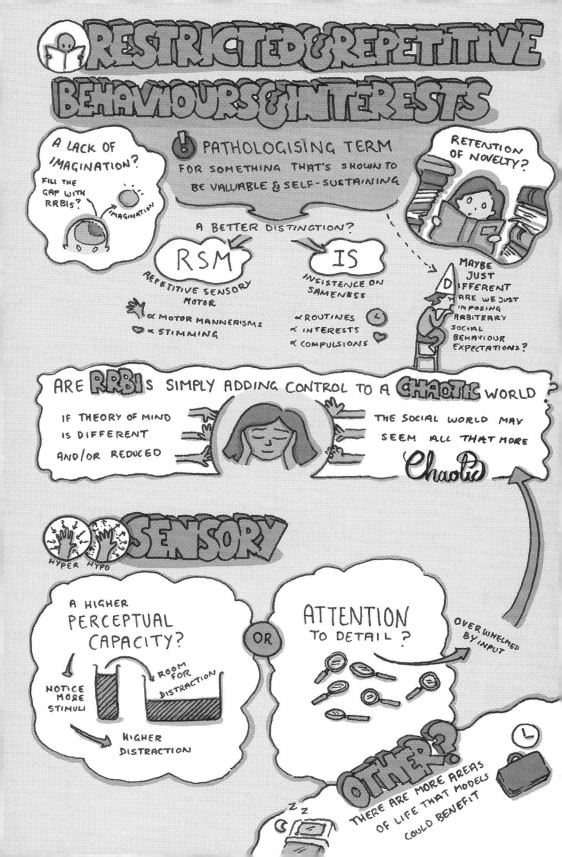

5 Autism at the cognitive level
What makes a good theory?

A T THE START of this book, we framed our approach in terms of different levels of explanation. We have so far attempted to give a fairly concise, descriptive account of the behavioural and biological features of autism as currently conceived. However, the bulk of the book focuses on the intermediate level – the cognitive level. Cognitive theories are the explanatory models that attempt to link biological heterogeneity with behavioural heterogeneity via cognitive simplicity (if only!). Given the vast complexity and variability in the autism constellation at both biological and behavioural levels, the cognitive level may be our best bet for encapsulating autism in a meaningful and concise manner. For example, differences in social interaction can manifest very differently depending on age, presence of intellectual disability (or not), environment, personality, gender and so on. And yet we may attempt to explain all these multiple presentations via shared cognitive roots.

Here we will consider three, key, observable domains of autism, exploring how these have been represented at a cognitive level, in order to introduce key terms, methods and concepts. Later chapters will interrogate the evidence for and against different theories, but here we focus merely on defining and describing the cognitive level of explanation. We will also provide an overview of the potential value of cognitive models and a framework for critical appraisal of psychological theory. Note that we use 'cognitive' and 'psychological' virtually interchangeably – cognitive here encompasses the processing of emotional information as well as learning processes and skills such as executive functions, memory and language.

1. Understanding social interaction and communication at the cognitive level

Social interaction and communication challenges are often characterised at the cognitive level as manifestations of a difficulty with 'mentalising' or 'Theory of Mind' (ToM). These terms both describe the everyday ability to recognise, represent and interpret the mental states (e.g. beliefs and intentions) of others. The published literature gives strong primacy to this domain, as a focus of both experimental research and as a support target. Despite the well-recognised complexity and multi-factorial consequences of autism, frequently, it is viewed in terms of social differences. As a result, a significant majority of experimental and qualitative research, and of autism-specific supports, focus on the social domain.

Mental states encompass a wide range of beliefs, thoughts and feelings which we have taxonomised as shown in Figure 5.1. The category of mental state cognitively underpinned by ToM is the *propositional attitude* – examples include believing, intending and pretending. These are important in psychological accounts, because keeping track of other people's propositional attitudes requires meta-representations: representations of representations. Meta-representations allow us to form a mental picture of the world not just as it is, but as it might be in the mind of another person (more on these in Chapter 6). However, there are other types of inner state which are important for social interaction, but don't require meta-representation. *Emotional states* include happiness, sadness or anger, and also more complex feelings like jealousy, embarrassment and tenderness. Recognising emotional states does not require ToM – but thinking about *why* someone seems angry might require inferences about their beliefs. Seeing that someone is angry, doesn't require meta-representation, but working out that "she is angry that I forgot her birthday" and also "I don't need to apologise because actually I have a surprise party planned, but she doesn't know that", does need ToM. Hard-to-interpret

FIGURE 5.1 A taxonomy of mental states

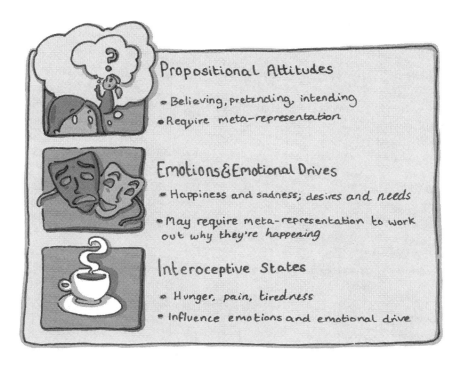

Propositional Attitudes

• Believing, pretending, intending
• Require meta-representation

Emotions & Emotional Drives

• Happiness and sadness; desires and needs
• May require meta-representation to work out why they're happening

Interoceptive States

• Hunger, pain, tiredness
• Influence emotions and emotional drive

emotional cues like conflicting facial expression and speech (e.g. "I really detest this cake" while raising one eyebrow, smiling and reaching for another slice), or ambiguous emotional signals might be elucidated using meta-representational information about what the person thinks or believes.

Underneath emotional states we find *emotional drives*, which can be further sub-divided into simple (e.g. wanting a coffee) and complex (e.g. wanting that the next café serves a good espresso). Again, interpreting others' emotional drives might involve meta-representation (e.g. "she is walking that way because she thinks there is a coffee shop there, but I know that there isn't"). *Emotional drives* overlap with *emotional states* but are more closely tethered to specific behaviours. They, in turn, are often founded on the most basic type of internal state – an *interoceptive state*, or physical sensation, such as hunger, pain or tiredness. It is important to remember that the psychological term 'ToM' in its original sense refers only to those mental states that require meta-representation. As we can see, this involves only one category of inner state, though in the real world understanding propositional attitudes interfaces with our interpretation of a much wider range of behaviours and feelings.

Chapter 6 includes a more detailed examination of how difficulties understanding mental states may explain a range of social communication differences in autism. In brief, one possibility is that difficulty spontaneously constructing or holding meta-representations in mind prevents autistic people from readily understanding other people's beliefs and intentions. We will see how this might in turn interfere with a range of social interactive skills – pretending during play, understanding referential aspects of language (e.g. the difference between "my cup" and "your cup") or telling a story.

2. Measuring social cognition

A range of tasks has been used to measure mentalising in the psychological literature, most of them requiring the participant to track someone's mistaken or false belief (Wellman et al., 2001). This has been considered the litmus test for mentalising because it requires attribution of a belief that is different from the participant's own belief (and reality). The classic 'false-belief' test is the Sally-Anne task, illustrated in Figure 5.2. In this task, the experimenter tells a story using two puppets, Sally and Anne. Anne moves Sally's ball while Sally is absent from the scene. The participant must identify where Sally will look for her ball when she returns – the correct answer is that she looks in the place where she left the ball: Sally has a false belief that it is still in the basket, even though (as the participant knows) it is actually in the box.

A wide range of other tasks have been used to test mentalising. These include false-contents tasks, like the Smarties Task, where a child finds out that a tube of sweets actually contains crayons, but must correctly predict that someone else would guess it contained sweets. The false-photograph task was developed to capture meta-representations in a non-mentalising context. In this task, the child

FIGURE 5.2   The Sally-Anne task

Reproduced from Uta Frith, 1989 with kind permission of the author and of the artist, Axel Scheffler.

has to hold in mind the dual representation of a doll's clothes now (red dress) and in a photo taken earlier (green dress). For older children there are second-order false-belief tasks. These involve stories where one character has a false belief about another character's belief – e.g. Mary thinks that Jon doesn't know where the ice-cream van has gone (but actually Jon does know). For adults, tasks like the *Strange Stories* present realistic scenarios (in written vignettes, Happé, 1994, or more recently short films; Murray et al., 2017) which require mentalising to interpret the non-literal utterance or ambiguous action of the characters, such as telling a white lie about an unflattering haircut or using sarcasm.

3. Mentalising and emotion

What about differences in perceptual exploration and identification of emotional expressions from faces, body language and stories? If we find differences here, this suggests that there's something going on in autism that extends beyond meta-representation specifically. While there is evidence of autistic differences, many studies report no difference (Uljarevic & Hamilton, 2013), and there is burgeoning evidence to suggest that some emotion recognition difficulties are due to co-occurring alexithymia – difficulty recognising what emotion you are feeling – rather than to autism (Bird & Cook, 2013). Furthermore, it is not clear whether emotion recognition in autism relies on different mechanisms to those found in neurotypical groups, nor whether such differences are fundamental to autism, or merely a result of reduced or different interpersonal experience (Harms et al., 2010).

Recent data have also begun to reveal that neurotypical people struggle to recognise and interpret the emotional reactions of autistic people, even while rating them as equally intense and expressive (Brewer et al., 2016; Sheppard et al., 2016). At the interoceptive level, there is evidence that some autistic people may experience even fundamental states, such as hunger and pain, differently from the general population (DuBois et al., 2016; Moore, 2015). Alexithymia has been linked to altered interoception, as part of a wider difficulty identifying how you feel inside (Murphy et al., 2018). Understanding more about interoception in autism may be important for elucidating sensory sensitivities and experiences, as well as differences in the social domain. Given the fact that there are probably differences between autistic and non-autistic people in how they experience, express or perceive emotional states and interoceptive states (even though we haven't quite pinned these down), it seems that our cognitive explanations need to explore more than just meta-representation to explain the social features of autism.

At the same time, it is essential to emphasise that if people with autism have problems knowing what other people are thinking, that doesn't mean they do not care how they feel. There is a dissociation between the skills required to comprehend the mental states of other people (mentalising), and emotional empathy. An example is illustrated in Figure 5.3. A mother was crying after the family cat had died. Her autistic son went and searched through all of his toys and found a hard, plastic figurine with a human body and a cat's head, from the children's cartoon show, *Thundercats*. In an attempt to comfort his crying mother, he prodded her gently with the figurine and, when she ignored him, finally held it up very close to her eye, pressing it into her face. This didn't have the effect of comforting the mother, but it seems clear that the boy was motivated by empathy and a strong desire to help, even though his solution (while logical) didn't really work.

Thus, we can see a dissociation in autism between knowing what someone thinks, which may be hard, and caring and feeling with them, which comes naturally. The same distinction is apparent in a very different group; those with psychopathy. Psychopaths are the opposite of autistic: they are good at telling what you are thinking and may use that to manipulate you, but don't give a damn about your feelings. In autism, *feeling* empathy must also be distinguished from *expressing* empathy – the latter may prove challenging for some autistic people, especially if expected to act in narrowly defined, normative ways to show they care. Finally, we should note that it is also possible that many, if not all, of the social domain differences observed in autism, may in

FIGURE 5.3 An illustration of mental state mis-understanding, with good emotional empathy, in real life

fact be underpinned cognitively by non-social explanations – this theoretical angle is explored in Chapter 8.

4. Understanding restricted and repetitive behaviours and interests at the cognitive level

The first point to reiterate here is that the term "restricted and repetitive behaviours and interests" (hereafter, RRBIs) is not popular among the autistic community, for understandable reasons. It pathologises a set of behaviours that vary widely in complexity and function, and give great pleasure and comfort to many. It is true that some RRBIs can present serious disadvantages – self-injurious behaviour falls into this diagnostic domain, but even in that case, simply forcing someone to stop a self-injurious behaviour can do more harm than good. In other cases, it is important to reflect on whether our judgements of RRBI result from adherence to unnecessary and to some extent arbitrary social expectations of behaviour. Despite these considerations, we will use the term RRBI in this book to enable correspondence between our discussion and the wider psychological and clinical literature.

The cognitive level explanation of RRBIs is (even) less clear cut than for social and communication differences associated with autism. Lorna Wing characterised these as a consequence of a failure of imagination (notably pretend play) in autism – for her, repetitive behaviours traced their roots to a failure to think of anything else to do. Another possibility was that RRBIs were the flipside of reduced engagement with the social world. They filled the space that would otherwise normally be taken up by interpersonal interactions. In both accounts, RRBIs take root through lack of an alternative. However, this is no longer the prevailing explanation. More recent characterisations of RRBIs seem to have reversed the hypothesised causal link between imagination (itself a poorly defined and hard to measure construct in psychological terms) and these behaviour patterns. It is now recognised that RRBIs are themselves motivating and self-sustaining, and may promote a particular form of creativity. In fact, there is increasing interest in, and awareness of, the imagination and creative talents of autistic people (Diener et al., 2014; Pring et al., 2012).

Why might RRBIs be so rewarding for someone with autism? One possibility is that they are a behavioural manifestation of anxiety – perhaps a response to the experience of operating in a social world which is hard to comprehend. RRBIs might serve to add an element of control to the world, thus reducing anxious feelings. There is some evidence supporting this account. Measures of anxiety correlate highly with measures of RRBIs in autistic groups, and both RRBIs and anxiety may be linked to an underlying psychological construct called *intolerance of uncertainty* (Wigham et al., 2015). If autistic people have high intolerance of uncertainty, this could cause anxiety, especially in social situations. This is because, if you struggle to represent other people's mental states and thus predict their behaviour, social situations probably involve high levels of uncertainty. To reduce uncertainty and anxiety, you might engage in predictable, familiar actions or routines. Comforting repetition may also not become boring if, as psychophysical studies suggest, habituation to familiar or repeated stimuli is reduced or even absent in autism (Sinha et al., 2014). Reduced habituation might mean that both pleasant and unpleasant sensations retain their initial fascination/repellence for longer, resulting in both RRBIs and sensory sensitivities.

RRBIs may also be related to patterns of ability, seen when running neuropsychological batteries of assessments with autistic people. A so-called uneven profile of abilities is often apparent, with enhanced or preserved skills in aspects of performance IQ relative to scores on verbal IQ tests. An area of autistic strength (e.g. attention to detail) may be instrumental in developing a particular interest (e.g. collecting thermostats). It is thought that enhanced visuo-spatial skills may explain some common areas of interest and expertise in autism, such as STEM subjects (science, technology, engineering, maths) or train spotting. Alternatively, an intense and focused interest might create the enhanced skill via a process of repeated practice and specialisation. Thus the causal primacy of cognitive abilities like attention to detail and RRBIs remains unclear. Another factor which muddies the waters in terms of determining causal precedence, is that having enhanced attention to detail seems a necessary pre-requisite for high levels of 'insistence on sameness'. After all, it's hard to get stressed about small changes in your environment if you don't notice them. To put it another way, a high level of attention to detail might result in a manifestation of insistence on sameness that is particularly hard to accommodate, since even tiny changes to the environment will be detected and cause distress.

In the future, it might help our cognitive models if we divide RRBIs into two factors that reliably emerge at the behavioural level:

> Repetitive sensory motor (RSM) behaviors and insistence on sameness (IS) behaviors . . . RSM behaviors are characterized by repetitive use of objects, complex motor mannerisms, and sensory seeking behaviors . . . IS behaviors include rituals, compulsions, and resistance to change in routines.

(Hundley et al., 2016, p. 3449)

Hundley and colleagues point out that while repetitive sensory-motor behaviours are associated with younger ages and lower IQ, insistence on sameness is either increased with age, or independent of that factor. Another way to further our understanding of RRBIs is to adopt more qualitative and creative methods to understand how RRBIs operate and are experienced in the lives of autistic people (e.g. Dickerson et al., 2007).

5. Understanding sensory, and other features, at the cognitive level

Sensory aspects of autism include both hyper (over) and hypo (under) sensitivity. At the cognitive level they may be understood within an attentional framework by positing a relationship between detail focus and patterns of sensory sensitivity. For example, a focus on the details of a sensory input – like the presence of a specific frequency in a complex audio stimulus like the sound of a hoover – might make that sound especially unbearable. As with other domains of interest, the causal links in this case are opaque: is attention to detail a manifestation of sensory sensitivity, or a consequence thereof?

Sensory symptoms can also be linked, at the cognitive level, with some RRBIs, especially physical ones like flapping or rocking. This explanatory framework characterises RRBIs as a way to screen-out unwanted input by overwhelming the system with self-stimulatory behaviour: e.g. I can't hear the humming of the lights if I am totally focused on the sensation of flicking my fingers in front of my eyes. The same system may be used by people who experience chronic hypo-sensitivity and use self-stimulation to provide more input to an under-stimulated system. Some autistic people have talked about needing weighted vests or blankets, or tight clothing to help them identify the edges of their body in space.

One interesting line of research suggests that autism may be characterised by increased perceptual capacity, which – at first sight paradoxically – leads to greater distraction by task-irrelevant stimuli (Remington et al., 2009). The idea is that we are less distracted when all our perceptual capacity is fully engaged by a task with high 'perceptual load' (e.g. spotting a target among very similar items), but when the task becomes simpler (the targets are easy to spot), distraction by irrelevant stimuli increases. High perceptual capacity in autism might result in irrelevant sensory stimuli intruding on attention more easily, leading to unwanted distraction by sensory stimulation.

There are multiple other experiences, common to many people within the autistic community, that do not have their own cognitive explanation. In fact, it is a frequent objection among autistic people, and those who support them – like their parents – that some of the most pressing issues in their lives are under-studied by scientists. Where, they ask, is the research on potty training? On sleep? On employment skills? And they are right that a tiny minority of research focuses directly on these issues, which have an unquestionably strong impact on people's lives. On the one hand, some of these issues may not be autism specific and so are addressed by research in other domains (e.g. trials of melatonin for sleep). On the other hand, one would hope that *all* autism research that improves our psychological theories will contribute to understanding and addressing these practical issues. Taking sleep as an example, again, understanding why autistic people struggle with sleep may involve understanding anxiety and stress. If these, in turn, are a result of operating in a social world organised according to neurotypical expectations that are often bewildering, any research that attempts to understand and better accommodate the social differences between people with and without autism is actually relevant (in the long run) to improving sleep problems in autism.

6. What to look for in a psychological theory

This chapter has introduced some of the key terminology and concepts that we use to describe features of autism in cognitive terms. Subsequent chapters will take an in-depth look at different sorts of theories that have been put forward to account for autism, examining the evidence for and against in each case. One final step before we proceed however, is to agree what to look for in a psychological theory. What work must a theory do for us? How can a theory open our eyes to facts, and how can we avoid being blinded by our preconceived notions? Table 5.1 summarises what we might look for in a good theory of autism.

Think back to Chapter 1, when we described how autism could be a condition with multiple biological and behavioural manifestations, united by a common cognitive dimension. If several features co-occur reliably, the most parsimonious explanation is that they are caused by the same underlying differences. Despite the huge variety within the autism constellation, and changes in our formulations of the diagnosis, autism is defined by the co-occurrence of social and communication differences with RRBIs. Thus it is possible, perhaps even probable, that a single cognitive characterisation could underlie these diverse features of autism.

It is worth highlighting that, while a good theory should give a causal account it should not be construed that this means these theories advocate for autism 'cures'. Understanding what comes first can help with understanding and support and does not imply a preventative agenda. A good theory should also be supported by high-quality evidence. It is important to be clear that this doesn't preclude the use of qualitative methods – it is essential in research that

TABLE 5.1   What to look for in a good autism theory

1	Concrete predictions, which generate rigorous tests
2	An interpretation, not just a simple description, of the evidence
3	Detailed explanation of the *pattern* of characteristics in the autism constellation
4	A causal account
5	Alignment with basic scientific truths, including what we know about typical development
6	Informed by community perspectives and priorities

the selected method is a good match with the question being asked. For many questions, qualitative research methods are the most appropriate and can provide unique opportunities to probe, for example, the nature of the social construct of autism (O'Reilly et al., 2017) or practical ways to make a community setting more autism-friendly (Fletcher-Watson & May, 2018). In other cases, qualitative research offers rich complementary information about phenomena identified experimentally, or raises new questions for quantitative investigation (e.g. Losh & Capps, 2006 on experiences of emotion in autism). However, when quantitative techniques are required, it is right to expect the highest standard of evidence. Anything less risks selling the autistic community short, by providing a wobbly foundation for policy and practice.

In 1994, when this book was first published, adequate sample sizes, comparisons across syndromes and high-quality methods, such as RCTs and longitudinal studies, were few and far between. Now that the research field has grown-up, we will be focusing on high-quality studies and especially systematic reviews and meta-analyses wherever these are available. At the same time, we recognise that new ideas are coming up in autism research all the time. These are often initially tested in small experimental studies, which can be strengthened by the use of clever experimental methods, including well-designed control tasks, and measurement of potential confounders.

Where good quality evidence is available to support a robust theory, this can influence both behavioural and biological levels of understanding, and in turn shape best practice in schools, clinics and communities. Psychological theories can provide a supporting framework for the interpretation of biological data (neuroimaging, genetic profiles) and help develop translational measures that increase the impact of research with animal models. A strong theory can flag what behavioural features are distinctive to autism and important for diagnosis or measurement over time. Where there are challenges, psychology directs our attention to the underlying problem (e.g. anxiety) rather than placing the emphasis on the surface behaviour (e.g. head-banging). If we move towards comprehension of the deep underpinnings of autism this can lead to greater empathy, patience and understanding from would-be allies. In addition, good quality research can highlight what's *not* different in autism – what's common to all of us and how we can use this information to develop shared understanding and opportunities?

A key part of the quest for a psychological theory is robust and unbiased examination of assumptions. It is instructive to ask yourself (if, like us, you are a neurotypical Brit), is life for an autistic person a bit like life for me if I found myself plonked down in rural Japan? What would I do there that would be typically autistic? Probably fail in your attempts to communicate and misunderstand people a lot, sometimes cause offence, be highly stressed, struggle to make friends or get a job, adopt fixed routines and copy others, as coping strategies. And if you also look obviously different, you would have it relatively easy. The Japanese folk around you would realise you haven't a clue, forgive your faux pas as due to ignorance rather than bad intentions and adapt their behaviour to accommodate your needs. Autism, as a hidden disability, confers no such opportunity. Throughout this book, we try to adopt neutral terminology, emphasising *difference* rather than *deficit* – while recognising the disadvantages that being autistic may bring in a neurotypical world. In any attempt to explain autism that follows, we ask readers to bear in mind that we work within a paradigm defined by a non-autistic majority who have developed social rules and traditions that work for them. Reflecting on this position is an essential part of ensuring that we are not too quick to translate an autistic *difference* into an autistic *deficit*, simply because it doesn't fit with those norms.

7. Current debates

Summary

The diagnostic and behavioural features of autism can be interpreted via cognitive frameworks to provide simpler models to make sense of a seemingly diverse set of behaviours in a (relatively) unified way. Examples include: describing social features of autism in terms of meta-representation, linking restrictive and repetitive behaviours with attention to detail and understanding sensory sensitivities in the context of increased perceptual capacity. A robust psychological theory can connect lived experiences and biological data into a coherent model with implications for best practice.

Big questions

There has been, historically, an overwhelming focus on the social and communication domain in psychological literature. Is it warranted? Does this correspond with the primary needs of people with autism? Or is it more aligned with researcher interests – for example, using autism as a 'window on typical development'?

How can we link cognitive research more clearly to community priorities? Are the connections we might write about in academic papers likely to come to fruition? How can we ensure that psychological research follows through, by delivering theoretically informed and evidence-based supports for the community?

What are the causal relationships between different features of autism? Is it possible, or desirable, to identify features that are drivers versus consequences of autistic development? For example, are RRBIs a typical response to living in a social world that is confusing and stressful? Or a fundamental part of a uniquely autistic experience?

COMMUNITY CONTRIBUTION: DR CLAIRE EVANS-WILLIAMS – *AUTISTIC PERSON, AUTISM ADVOCATE AND CONSULTANT CLINICAL PSYCHOLOGIST*

There are more things in heaven and earth Horatio, than are dreamt of in your philosophy.

(Shakespeare, 1603)

Upon completion of this chapter, the prudent reader may engage in a critical reflection on the merits and short-fallings of Autism *theory*. In so doing, one should consider the ubiquitous challenges and limitations associated with *theorising* about human cognition, emotion and behaviour. Not only do human beings abound with rich diversity in culture, language and belief systems, we are, by our very nature, inherently (biologically, psychologically and socially) complex. A conclusion may be that it is not advantageous to presume the essence of Autistic-*ness* can be captured and reduced to a single unitary psychological theory.

Theory can offer useful definition, structure and fixed boundaries of categorisation. By all means, let us profess that (the access to, and knowledge of) theory can be a convenient pragmatic tool and a comforting lynchpin when systematising large chunks of complex information. In my everyday professional practice, theoretical models of Autism can, for example, enable identification of thresholds of cognitive states, which can simplify the process(es) of universal recognition, and communication in both clinical practice and research settings. However, the narrow and finite dimensions of psychological theory cannot speak to the magnitude of autistic heterogeneity. There is a real threat to the fidelity of autism research and practice if we blindly subscribe to theory. For instance, expressed beliefs such as "autistic people can't feel empathy", or "autistic people don't have the ability to mentalise" and "it's impossible to be in a caring profession if you're autistic" are damaging to the autistic community and likely derived from out-dated autism theory.

A rudimentary glance over the past 70 years of autism research uncovers a history that can be labelled as progressive at best, and turbulent at worst. Our collective knowledge and understanding of autism, as expressed through current psychological theory, is perhaps most sensibly categorised as transient, momentary and imperfect. The authors wisely highlight "*new ideas are coming up in Autism research all the time*" and so, amidst the frequent evolution of novel research hypotheses, experimental paradigms, and theoretical perspectives there is but only one certainty of which we can be sure: The human-*ness* of autistic people (their families, friends and carers) transcends anything a theory has to offer. Only by opening up to the lived experiences and lifelong narratives of autistic people may we achieve an understanding of what it means to *be* autistic.

Recommended reading

Adams, J. (2017). *Active but odd: An unswerving 'compulsion' to create*. Blog post published at Museum for Object Research, www.museumfor objectresearch.com/jon-adams/

Baron-Cohen, S., Tager-Flusberg, H., & Lombardo, M. eds. (2013). *Understanding other minds: Perspectives from developmental social neuroscience*. Oxford: Oxford University Press.

Frith, U. (2008). *Autism: A very short introduction* (Vol. 195). Oxford: Oxford University Press.

Grinker, Roy Richard. (2007). *Unstrange minds*. New York: Basic Books.

A GOOD MODEL MUST BE...

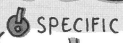 CHALLENGES TO THEORY OF MIND

UNIVERSAL

SOME AUTISTIC CHILDREN PASS THEORY OF MIND TEST!

WHY?

- CONFOUNDABLE TEST?
- DEVELOPMENTAL DELAY?
  ↳ LIKE A SECOND LANGUAGE

- PROCESSING DIFFERENCE?
  ↳ CORRELATION IN AUTISM

IQ → THEORY OF MIND

PRIMARY

DOES IT EXPLAIN RRBIs?

FILLING THE GAP LEFT BY THEORY OF MIND?

A COPING MECHANISM FOR ANXIETY FROM LACK OF THEORY OF MIND?

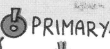

SPECIFIC

THEORY OF MIND DIFFICULTIES SHOW UP ELSEWHERE

- SCHIZOPHRENIA (OVERACTIVE)
- DEAF CHILDREN IN NON-SIGNING HOMES
- CHILDREN UNDER THREE YEARS

CONCEPT OF ToM IS ALSO BECOMING ENRICHED

DESIRE REASONING → TEASING, JOKING → SALLY-ANNE

DEVELOPMENTAL TIMELINE

EXECUTIVE FUNCTION

THE ABILITY TO INHIBIT A PREPONENT

SORT!
STOP!
SORT!

ALTERNATIVE THEORY

POINT TO WHERE IT'S <u>NOT</u>

CHALLENGES TO EXECUTIVE FUNCTION
↳ SPECIFICITY:
- ALSO EVIDENT IN ADHD

BEWARE OF ASSUMPTIONS

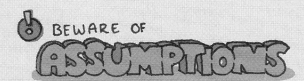

PERFORMANCE 'GAP' IN AUTISTIC PARTICIPANTS DISAPPEARED WITH OUT OBSERVER

AUTISTIC PARTICIPANTS SEEM LESS SUSCEPTIBLE TO 'AUDIENCE EFFECTS'

OUT-GROUP STATUS

A LOT OF AUTISTIC BEHAVIOUR COULD BE EXPLAINED BY FEELING 'SEPARATE' FROM THE EXPERIMENTER

NOW PLEASE SORT THESE SHAPES

NEUROTYPICAL PARTICIPANTS ALSO STRUGGLE TO INTERPRET ANIMATIONS CREATED BY AUTISTIC PARTICIPANTS

6 Autism at the cognitive level
Primary deficit models

THE FIRST ATTEMPTS to understand autism within a modern psychological framework came in the 1980s. Autism was more narrowly defined at that time (in the *DSM-III*) and still considered a relatively rare condition. Research was framed by Wing's "triad of impairments" framework – social interaction, communication and imagination – which was represented in the *DSM-III* as a triad of social interaction, communication and RRBIs. Nevertheless, psychologists aimed to determine a single, underlying difference that could explain all the diverse features used to diagnose autism. Three commonly accepted criteria for assessing the primacy of a specific feature are universality among people with the condition, specificity to that condition and causal precedence in development. In addition, any such theories of autism must steer a course between explaining too little – in effect merely describing features – and explaining too much. Autistic people show a strikingly uneven profile of abilities, with superior skills which require explanation just as much as do areas of difficulty. The challenge was to pinpoint pivotal psychological skills, significant enough to explain the differences between people with and without autism, but nuanced enough to allow for uneven profiles of ability.

Today, we do not characterise autism in terms of deficit or impairments, but as a pattern of differences which present advantages and disadvantages in relation to neurotypical social norms and expectations. However, these early, primary deficit models were formulated in a context where autism was almost universally seen as an impairment. Rather than whitewash this historical fact, we choose to use the term 'primary deficit' to describe these explanatory frameworks (though their more modern iterations could be characterised as 'primary difference' models). It should be noted that they represented a significant advance on earlier notions that autistic children were fundamentally uninterested in others and/or suffering from childhood psychosis. They were also formulated based on work mainly with children with autism and intellectual disability, often with additional language impairments – young people with a clear and significant need for support. Another key fact about this time in psychology is that we tended to adopt a modular view of brain-behaviour relationships when attempting to explain developmental phenomena. Many psychologists were looking for some discrete ability which was 'switched off' in autism but switched on in everyone else. This notion now seems out-dated – psychology today is engrossed by the multiple interacting factors that contribute to every developmental milestone and group difference. Nevertheless, we can learn a great deal from these early attempts to characterise autism at the cognitive level.

1. The Theory of Mind model

The term 'Theory of Mind' (ToM), referring to the ability to attribute independent mental states to oneself and others in order to explain behaviour, was coined by Premack and Woodruff (1978) in the context of exploring chimpanzee social cognition. The attributed mental states were 'independent' both of the real world state of affairs (because people can believe things that are not true) and independent of the mental states other people have (because you and I can believe, want and pretend different things from one another). The philosopher Daniel Dennett (1978) pointed out that only understanding and predicting a character's behaviour based on a *false* belief could demonstrate ToM conclusively, since otherwise the real state of affairs (or the participant's own beliefs) would be sufficient to pass the task without the need to postulate mental states at all (Dennett, 1978). Thus the Sally-Anne, false-belief task (shown in Figure 5.3, previous chapter) was the litmus test used by Uta Frith, Alan Leslie and Simon Baron-Cohen to assess ToM in autism (Baron-Cohen et al., 1985). In this seminal paper, a significantly higher proportion of the autistic group answered incorrectly on the false-belief task, compared with typically developing and learning disabled groups. The ToM account of autism – which posited a meta-representational deficit as the defining feature of the condition – was born.

The original version of this book, written when the resulting landmark paper was still relatively new, devoted much of a chapter to describing how the ToM account connected Alan Leslie's theory about the meta-representational underpinnings of pretend play, with the observation, by Lorna Wing and others, that pretend play was largely absent in autism. Now the ToM account of autism is over 30 years old, and the original 1985 paper has more than 8,000 citations on Google Scholar as we write! The theory has had enormous influence on research, but also permeated thinking about autism by teachers, parents and clinicians. Why? Perhaps because, in its original form at least, it made clear and specific predictions about what aspects of 'doing social' would be hard for autistic people, and – just as importantly – which would be easy.

The ToM explanation of autism allowed researchers to make clear cuts between what appeared to be very similar behaviours – 'carving nature at the joints' according to a precise theory about the underlying cognitive 'bone structure'. For example, Attwood et al. (1988) found that in autism the clinically noted reduction in use of gestures actually applied only to those gestures that normally influence mental states (e.g. expressions of consolation, embarrassment and goodwill), whereas children with autism showed as many gestures that manipulate behaviour (e.g. signals to come, be quiet, or go away) as did comparison participants with learning difficulties. Similarly, Baron-Cohen (1989) found that a group of autistic children did not use or seem to understand pointing for the sake of sharing attention (protodeclarative pointing) but were able to point in order to get a desired object (protoimperative pointing). Other fine cuts have been made between, for example, understanding seeing versus understanding knowing (Perner et al., 1989; Baron-Cohen & Goodhart, 1994) and recognising happiness versus recognising surprise (Baron-Cohen et al., 1993). Such distinctions in the smooth continuum of everyday behaviour would appear to be hard to derive from or explain by other psychological theories of autism (e.g. primary problems in social motivation – see Chapter 7 for more on this).

The other major appeal of the ToM account of autism was its apparent ability to explain all of Wing's triad. The hypothetical developmental sequence went as follows: autistic children start out with an inability to meta-represent, apparent in a lack of pretend play; social differences then arise because meta-representation is required to understand people as agents with independent minds; thus, the characteristic communicative profile of autism would follow from an inability to represent intentions, or to recognise utterances as conveying a speaker's thoughts.

2. Variants of the Theory of Mind model

The ToM model of autism became extremely influential in autism research and continues to be a central component of a lot of teaching and training about autism. Regardless of the detail of whether its hypotheses have been upheld by the evidence (more on that next), there's little doubt that talking about autism in terms of difficulties understanding what other people are thinking is a useful conceptualisation for neurotypical people new to the condition. Uta Frith's influential 1989 book 'Autism: Understanding the Enigma' brought the ToM account of autism to a wider audience, including parents and teachers. Following its initial break-through moment, ToM-based accounts began to diversify and competing versions arose. Many of these aimed at trying to identify the developmental precursors to false belief understanding, following Alan Leslie's groundbreaking work (Leslie, 1987).

Simon Baron-Cohen's monograph, *Mindblindness* (1997), presented a model of the cognitive components of ToM, incorporating first an eye-direction detector and an intention detector. In the model, these two psychological components caused children to attend to other people's eyes and intentions, which was necessary in order to develop an understanding of mental states in dyadic interaction contexts. Together these skills combined to provide the basis of a Shared Attention Mechanism, enabling triadic interactions between two people and a third shared focus (e.g. a father and daughter looking at a butterfly together). This mechanism provided the foundation of the ultimate ToM

Mechanism required for understanding of mental states. For Baron-Cohen, the root of autism was a failure to develop and display shared attention, and this was supported by evidence that lack of shared attention was a reliable pre-diagnostic marker (Baron-Cohen et al., 1992).

Other variants on the ToM model asked *how* a child with typical development built this set of skills. Many rival theories arose (see Carruthers & Smith, 1996 for a range of relevant chapters). Theory-theory purported that children acted like little scientists, making hypotheses about the actions of those around them and testing them against reality. In this way, children would learn to predict how people would behave under certain conditions and extrapolate a complex set of rules about behaviour and beliefs. Others argued that the young age at which children understood false beliefs, and the relative universality of that early understanding, was incompatible with conscious reasoning as the route to ToM. Instead, Alan Leslie and others proposed that children were innately predisposed to develop the meta-representational ability underlying pretending and reasoning about others' mental states. Meanwhile, simulation-theory suggested that the basis of ToM was an identification between the child and those around them – an awareness that other people are "like me". This enabled the child to simulate another's behaviour by asking themselves what they would do in a particular situation.

3. Challenges to the Theory of Mind model: universality

In every study using ToM tests, including the original 1985 paper, some autistic people are found to pass. How can we explain this test success? The first question is whether those autistic participants who pass ToM tests are using the same sort of automatic and intuitive mentalising as do neurotypical participants, or instead figuring out what others think via another route? If the latter, then difficulty intuitively representing other's mental states may still be universal to autism, and a good explanation for social and communication differences.[1] If, on the other hand, we believe that some autistic people can represent mental states, but still show the social and communication features of autism, then a second possibility is that a delay in acquisition of mentalising abilities reverberates across the lifespan, causing persistent differences in interaction. Delay could disrupt the normal coordination of the mentalising system with other abilities during development and potentially interfere with

---

1   It seems important to reiterate here that an "inability to represent mental states" for an individual, or an entire population, should not be taken to imply that an autistic person does not care about or have an interest in other people. We simply mean that the underlying, automatic representational mechanism used by the non-autistic population for 'mind-reading' may not be 'wired in' for autistic people.

years of formative social experience. A parallel might be drawn with learning a second language in early versus later life; the latter rarely results in totally fluent, accent-free use. The second language analogy is helpful, perhaps, because speaking a second language learnt late can be enjoyable or frustrating, can be exhausting and harder when you are tired; all things that may apply to the social understanding that autistic people develop through their own efforts later in life.

A highly intelligent young woman with autism told Francesca that, when tested on the Sally-Anne task, she had wanted to answer 'box', where the ball really was, but remembered that when psychologists ask questions there are always tricks, so she said the opposite, 'basket', thereby passing the test! Many autistic people describe consciously working out what is going on in social situations and say that this feels like doing mental arithmetic. There is evidence that some autistic people have managed to "hack" a solution to ToM tasks, thanks to experience, and using general problem-solving skills (Frith et al., 1991). Such hacking may be relatively inflexible, allowing success on simple, artificial ToM experiments, but without the flexibility and automaticity required in real life. Various attempts have been made to create ToM tests that are more ecologically valid, less easy to hack and therefore more representative of the real-life social difficulties many autistic people experience.

The Strange Stories (Figure 6.1) were an early attempt to present complex real-world vignettes that require mentalising in order to understand the speaker's intention behind a non-literal utterance (Happé, 1994); they have more recently been turned into video-based tasks (Brewer et al., 2017; Murray et al., 2017). The Frith-Happé Triangles Animations, inspired by the work of Heider and Simmel ask the participant to interpret the actions of abstract moving shapes (Abell et al., 2000). The descriptions participants produce are analysed for evidence that the animations have been spontaneously interpreted as intentional, marked by use of mental state terms. These tasks have revealed a persistent reduction in mentalising in autistic adults without learning disability, though exceptions to the rule remain. Further evidence of subtle differences between autistic and non-autistic approaches to mentalising comes from implicit ToM assessment via eye-tracking (Schneider et al., 2012). In these experiments, people watch a sequence of events from a Sally-Anne type scenario, while their eye-movements are recorded. When the 'Sally' character returns to collect her hidden toy, neurotypical people tend pre-emptively to fixate where they expect her to look first, based on her false belief. Autistic participants tend not to do this, even when they pass the explicit verbal false-belief question (Schuwerk et al., 2015).

We have reviewed, two possible interpretations for the fact that many autistic people pass ToM tasks: one is that people may grow out of differences seen in childhood and another is that people can learn strategies to tackle

FIGURE 6.1   Some examples of the *Strange Stories*

Example of a Double Bluff story
During the war, the Red army captures a member of
the Blue army. They want him to tell them where his
army's tanks are; they know they are either by the sea
or in the mountains. They know that the prisoner will
not want to tell them, he will want to save his army,
and so he will certainly lie to them. The prisoner is
very brave and very clever, he will not let them find
his tanks. The tanks are really in the mountains. Now
when the other side ask him where his tanks are, he
says, "They are in the mountains".
Q: Is it true what the prisoner said?
Q: Where will the other army look for his tanks?
Q: Why did the prisoner say that?

Example of a Persuasion story
Jill wanted to buy a kitten, so she went to see Mrs.
Smith, who had lots of kittens she didn't want. Now
Mrs. Smith loved the kittens, and she wouldn't do anything to harm them, though she couldn't keep them all
herself. When Jill visited she wasn't sure she wanted
one of Mrs. Smith's kittens, since they were all males
and she had wanted a female. But Mrs. Smith said, "If
no one buys the kittens I'll just have to drown them!"
Q: Was it true, what Mrs Smith said?
Q: Why did Mrs. Smith say that?

ToM problems. While we know that some delay in ToM seems inevitable
(there is no evidence to date of pre-schoolers with autism passing ToM tasks),
so far there is no evidence available that can categorically distinguish between
the "different strategy" and the "developmental delay" interpretation. Both
accounts predict that autistic people should be able to solve ToM tasks when
they are simple, but that a dis-fluency in application of mentalising should
be apparent in more complex tasks and everyday life. One way to disentangle
these accounts is to use longitudinal data which can tell us whether ToM task
performance is predicted by age or intellectual ability. If ToM task success
comes with age, that suggests a developmental delay account, but if ToM task
success is more closely related to IQ then we might lean more towards an
alternative strategy account. That said, delayed and different are not strictly
alternatives – for example, early delays in ToM might lead to the development
of different strategies later in life.

  When there is evidence that IQ influences ToM scores, this also invites
a third interpretation – that mentalising is hard for autistic people because
of an additional processing difficulty. We know that the intellectual capacity

required to mentalise is not especially high – in typical development a mental age of four years is sufficient to pass standard ToM tests and to demonstrate this ability across a range of different tasks (Gopnik & Astington, 1988). In fact, implicit tasks are passed much earlier (see Chapter 7). Participants with learning disability, too, pass these tasks despite relatively impaired general intellectual and problem-solving abilities (Baron-Cohen et al., 1985). Data from the false-photograph task (see Chapter 5 and Figure 6.2 – in this task, the child has to hold in mind the dual representation of a doll's clothes now and in a photo taken earlier) seemed to show that autistic children who struggle with mentalising can manage meta-representation outside the social domain. On the other hand, other work comparing verbal, non-verbal and non-social meta-representational tasks suggests that autistic children may have a generalised difficulty extending beyond mentalising specifically (Iao & Leekam, 2014). Consideration of domain-general information processing differences in autism will be addressed further in Chapter 8.

FIGURE 6.2   The false photo task

Reproduced by kind permission of the artist, Axel Scheffler.

Why does all of this matter? We want to be clear on why determining the root of the apparent, if not consistent, autistic difficulty with mentalising is important to psychologists. First, let us assume that being able to envisage, interpret and act upon the mental states of others is useful (this is not necessarily the case – more on this later in the chapter). Second, let us assume that the autistic community agree it is desirable for children to learn to apply this skill, in order to get by in a largely non-autistic world. In that case, we would want to understand the best way to teach mentalising skills to children on the spectrum. The best way to teach would probably be to help them replicate a strategy which had already been applied and honed by autistic people before them; which means understanding how that strategy works is a pre-requisite for teaching. One starting point is to examine more directly the ways in which autistic people think about mental states. In one innovative study, Edey and colleagues (2016) showed that, when asked to produce animations representing different mental states, the films made by autistic people were not just different to those created by neurotypical people, but also that neurotypical viewers struggled to interpret those films. This kind of work may be the key to supporting young autistic learners but also helping non-autistic people to confront their own role in the social communication barriers between people with and without autism.

4. Challenges to the Theory of Mind model: specificity and primacy

As well as problems with the universality of mentalising difficulties in autism, it has also been suggested that ToM difficulties are found in other groups apart from autism. If mentalising can be disrupted without resulting in the behavioural features of autism, this would seem to threaten its proposed causal role. Acquired or later life mentalising problems have been reported in many other clinical groups, including those with strokes leading to brain damage in the right hemisphere, and individuals with schizophrenia, who show over-attribution of mental states that may relate to paranoid delusions. In addition, three key groups in whom traditional false-belief failure has been shown *developmentally* are typically developing children under 3 years, children with learning disability (but not autism) and children born deaf into non-signing homes.

In all three cases, unlike in autism, failure on false-belief tasks is not commensurate with social difficulties in everyday life. For this reason, it is plausible that task failure is not due to problems attributing mental states per se, but to aspects of the task demands, such as executive control. After all, 2-year-olds talk about mental states, and deaf and learning disabled children make friendships in the usual way. Importantly, when task demands are reduced, for example using implicit false-belief tests measuring spontaneous looking behaviour, typically developing toddlers show evidence of tracking mental states as young as 15 months (Scott & Baillargeon, 2017; Setoh et al., 2016). Simple tests like the penny-hiding game – where a child gets to guess which hand an adult is hiding a coin in and then has a go at being the hider – also show that ToM operates more typically in those with intellectual disability but not autism, compared with those with both (San José Cáceres et al., 2015).

The originators of the ToM account set themselves a high bar by setting out to identify a primary deficit. Even if mentalising is universally challenging for autistic people, is this really the *primary* difference? One challenge is that for ToM to have a primary role in explaining autism, it needs to explain other features as well as social and communication differences. Some authors have proposed that RRBIs infiltrate the cognitive space that would otherwise be occupied by a rich database of social knowledge, built on early mentalising abilities. Keen interests in, say, Finnish architecture or bicycle maintenance simply absorb the resources that most non-autistic people give over to recording and processing details about other people. Another possibility, reviewed already in Chapter 3, is that RRBIs are a way to manage the anxiety that results from having to operate in a hard-to-comprehend social world. One prediction that results from these proposals is that RRBIs should be at their most intense when ToM difficulties are most profound. While some papers do find associations between ToM and RRBIs (e.g. Jones et al., 2018), the general lack of association offers further support for the 'fractionated triad' approach to understanding autism at the cognitive level (Brunsdon & Happé, 2014).

Another challenge for ToM models is to determine the point in the developmental process at which the autistic and non-autistic pathways divide. As the ToM model was extrapolated – both in the study of autism and in investigations of typical development – a richer developmental sequence was revealed, making it harder to determine this point (see Figure 6.3).

FIGURE 6.3   An approximate developmental sequence of milestones relating to Theory of Mind

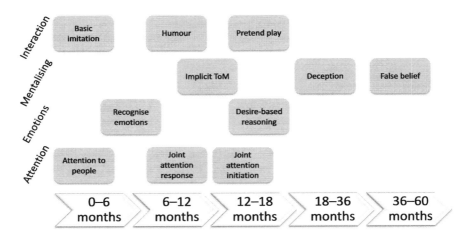

A significant factor in this process is the diversification of ways to measure ToM. Although the false-belief task remains the 'gold standard', a range of experiments reveal ToM-relevant abilities that precede false belief in development. An example is desire-reasoning tasks in which children as young as 18 months can correctly recognise that someone else might have different wants – in this case a preference for broccoli rather than biscuits – than their own (Repacholi & Gopnik, 1997). Other studies have illustrated implicit mentalising-in-action when children from two-and-a-half years are able to lay a false trial in order to deceive others (Chandler Friz & Hala, 1989). Vasu Reddy pioneered research into early humour, showing how toddlers can make jokes and tease people in a way that seems reliant on a rudimentary mentalising ability (Reddy, 1991). Thus the capacity to represent the mental states of both oneself and others, or of reality and appearance, is evident from very early in development.

In addition, mentalising skills have been associated with other early developmental milestones, such as attending to people, joint attention with others, imitation and recognising emotions (Baron-Cohen, 2000). Joint attention has been described as a 'pivotal skill' in development that is often significantly delayed in autistic children (Charman, 2003). This term describes the three-way, or triadic, attention that can take place between two people and a shared external object. For example, when a mother points to an airplane in the sky and says, "Look!", and her son looks up at her and then at the plane, and she looks back at her son and so forth . . . that's joint attention. Likewise, imitation has been hypothesised to play a key role in development, providing a foundation for much learning but also a way to connect emotionally with others (Meltzoff, 1990). Figure 6.3 shows an approximate timescale of ToM-related abilities in typical development. As ever, the causal relationships here are hard to disentangle – a series of skills become apparent over a narrow developmental period and the extent to which one might be dependent on another remains uncertain.

This enrichment of our concept of ToM has given rise to some developmental models of autism. When mentalising was judged only by standard false-belief task success, the primacy of mentalising problems in autism seemed problematic; after all, children often show signs that they are autistic before they are old enough to take ToM tests. However, over recent years the use of looking-based tests of so-called implicit false-belief attribution suggests mental state tracking at 18 months (Senju et al., 2011) and even younger (see review by Scott & Baillargeon, 2017, but also Heyes, 2014 for a debate regarding interpretation of these findings). Now the emergence of mentalising no longer looks too late to play an early and causal role in, at least, the social and communication features of autism. On the other hand, work with cohorts of infants with a high-likelihood of later autism diagnosis has demonstrated few reliable behavioural markers of autism before age 12 months. Whether a narrow focus on meta-representation can explain the rich and complex developmental sequence in autism will be explored in more detail in the next chapter, where developmental models of autism are considered.

5. Alternatives to the Theory of Mind model

One other cognitive capacity that has been proposed as the primary deficit explaining autism is executive function. Executive functions are subject to a range of subtly different definitions, but they encompass those 'oversight' abilities, reliant on frontal lobe function, which pervade any complex/novel task. Examples of executive functions, include planning, inhibition and working memory. There is considerable evidence that many autistic people have executive function difficulties (Hill, 2004), but are these a candidate for a "primary deficit"?

To be convincing in this field, an executive (dys)function model of autism must explain the social difficulties apparent in the real world, as well as those operationalised in false-belief tasks and other ToM measures, by recourse to a more general process. After all, executive functions operate across both social and non-social contexts. Some authors propose that an autistic child's performance on false-belief tasks does not reflect a mentalising deficit, but rather a specific difficulty in overcoming the perceptual salience of the object in the real location. One test of this hypothesis examined the effect of a competitor on performance on a "windows task". In this task, the child simply had to point to one of two boxes, into which she alone could see, via a small window. On each trial a sweet was placed in one of the boxes, and if the child indicated the *empty* box, she won the sweet. In the competitor version, an ignorant second player searched in the indicated box and kept any sweets they found – so that the same response (pointing at the empty box) resulted in the child being rewarded with a sweet, but this time in the social context of "deceiving" the competitor. Hughes and Russell (1993) found that autistic children struggled with the 'windows task' in both conditions and concluded that their difficulties with deception did not spring from an inability to mentalise, but from a failure to inhibit action to the object.

Subsequent studies (e.g. Hughes et al., 1994) showed that on a number of non-social tasks – Tower of Hanoi, detour reach task – most children with autism do show some difficulty with acting away from the object or inhibiting a prepotent (previously rewarded) response. However, the debate about the primacy of executive function versus mentalising difficulties in autism is not so easily resolved (for an interesting examination of the developmental relationship between these abilities, see Wade et al., 2018). One meta-analysis of studies in typical development suggests that executive functions have a role to play in false-belief understanding, but not other aspects of ToM (Devine & Hughes, 2014). Early individual differences in executive function have been found to predict later false-belief performance, but not vice versa, which may suggest a developmental primacy of executive function – assuming that measures of the two constructs are of equal developmental sensitivity. However, the presence of ToM difficulties along with intact executive function has been found in autistic children, suggesting that executive difficulties do not underpin mentalising difficulties in this population (Pellicano, 2007).

The relation between executive function difficulties and social interactive behaviours in the real world (as opposed to ToM task performance) has not been adequately probed, but there is some evidence that executive function problems do link to social interactive and communication difficulties beyond the lab (Happé et al., 2006). On the other hand, this same paper showed that executive function difficulties are more severe and persistent in children with ADHD than children with autism. One requirement of a 'primary deficit' model for autism is that it ought to be able to explain what is unique about the autistic profile – something traditionally undermined by the presence of overlapping but more intense executive function difficulties in a distinct condition. However, if autism is a composite of cognitive features (as suggested in the fractionated triad account), not all the 'ingredients' need be unique to autism.

Can executive function difficulties explain other features of autism? Certainly many autistic people report difficulties with real world tasks that rely on executive function, such as planning their personal schedules or dealing with changes to a regular journey. Attempts have also been made to trace the roots of RRBIs to an executive function cause. One such is a suggestion that autistic people find generalisation and generativity difficult – these are the cognitive underpinnings for the transfer of knowledge across contexts and spontaneous generation of new content and solutions. It is proposed that such limitations might translate into a tendency to engage in the same behaviour repeatedly, across multiple settings. However, a recent study exploring ToM, executive function and diagnostic features of autism in a large group (n = 100) of diagnosed adolescents demonstrated links between ToM and autism profiles (including RRBIs), and between ToM and executive function, but not between executive function and autism behavioural profiles independently (Jones et al., 2018). One possibility is that executive function difficulties are not a core part of autism at the cognitive level, but that these may co-occur with autism quite often and that such executive function challenges make it harder for an autistic person to mask, strategically accommodate or compensate for their social and communication differences. Conversely, an autistic person with good executive functions might be getting by at school or at work using a series of rules, switching between these in response to changing contexts, relying heavily on working memory, attention, flexibility and planning. It is possible that competence in executive functions is one of the things that separates those who aren't readily identified as autistic – including many women and girls – from their autistic peers. The same compensatory phenomenon might be apparent in a range of other conditions that diverge from typical development, as suggested by Mark Johnson (Johnson, 2012). Of course, the negative consequences of some such compensatory efforts, such as camouflaging, can be exhaustion, burn-out or worse (Hull et al., 2017).

6. The role of primary deficit models

Neither of the two models presented here has fully achieved what it set out to do – to provide a simple, cognitive-level explanation for a diversity of biological and behavioural features found in autism. Autistic performance on the various measures created to assess ToM in particular, but also executive function, remains complex. It has not yet been possible to disentangle the various ways in which an autistic person might address a ToM task. One of the reasons that data are lacking on this is that, since the introduction of the ToM model, the science has begun to focus on more nuanced, developmental theories of autism. While many of these have their roots in ToM, incorporating mentalising as part of an important array of social cognitive abilities, the focus on false belief in particular has lessened.

Despite the terminology of 'deficit' and the determination to encapsulate the variety of autistic experience in a single cognitive label, we must acknowledge the beneficial descendants of this body of work. Mentalising remains a useful shorthand for a non-autistic person encountering autism for the first time. Considering that someone else might not easily comprehend your intentions or beliefs (even though they are interested in and concerned for you) can help neurotypical people to adapt their behaviour in ways that autistic people may find useful – e.g. be more explicit about their thoughts and feelings, make their language more literal and precise.

A desire for parsimony – with authors postulating the minimum number of underlying psychological features necessary to account for a behavioural pattern – is prevalent throughout psychology. However, it may be more convincing in the case of autism to propose multiple primary differences, at the psychological level as at the genetic and behavioural levels (Happé et al., 2006). A co-occurrence of multiple differences, unconnected at the psychological level might be explained by the spatial proximity of their biological substrates in the brain or by a single but pervasive difference in brain function or connectivity. If this is the case, it may be futile to look for a single psychological marker of autism. The 'fractionated triad' account argues for different psychological factors impacting different aspects of the behavioural phenotype of autism, underpinned by largely independent genetic influences (Brunsdon & Happé, 2014).

7. Questioning assumptions about cognitive performance in autism

There are also other ways altogether to interpret these attempts to determine the psychological features of autism. One recent study examined the role of audience effects – the performance-enhancing impact of being watched by another person – on false-belief task scores in children with and without autism (Chevallier et al., 2014). The study revealed that the usual 'performance gap' between typically developing and autistic children was eliminated when there was no observer. The authors conclude that some behaviours that have been considered characteristic of autism may derive from a lack susceptibility to audience effects rather than an underlying difficulty with the task itself.

Further, indirect evidence for this interpretation comes from parallels between patterns of data derived from studies with autistic children, and studies of in-group and out-group effects in typical development. For example, multiple studies find evidence that autistic children show less spontaneous imitation, and less fidelity in imitation, than children without autism (Williams et al., 2004). However, the same effect is seen when typically developing children are organised into two arbitrary groups (a "minimal group paradigm") – children as young as 14 months old are less likely to imitate peers from the other group (e.g. Buttelman et al., 2013). When we use this result to frame our interpretation of autism research, suddenly we can see that a lot of autistic behaviour could potentially be understood in the context of feeling separate from, or different to, the experimenter. And of course, because experimenters in the field are rarely autistic themselves, this is a perfectly accurate and reasonable judgement of the situation.

8. Current debates

Summary

Late 20th century models of autism strove to identify a single core cognitive feature of autism that could explain all surface behaviours observed. These models were to some extent victims of their own determination to explain autism in one neat theory, as they could not adequately address the variability among people with a diagnosis, or explain features of autism whose importance researchers were only just beginning to acknowledge (e.g. sensory sensitivities). These theories, ultimately, explained too little.

In addition, much of this work adopted a view of autism that is no longer an acceptable approach, describing autism in terms of deficit and disregarding the strengths of, and contributions made by, autistic people. Nevertheless, these models have driven the field forward by drawing attention to fascinating aspects of typical and autistic development (how *do* we understand other people's minds?). By identifying features of autism which were outside the reach of these attempted explanations, these researchers exposed the heterogeneity and complexity which is now a focus of much research and community interest.

Big questions

What is next for ToM? This construct is still used widely in research, often to explore connections with other variables – ToM and gender, ToM and employment, theory of mind and quality of life. Given the limitations of the construct as an explanation for the wide range of experiences within the autistic constellation, is it still useful? Or is a focus on ToM now merely a habit in the field?

Can autistic performance on ToM tasks be explained largely in terms of in-group and out-group or audience effects? And, if we adopt this framework, what does it mean for our understanding of typical social behaviours? It is reasonable to question whether mentalising and its consequences are necessarily a positive influence in our society. For example, in-group effects can lead to prejudice and unconscious bias, and obligatory mentalising mechanisms may be counter-productive for originality.

Some autistic people report having too much insight into other people – detecting every detail of someone's behaviour, as well as feeling empathy very strongly. If so, it is possible that we have our models of autistic and non-autistic social skills entirely the wrong way around. Perhaps non-autistic people are relatively poor observers of human behaviour, and this gives us the ability to respond quickly and fluently, because we are only using the gist of the social situation to guide our decisions. Meanwhile autistic people are burdened with an unfiltered representation of every detail that prevents them from making handy generalisations or using holistic approximations to guide their social behaviour. We will return to this theme in Chapter 8.

COMMUNITY CONTRIBUTION: HARRIET AXBEY – *AUTISTIC TRAINEE TEACHER*

While I struggle understanding peoples' thoughts and actions, I have also dedicated a lot of my time to 'learning social', much like learning a language as described in this chapter. Therefore, in the same way that a newcomer to English might have more knowledge of prepositions and the passive voice than a native speaker, I often see intricacies in interactions that others miss because of this active learning process. But I will always have an 'accent' preventing me from fully integrating, and the constant practise and repetition of this learning is indeed frustrating and tiring.

The primary deficit model was damaging, especially in schools, as it paved the way for interventions aimed at making autistic individuals 'normal'. When I read about the early deficit models, I feel angry, as these have left an imprint in people's minds. The idea that something is 'missing' infers that it can be added or fixed at a later date, and although the neurodiversity model is working to amend these preconceptions, they have spawned many inappropriate interventions such as applied behavioural analysis (ABA). When people tell me they are engaging their children in these kinds of therapies, or in diet treatments like the gluten-free, casein-free approach, what I hear is that they feel that their child, and I, are not good enough as we are. That we need to be cured, fixed, tempered, basically changed to be more acceptable as human beings.

The primary deficit assumption that autistic individuals 'overreact' or 'misinterpret' all situations must be addressed as this could lead to serious problems. When I was at school I raised a potentially very serious child protection issue with a teacher; I was later told that I had overreacted to the information I had heard because I was autistic and that it was not being followed up because of this. Now, I don't know if there was anything behind the 'banter' I had heard in the common room, but I do know that my instincts were being questioned because of my diagnosis.

I welcome the idea of neurotypical ToM being taught by autistic individuals who have already mastered it. I think I would have gained a lot more from someone sitting me down at nine years old and telling me: there's nothing wrong with you; you're just different. These are the problems you are going to face, but it will get better.

Recommended reading

Baron-Cohen, S. (2000). Theory of mind and autism: A fifteen year review. *Understanding Other Minds: Perspectives from Developmental Cognitive Neuroscience, 2,* 3–20.

Beardon, L. (2008). Is Autism really a disorder part two – theory of mind? Rethink how we think. *Journal of Inclusive Practice in Further and Higher Education, 1,* 19–21.

Johnson, M. H. (2012). Executive function and developmental disorders: The flip side of the coin. *Trends in Cognitive Sciences, 16*(9), 454–457.

Leslie, A. M. (1987). Pretense and representation: The origins of "theory of mind". *Psychological Review, 94*(4), 412.

Scott, R. M., & Baillargeon, R. (2017). Early false-belief understanding. *Trends in Cognitive Sciences, 21*(4), 237–249.

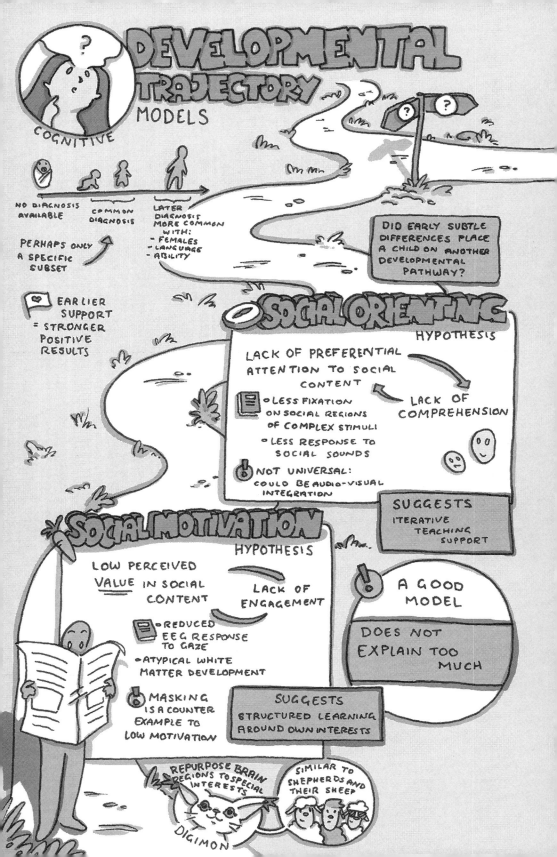

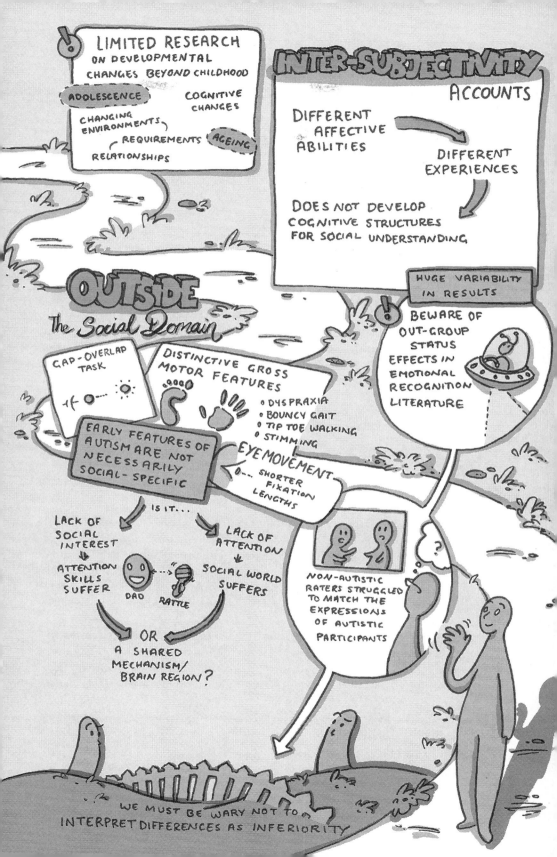

7 Autism at the cognitive level
Developmental trajectory models

AS WE HAVE seen, Theory of Mind (ToM) was originally conceptualised in a fairly modular fashion: as a skill which appeared at a specific developmental time point (ultimately marked by the ability to pass false-belief tasks) and that could either be present or absent. However, updated accounts of social cognitive development situate false-belief task success within a more complex developmental trajectory. This incorporates both early examples of ToM, such as implicit belief tracking and desire reasoning, and related behaviours such as joint attention and emotion recognition.

Rather than focus on a single deficit (failure to switch on ToM) marked out by a simple test (false-belief comprehension) developmental theories of autism posit that early, subtle differences in the child's relationship with their environment place them on an unusual developmental pathway that leads to a pattern that makes up the diagnostic features of autism (Happé, 2015).

1. Early signs of autism

As mentioned in Chapter 3, diagnosis of autism is possible from early childhood. The average age of reported diagnosis in a large European survey was 42 months (Salomone et al., 2016), though the range varied from 34 to 50 months when comparing between European countries. In addition, this sample were only aged up to 7 years old, and many autistic people are diagnosed much later, including in adulthood. Diagnosis can also happen before 3 years old, but there are question marks over how reliable such diagnoses might be. Salomone and colleagues showed that being female and having better language are associated with later diagnosis, suggesting that those children diagnosed very early may represent only a sub-set of the autism constellation. This may be compounded by the influence of socio-economic and ethnic factors on access to specialist diagnostic services (Daniels & Mandell, 2014). Another possibility is that when diagnoses are offered very early in development, these are not stable over time (Bieleninik et al., 2017). At the time of writing, there is no reliable way to diagnose autism in the first year of life.

This is largely because, as we have seen, diagnosis at any age relies on observation of a pattern of behaviours across multiple contexts, ideally by a multi-disciplinary team. There is no single biological or behavioural marker with a robust positive predictive value for autism. Instead, there exists a range of early, parent-report screening tools (e.g. the Checklist for Autism in Toddlers, the Early Screening for Autism and Communication Disorders and the Autism Parent Screen for Infants) or direct observational protocols (e.g. the Autism Observation Scale for Infants, the Autism Diagnostic Observation Schedule – Toddler Module) to facilitate early screening. These tools rely on so-called 'red flags', which are lists of behaviours such as following a point or responding to their name being called, that are reduced (or, for some behaviours, e.g. spinning objects, increased) in children who later receive an autism diagnosis relative to the general population.

Theoretical accounts of autism reviewed in this chapter interpret these early, small disruptions to the typical developmental process as having larger downstream effects, which are eventually recognisable as autism. Waddington's epigenetic landscape, shown in Figure 7.1, is a useful visual metaphor for this process. Although the landscape was initially put forward as a way to understand the actions of genes across the lifespan, it can also be used to conceptualise how early subtle differences can result, over time, in a radically different approach to the world, such as found in autism. In the image, the ball can represent the child and his or her development, which unfolds like a slow, downhill roll. Small differences in the starting position, direction or speed of the ball, or tiny bumps along the way, could result in the ball following paths that diverge over time to become radically differentiated. The hills which

FIGURE 7.1 Waddington's epigenetic landscape

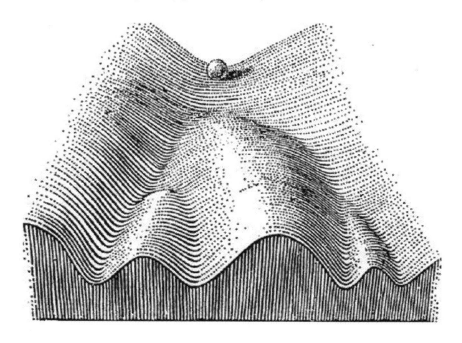

separate each path can represent the significant effort required if one were to attempt to move, later in life, from one path to another.

2. Studying early signs of autism

There is great interest in how autism is manifest in the first year of life and even pre-natally. For some, this effort is aimed at discovering a potential 'cure' for autism or even introducing pre-natal screening, highly controversial and ethically debatable aims (see this chapter's Current Debates section for more). However, the majority do not endorse this viewpoint but are still interested in early autism development, and there are many good reasons for this focus. Parents often report distress over the long, complex and sometimes upsetting process of seeking a diagnosis. In a recent international survey, Sue and colleagues uncovered large gaps between the age at which parents first raised concerns and mean age at which diagnosis occurred (Fletcher-Watson et al., 2017). In some cases, parents may struggle to have their child's needs recognised by clinical services, especially if the child is cognitively able and/ or skilled at masking. Likewise, autistic people who receive a diagnosis in later life often regret the time it took to identify their autism – in a recent qualitative study of the experiences of autistic women and girls, nearly every person interviewed wished they had known earlier (Sedgewick, personal communication). Robust, biological early diagnostic markers would permit rapid, reliable diagnosis early in life, with potential benefits for autistic people, their families and also for society in areas like planning service provision. Early diagnostic markers would also allow proper investigation of any putative environmental factors contributing to outcome, and help put paid to scaremongering media reports about the supposed causal role of screen time or radio waves in autism.

There are also more purely scientific reasons to search for concrete diagnostic markers to further our understanding of how different developmental domains interact. For example, as we will see in more detail next, there is ongoing discussion of how social cognitive skills relate to 'domain-general' (i.e. not specifically social) abilities. Are differences in attention to social content in a stimulus related to general attentional processes? Do our social interactions in the real world rely on a fully operational attention system or, conversely, do they provide a training environment for that attentional system to develop? Likewise, in the previous chapter, we raised the question of how executive functions might act as a compensatory mechanism for some autistic people. In terms of autism, diagnostic markers might also provide a basis for starting to understand heterogeneity in autism, resolving the issue highlighted in Chapter 3 that division of autism into meaningful sub-groups is virtually impossible while we are reliant purely on behavioural diagnosis.

For a long time, the main method adopted to try to identify the earliest signs of autism was retrospective parental report and video analysis. In these studies, researchers asked parents about their child's earliest months and years, and gathered home video footage of children who had later received an autism diagnosis. Attempts were made to standardise the samples, for example, by focusing on videos of a child's first birthday party. The method was far from perfect, but despite the lack of control and objectivity, retrospective analysis produced some important findings about early features of autism, including reduced smiling and orienting to name around 12 months (Palomo et al., 2006). Other studies focused on clinical records, finding higher levels of reported concerns in routine infant and toddler screening tests, specifically in the social domain, for children who later received an autism diagnosis (Johnson et al., 1992).

More recently, the focus has switched to prospective studies, which permit the use of experimental methods and uniform classification of all participants. The most established method of prospective research is to recruit parents who already have an autistic child, who are now having a new baby. These younger siblings have about a 20% chance of receiving an autism diagnosis, meaning that researchers can recruit, for example, 100 families and reliably gather early years data from a sample of 20 children with autism. Given an estimated prevalence of 1% in the general population, it would require recruitment of 2,000 families to achieve the same group size if recruiting from the general population. The first of these autism-sibling studies began to yield data in 2005, when Lonnie Zwaigenbaum and colleagues reported on 65 younger siblings who had been – at that point – followed up to 24 months (Zwaigenbaum et al., 2005). More recently, the field has begun to be augmented by work with other high-likelihood groups, including children of autistic mothers and infants born premature. Specific findings from these studies will be mentioned next, as we consider a range of theoretical models in turn, but a recent review of results suggests that while many group differences have been found, the field requires more replications before any test could begin to achieve candidate marker status (Jones et al., 2014).

Although sibling studies, and work with other high-likelihood infant groups, represent a significant methodological improvement on the retrospective work that went before, this literature remains beset by limitations. One key issue is the potential generalisability of findings. It is unclear to what extent findings from an infant-sibling group would generalise to autistic children born into families without existing autism experience, or this pattern of genetic predisposition. The specificity of results is also a problem. To date, no published sibling studies have recruited a relevant control group, such as children with a learning disability or a genetic susceptibility to (for example) dyslexia or ADHD (although this latter group is currently being recruited and studied as we write). While some of the cohort may follow neurodivergent pathways without being autistic, permitting some comparison to be made between atypical outcomes, larger numbers are needed to determine the specificity of findings to later autism diagnosis. At the time of writing, when long-term infant cohort studies are still relatively few and far between, this issue is compounded by the drive to publish early – many papers report merely on cross-sectional comparisons of high-likelihood versus low-likelihood groups rather than wait for longitudinal data on diagnostic outcome. Even when outcome data are available, these will normally have been collected at the earliest reasonable time point (often 36 months, but sometimes as young as 18 months) – raising the likely possibility that these children actually represent a sub-set of the constellation, with a specific combination of autistic features amenable to early diagnosis. We know that many autistic children don't stand out until much later, and as yet, we have little data from later diagnosed participants in infant-sibling studies, which may relate to variability within the autism constellation.

The field also needs to meet some steep statistical challenges before a robust early marker can be identified. It is well known that any early marker must demonstrate adequate sensitivity and specificity in a study with a large enough sample size to limit confidence intervals to an acceptable range. But less widely acknowledged is the importance of a test being both reliable and straightforward to administer, and the fact that the predictive value of any marker is adjusted according to the baseline prevalence of a condition in the general population. The percentage of false positives might be low, but if the number of people who do not have a particular condition is high – in this case, 99/100 individuals at current best estimates of prevalence – even a low false positive rate could translate into a large number of people being misdiagnosed. These complex statistical concepts have been superbly summarised and helpfully modelled online on the Spectrum blog (see "Further Reading") and are represented in Figure 7.2.

3. The social orienting hypothesis

We have seen that there is still no robust, reliable early marker of autism, either cognitive or biological. However, there are a number of theoretical accounts that make predictions about where such a marker might be found. The first of these is the social orienting hypothesis, which predicts that the earliest signs of autism should be a lack of preferential attention (across all sensory domains) to social content in the world. This account supposes that a basic mechanism that prioritises attention to social content, starting with simple orienting to faces and voices, is disrupted in autism. The child attends less to social content, missing out on opportunities to learn about social behaviour and develop language. Soon, a lack of comprehension of the social world starts to reinforce the attentional difference – children may choose to spend time and attention on non-social activities, which are more comprehensible and therefore enjoyable. This developmental pathway results in the social interactional and communication differences that are characteristic of autism.

This hypothesis was originally based on two different sources of data. Dawson and colleagues showed that autistic children at young ages were less likely than typical and learning disabled children to orient to social

Chapter 7 Developmental trajectory models 107

FIGURE 7.2 Statistical challenges of identifying a biomarker for autism

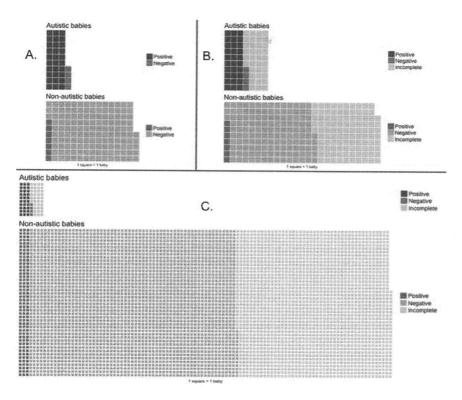

Panel A shows results of one attempt to identify autism using markers of early brain development (Hazlett et al., 2017). Here the data look like they have fairly good levels of precision. In Panel B, we see how different the data look when the number of incomplete scans are taken into account – this gives us a lot less confidence in the practical potential of the marker. Panel C extrapolates the data according to the population base rate. We can see that, if applied in practice, this test would result in unacceptably high numbers of false positives: infants diagnosed with autism who are not autistic. Provided by kind permission of Jon Brock.

sounds – their name being called and clapping (Dawson et al., 1998). In the visual domain, Klin used eye-tracking with a small group of autistic adults to demonstrate that autism was associated with differences in looking patterns (Klin et al., 2002). Specifically, the autistic group showed less fixation on the social regions (e.g. face, eyes) of a complex stimulus (excerpts from a movie).

What about data from infancy? It is uncontested that infants (including non-human infants, even chicks!) show a preference for looking at faces, or face-like stimuli, from birth. In fact, recent data have revealed that this may even be in evidence pre-natally, as infants in the womb orient to face-like light patterns projected onto the mother's body (Reid et al., 2017) – though replications are needed to confirm this preliminary finding. Turning to autism,

Klin and colleagues have replicated their adult finding with toddlers, showing less attentional bias towards faces compared with typical and learning disabled groups (Chawarska et al., 2010; Jones et al., 2008). In a study with typically developing twins, they also demonstrated that such looking patterns appear to be under genetic control (Constantino et al., 2017).

So far, so good, but there are complications. There are a number of findings that suggest intact social attention and orienting among adults and children in the autism constellation, casting doubt on the social orienting hypothesis (see Guillon et al., 2014 for a review). Indeed, the British Autism Study of Infant Siblings found no differences associated with later autism diagnosis in looking patterns to social and non-social content in a static image array (Elsabbagh et al., 2013). There are a number of ways we might probe the apparent disparities in the literature. Sue and colleagues found subtle differences in the *timing* of eye-movements when viewing naturalistic, but static, social stimuli (Fletcher-Watson et al., 2009). Other studies have suggested that the looking preferences of autistic toddlers are dictated by episodes of audio-visual synchrony rather than social content (Klin et al., 2009), though this finding, too, is contested (Falck-Ytter et al., 2017). A problem with much of this literature is that stimulus complexity is not well captured or controlled. There is evidence that the greatest group differences arise when more ecologically valid stimuli are used (Frazier et al., 2017), but this raises the question of whether the ultimate cause of different looking patterns is specific to the social domain, or rather an information-processing difficulty. The use of video stimuli that feature cuts between camera angles may be particularly problematic when it comes to interpretation of data, since a delay in oculomotor movements or in information processing could be mistaken for a difference in top-down attentional preference (Ames & Fletcher-Watson, 2010).

One way to attempt to resolve these equivocal findings is to probe differences in attention developmentally, rather than cross-sectionally – mapping the timeline of specific behavioural patterns and their effects. One recent high-profile paper charted looking patterns in an infant-sibling group with repeated testing, using eye-tracking, over the first six months of life (Jones & Klin, 2013). The authors reported significant differences between children who were, and were not, later diagnosed with autism in the *trajectory* of looking patterns over time. However, taking each data collection point independently, there were no group differences in looking times. Moreover, at the earliest time points, infants who later received an autism diagnosis actually showed higher proportions of looking time to social content – though this pattern was non-significant. This finding, combined with evidence that domain-general attentional differences *are* predictive of autism outcome, led Mark Johnson to argue that it was time to reject the social orienting hypothesis of autism (Johnson, 2014).

4. The social motivation hypothesis

A subtly different account of the developmental cascade resulting in autism places the emphasis not on attentional biases, but on reward value. The theory has a very similar structure to the social orienting hypothesis. Again, an innate mechanism is proposed, making social information inherently rewarding to infants. The earliest sign of autism in this scenario would be a reduction or absence of this tendency to find social information rewarding. This early small shift could result in reduced engagement with the social world over time, resulting in missed opportunities to learn normative interaction skills, and ultimately delivering the social and communication features of autism. As in the case of social orienting, an early bias might be self-sustaining–lack of social engagement, resulting in reduced social understanding, would undermine the already limited reward value of social information or contact.

This hypothesis continues to rely largely on data from adults, indicating fundamental differences in neural response to social stimuli. One argument emphasised by this theory is that the brain regions normally dedicated to developing social expertise become re-purposed in autism. A striking case study comes from a young man with autism who showed a neurological specialisation for recognising Digimon characters in regions typically reserved for recognition of human faces (Grelotti et al., 2005). However, it's worth noting that shepherds learn to recognise their sheep using similar brain regions, without anyone implying this shows reduced interest in people! There is also some limited data from infancy, for example, indicating a reduced EEG response to direct gaze in infants who later get a diagnosis (Elsabbagh et al., 2012) and atypical white-matter development in the same population (Wolff et al., 2012). However, these data do not specifically invoke a social motivation account, as they do not demonstrate specificity of disruption to brain regions underpinning reward. Nor indeed is it clear that there is any such thing as a 'social reward' system – meaning something distinct from the general reward system that can be activated by a range of stimuli; social, monetary, food and so forth (Lin et al., 2011). That said, recent data do show that reward value (indexed by rapidity of learning) varies with the social versus non-social nature of the stimulus and also whether it is more or less engaging for adults and children with typical development – a replication in autism would be of interest (Vernetti et al., 2018).

This theory clearly requires more direct testing in relevant populations, but even with more data, it is likely to be challenging to distinguish the social motivation hypothesis from the social orienting hypothesis. It is possible, perhaps even likely, that social attentional and social reward differences interact reciprocally across infancy. However, disentangling these is essential if we wish to understand the best way to support autistic children. Take, for example, a non-speaking child – what is the best way to help them develop their communication skills? The social orienting hypothesis suggests that iterative teaching might be appropriate. They have missed out on a number of natural learning opportunities, due to their different attentional focus at a critical developmental stage, but explicit teaching might enable them to expand their repertoire of communication skills, resulting in greater autonomy in the future. In contrast, the social motivation hypothesis suggests that the child's lack of speech may reflect a lack of motivation to engage with others. In this context, repeated skill teaching might have limited value – especially in a framework where success is rewarded with social feedback, like smiles, praise and high fives. Instead, we might wish to structure the learning around the child's personal interests, while providing an alternative way to communicate, such as a voice-output communication aid.

A challenge to the social motivation hypothesis comes from the reports of autistic people themselves, as well as independent observations. Children's attachment to parents/caregivers is not affected by autism (Teague et al., 2017). Many autistic adults show a high motivation to engage with others, albeit in ways that do not always adhere to social norms. This is not a new observation – Lorna Wing originally characterised such children as "active but odd". The phenomenon is also apparent when one considers the high rates of self-reported 'camouflaging' among autistic people (Lai et al., 2017). Why would someone who does not find social engagement rewarding put so much effort into their relationships with other people? Difficulties navigating the social world, where these occur, often seem to arise from differences in social interaction style rather than a lack of motivation. One answer to this apparent conundrum might lie in considering the developmental timeline. If autistic people experience a reduced neurobiological reward in response to social content in infancy, this could have an impact on their developmental trajectory in relation to quantity, and therefore quality, of social interaction. However, this argument does not also require that an older autistic child or adult would still be un-motivated by social engagement. Indeed, individual differences in the period of time during which social reward systems were depressed could theoretically go some way towards explaining the sub-groups labelled aloof, passive and odd by Lorna Wing. However, firm evidence that infants later diagnosed as autistic lack social motivation is still wanting, and the absence of overt behavioural differences in social response in the first year of life is a striking finding from infant-sibling studies.

Returning to our criteria for what makes a good theory (see Chapter 5), both the social orienting and social motivation account run the risk of explaining too much. The developmental cascade does not allow, in any clear way, for the uneven profile of social abilities in autism. While autistic children often find it difficult to spontaneously intuit what someone else is thinking, they do show attachment to loved ones, emotion recognition and emotional empathy (unless they have an additional problem of alexithymia), as well some of the less noble aspects of human social processing, such as gender and racial stereotypes (Hirschfeld et al., 2007).

5. Intersubjectivity accounts

A very early theoretical model of autism, proposed by Peter Hobson, maintained that autism is primarily rooted in an affective and interpersonal difference (Hobson & Lee, 1998, 1999). Differences in the ability to perceive and respond to the affective expressions of others were hypothesised to lead to atypical social experiences in infancy and childhood, which in turn impacted later social understanding.

In common with other developmental models, this account is not consistently supported by the data: findings on differences between autistic and non-autistic people in viewing, identifying and responding to emotional stimuli are mixed at best. There are large individual differences between autistic people, and results change with age, intellectual level and specific study design (Uljarevic & Hamilton, 2013). Another source of evidence that may be relevant to intersubjectivity accounts of autism comes from studies of imitation. Like joint attention, imitation is thought to be a pivotal developmental skill underpinning explicit teaching and playing a role in forging social bonds. But, like emotion recognition, while imitation is frequently reported to be atypical in autism, methods and findings vary widely, and there are substantial individual differences (Vanvuchelen et al., 2011).

A significant question arising is whether we should interpret a lack of intersubjective identification between autistic people and non-autistic experimenters as a difference associated with autism, or as a typical manifestation of in-group effects? In Chapter 6, we discussed how some findings relating to imitation might plausibly be attributed to in-group and out-group status, rather than being autism specific. The same possibility applies to our interpretations of the emotion recognition literature. For example, Sheppard and colleagues created emotional stimuli by placing autistic and neurotypical people in one of four different social scenarios (Sheppard et al., 2016), such as being ignored or being told a joke. Their reactions were filmed and later these films were shown to non-autistic raters, who were asked to match the reactions to the scenarios. The results showed that raters struggled to match emotional responses of autistic people with scenarios, even though they rated those responses as equally expressive. In other words, this study reports a neurotypical deficit in recognising and interpreting the emotional expressions of autistic people. This echoes the work of Brewer and colleagues (2017, and see Chapter 6), which also demonstrated a mismatch between neurotypical and autistic expressions of emotional states – though in this case both autistic and non-autistic participants found autistic facial expressions harder to read. Moreover, Komeda and colleagues (2015) demonstrated that autistic people show a stronger neural signal of empathy towards autistic characters than to non-autistic characters – and the opposite pattern was true for neurotypical participants. These findings suggest that we might explain some of the behaviours considered to be distinctive features of autism as, instead, a typical manifestation of the tendency to more readily and deeply engage with people from the same social group. This finding corresponds with some new social theories of autism, as well as with reports from autistic people, and we will return to this theme in more depth in Chapter 9.

6. Early development outside the social domain

All three of the theoretical accounts presented here attempt to explain autism by identifying an early, subtle difference in the way that autistic infants relate to the social world. However, some of the most robust early markers linked to later diagnosis are in the non-social domain. For example, the gap-overlap task is a measure of the ability of an infant to switch their attention from a central target which has just disappeared, to a peripheral target which has just appeared. It also measures, via the 'overlap' condition, how this ability is impacted when the peripheral target comes on while the central one is still present, and thus disengagement is required as well as switching. The association between gap-overlap task performance and later autism diagnosis has been replicated in different cohorts, though sensitivity and specificity of this marker has yet to be established (Jones et al., 2014).

Another domain receiving increasing attention is motor development. Autism in children and adults is associated with a number of distinctive gross and fine motor features including tip-toe walking, bouncy gait, dyspraxia and a range of repetitive behaviours in the motor domain (e.g. hand-flapping, body rocking, finger twiddling) often known colloquially as 'stimming'. Recently, early motor differences have also been detected at the level of eye-movements, with shorter mean fixation lengths in infancy being associated with later diagnosis (Wass et al., 2015). Micro-movements of the head, for example, as captured during neuroimaging, are being analysed in autism and other groups (Torres & Denisova, 2016). An innovative tablet-based study shows how distinctive motor movements in autism might be identifiable from game-play using machine learning (Anzulewicz et al., 2016). It is too early to draw firm conclusions from this literature, which is currently lacking large-scale and robust longitudinal data, but certainly the importance of early motor development should not be ignored in our efforts to understand autism.

How do we interpret these findings? One possibility is that the early features of autism are not social-specific. This feeds into a wider debate in development psychology on how skills required in the social domain relate to domain-general skills – we touched upon this in the review of executive function in autism in Chapter 6. On one hand, we might hypothesise that the social world permits intensive rehearsal of key domain-general switching (and other executive, or motor) skills. For example, attention switching and disengagement are required when rapidly moving your focus between your father's face and the rattle he is shaking. Perhaps frequent exposure to this sort of situation acts as a 'training ground' for the attention system. An infant without a great deal of interest in that situation, due to social attention, social motivation or intersubjective differences, might miss out on the chance to build up their attention skills. Alternatively, the causal direction could be the opposite. A child without an efficient attentional switching system might find that impedes their social interactions, leading over time to a divergent path in terms of social interactive behaviour. Another factor concerns the behaviour of the parent, of course. In the example noted earlier, if the child looks at the rattle but not her father's face, how will her father react? His behaviour will be shaped by hers, and vice versa. Both people in the dyad create a shared environment which may promote certain types of skills and behaviours more than others.

A third explanation also exists – that both social interactive behaviours and domain-general skills are subsumed by a shared mechanism or brain region which is the source of the difference. Some have proposed that self-other switching, that is switching between representations to do with the self (own emotions, beliefs, motor intentions, etc.) and those to do with others, might be a candidate mechanism in the development of autism (de Guzman et al., 2016; Sowden & Shah, 2014). Bedford and colleagues have further shown that a combination of markers of domain-general attention with social neuro-response plus direct observation measures provide the most robust early identifier linked to later autism diagnosis at 7 years old (Bedford et al., 2017). Their data are interpreted as reflecting an additive mechanism, resulting in a predictor of autism that relies on the presence of separately measured cognitive capacities that combine to increase likelihood.

One final question is whether determining the early causal associations between different features of autism is really necessary? If interactive scenarios, like playing with a parent and a rattle, involve both social and non-social skills, we can provide opportunities to develop both by simply creating more such opportunities in a suitably enjoyable and motivating way. A recent attempt to do just that found that early, parent-delivered, play-based intervention led to increased attention to parents, with longer-term positive effects on parental directiveness and child communication (Green et al., 2015, 2017). Crucially, the authors emphasise *"a strategy to mitigate developmental risks and modify prodromal symptom trajectories, rather than 'eliminate' a condition"* (2017, p. 1330, emphasis in original). Thus, while such early interventions require a robust ethical framework, they may have the potential – by delivering support in a critical window of development and enhancing key skills – to guide parents to tailor their behaviour, creating an optimal environment for the autistic child. This in turn could enable a higher proportion of autistic children to achieve greater autonomy and self-determination in the future.

7. Lifespan development in autism: beyond childhood

Theoretical accounts of autism reviewed here focus exclusively on early development in infancy but of course important developmental changes continue across the lifespan. Here we briefly mention two other key developmental stages: puberty/adolescence and old age (discussed at the behavioural level in Chapter 3). These are selected not because other life stages are unimportant – starting school, transitions from school to adulthood, finding a life partner and parenthood are all major life changes – but because these two stages are specifically associated with *cognitive* changes. The review is brief, again, not because these life stages are unimportant but because the published literature here is very limited.

At puberty, children experience changes across the biological, cognitive and behavioural levels. Biologically, there are well-known hormonal effects, but also neurological developments (Blakemore & Choudhury, 2006). Behavioural changes include transitions of school setting around the time of puberty, with new expectations, including the need to monitor a more complex timetable, maintain concentration for longer periods in class and manage independent study. Moreover, at this time, there are changing expectations of appropriate behaviour with regard to play, friendship and romantic relationships; for neurotypical teenagers, family often becomes less important and peer group relations much more influential. Occurrences of diagnosis of autism in later childhood and adolescence may be related to these contextual factors. As new, adult-like societal norms start to be applied, young people with autism may find their coping techniques stretched beyond capacity, revealing differences that were previously masked or accommodated. Qualitative work has revealed, for example, high rates of loneliness reported by autistic teenage boys (Lasgaard et al., 2010) and difficulties navigating sexual development (Dewinter et al., 2017). The challenges of the latter domain may be exacerbated by the high-prevalence of non-normative gender identification and sexual orientation among autistic people, and by the potential sensory impact of bodily changes. Adolescence is also a risky time in terms of mental health; social anxiety, eating disorders and depression often arise in the teens for neurotypical young people, and autistic young people are at higher risk for all of these (Simonoff et al., 2008).

For autistic adolescents who have significant support needs (perhaps due to learning disability and/or language disorder) and those who support them, this stage of life may produce different pressures. As non-disabled peers start to become more independent, parents and siblings can feel the stressful impact of having an autistic family member more acutely (Tsai et al., 2017). Hormonal changes may be related to increased frequency of self-harm or violence, made more challenging by increased size and strength. Beyond adolescence, as children grow into adults but support needs remain high, parents can start to worry about their child's long-term care and well-being (Griffith et al., 2012).

Some studies report on so-called optimal outcome where children with an early diagnosis no longer meet diagnostic criteria on standardised instruments later in life (Fein et al., 2013). However, there is some evidence that those individuals do still experience significant mental health difficulties, raising concerns that apparent change in diagnostic status is due to effortful compensation (Livingston & Happé, 2017) rather than a genuine change in underlying differences. Recent attention to risk of suicidal behaviour in autism has revealed that feelings of "not belonging" and being a burden to others are among the factors contributing to suicidality in autistic people (Pelton & Cassidy, 2017). In that context, further research is needed to characterise so-called optimal outcome and the autistic experience of intervention, and to determine whether it is a legitimate goal for early supports.

Biological, cognitive and behavioural changes associated with ageing are also well established in the general population (Hedden & Gabrieli, 2004). Behaviourally, people may retire from full-time work, leading to opportunities for travel, hobbies and voluntary work, but also a loss of daily structure and work-based social networks. There may also be a need to care for grandchildren, a spouse or sibling and even, as life expectancies increase, a parent. Retirement can also put pressure on social relationships including life partnerships, as couples begin to spend more time together after many years of working outside the home. A number of adults coming for first diagnosis of autism in their 60s and 70s have long-standing autism traits that have not altered, rather the scaffolding and enabling environment may have been removed if an enjoyed and well-structured job ends, or an understanding and supportive partner dies.

Cognitively, as well as the risk of dementia, ageing is associated with normal declines in memory, reaction time and other fundamental cognitive skills. We know shockingly little about physical and mental changes in autism associated with ageing (Happé & Charlton, 2012). Follow-up of children diagnosed by the narrow autism criteria of the 1960s or '70s, show continued need for substantial support, and even when social difficulties or repetitive behaviours are rated as having reduced, quality of life is disappointingly low (Howlin et al., 2014). Studies in the states suggest these adults have higher rates of almost all health problems (Croen et al., 2015). However, today's children are diagnosed according to far broader criteria, and we hope they are being raised in a more supportive society – there is reason to be optimistic that their life journeys will be far more positive. A study of adults coming for first diagnosis of autism found that older adults reported more autistic traits than younger adults, but did somewhat better on some neuropsychological tasks (Happé et al., 2016). The first cross-sectional group studies of older autistic adults also suggest that age-related declines in some cognitive functions may be less steep in autism than non-autism groups (Lever & Geurts, 2016), although longitudinal studies are necessary to rule out cohort or selection effects.

A research focus on early development makes sense in regard to some scientific goals, such as understanding the developmental causal associations between different cognitive domains and key behaviours. Although there is no single pot of autism research funding that must be shared out between projects and disciplines, investment in such studies necessarily limits what is being done to provide evidence-based support for autistic people at other life stages. Given that aiming to identify a cure or preventative measure for autism itself represents a moral bankruptcy (even if improving communication or preventing epilepsy is desirable), we know that there will always be autistic people in our world. In which case, improving and increasing research into lifespan issues must be an important priority for the future.

8. Current debates

Summary

A group of theories arose, alongside and following attempts to characterise autism in relation to a fixed deficit in the social cognitive domain, which adopted a more developmental perspective on autism. We characterise them here as social attention, social motivation and intersubjectivity accounts. These theories attempt to capture small, early adjustments to cognitive processes, which set the child on a developmental pathway resulting in large differences at the age when diagnosis becomes possible. The developmentally increasing differences between the autistic and non-autistic child may be accompanied by differences in expectations from adults and peers, which contribute to the identification of specific behaviours as 'symptoms' of autism. The search for consistent and specific early signs of autism continues but faces major statistical and methodological challenges. Meanwhile, autism research focusing on other life stages, such as old age, is in its infancy.

Big questions

The early autism research literature is beset by specific ethical issues (Fletcher-Watson et al., 2017b). It is essential to embed early autism research in a framework of engagement with community priorities. How will autistic children enrolled in longitudinal or early intervention studies feel when they grow up? If we find a reliable early marker of autism, what should we do with that information? Are justifications for early intervention before diagnosis legitimate, and if so, where do the boundaries lie between a support that enables autistic children to achieve their goals and a support that serves merely to suppress or 'normalise' the autistic child?

Parallel with this debate is a concern regarding the ethics of intensive monitoring or early interventions in high-likelihood populations for those who do not go on to get an autism diagnosis. Are infant-sibling studies inadvertently changing parenting in enrolled families, and if so, how? What message do such studies send about the need to change the development of autistic children, and the acceptable costs of doing so? Rather than aiming for autism-specific early interventions, should we instead focus on 'generic' supports that empower parents, enrich the early years environment and focus on global targets like school readiness and language?

The pressure for early findings from longitudinal studies may result in results that reflect only part of the autism constellation; will infant-sibling study results be very different once we know the outcome of the children at 8 or 18 years? How far do any such findings generalise to the autism constellation as a whole?

One final question for this field concerns the definition of "social" in the context of social orienting, social motivation and so on. Frequently, studies rely on looking patterns to static faces or videos of a single person talking or singing. In particular, looking at the eye region is interpreted as social, while looking at the mouth region is not. There is a risk here of a tautological argument, whereby any looking pattern exhibited by a child identified as autistic is automatically characterised as non-social, or even inferior. Researchers in this field need to be vigilant to ensure that results are interpreted without recourse to such logical fallacies and that group differences are recognised as differences, rather than being automatically interpreted through a set of normative values.

COMMUNITY CONTRIBUTION: ANN MEMMOTT – *AUTISTIC AUTISM ADVISER, PARENT AND BUSINESS OWNER*

Could autism be a result of differences in development over time? As an autistic adult, working nationally as an adviser, this is a subject for personal reflection. Some of the theories of autism focus on the idea that autistic people are broken versions of other people. For example, suggesting that we're bad at paying attention to social signalling from any others. In reality, I and my autistic colleagues find that we're pretty excellent at paying attention to autistic social signalling and fairly clueless about how to interpret social signalling of non-autistic people. Likewise, non-autistic people seem to struggle to interpret us correctly. It appears to be a difference in communication, not a deficit. From my perspective, I find time with other autistic people socially rewarding. I am also very keen to attempt to socialise with non-autistic people, but am frequently met with a baffling response from them. A different communication system at work, rather than a deficit? Similarly, the idea that we struggle with empathy is a tricky one. I find it generally easy to spot the emotional state of autistic people and empathise accordingly. But, I struggle to interpret the signalling of non-autistic individuals, so take extra time to process that. By the time I've done so, and responded, they're often already offended.

The question of how autistic people develop different skills over time is one we may not be close to answering, given the current lack of good research into adults. As a child, I was functionally non-verbal for the first ten years, rocking, flapping, spinning the wheels on toy cars. I was without doubt very autistic. I could sometimes speak words, but had no concept of their meaning. I could sometimes then speak phrases, with similar lack of clue as to what I was saying. Often, I could not speak at all, no matter how much effort I made, especially in any situation of sensory/social overload. Endless effort on my part has resulted in the communication skills we now see; I speak at conferences, study at the master's level, run a company. And yet words are still not my natural language, and I still fail to use them well in any stressful situation. Spoken words remain exhausting, whereas technology has been hugely liberating. I'm the same person. Am I 'broken' or not? I believe that autism is a difference and one that often has significant strengths for society.

Recommended reading

Beardon, L. (2017). *Autism and Asperger syndrome in adults*. London: Sheldon Press.

Blakemore, S. J. (2018). *Inventing ourselves: The secret life of the teenage brain*. New York, NY: Doubleday.

Fletcher-Watson, S., Apicella, F., Auyeung, B., Beranova, S., Bonnet-Brilhault, F., Canal-Bedia, R., . . . Farroni, T. (2017b). Attitudes of the autism community to early autism research. *Autism, 21*(1), 61–74.

Happé, F., & Charlton, R. A. (2012). Aging in autism spectrum disorders: A mini-review. *Gerontology, 58*(1), 70–78.

Johnson, M. H. (2014). Autism: Demise of the innate social orienting hypothesis. *Current Biology, 24*(1), R30–R31.

Jones, E. J., Gliga, T., Bedford, R., Charman, T., & Johnson, M. H. (2014). Developmental pathways to autism: A review of prospective studies of infants at risk. *Neuroscience & Biobehavioral Reviews, 39*, 1–33.

EMPATHISING & SYSTEMISING

ACCOUNTS

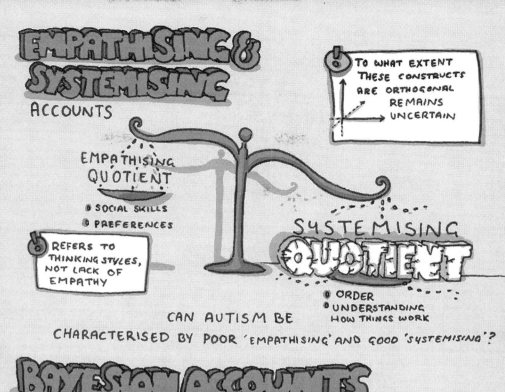

TO WHAT EXTENT THESE CONSTRUCTS ARE ORTHOGONAL REMAINS UNCERTAIN

EMPATHISING QUOTIENT
- SOCIAL SKILLS
- PREFERENCES

REFERS TO THINKING STYLES, NOT LACK OF EMPATHY

SYSTEMISING QUOTIENT
- ORDER
- UNDERSTANDING HOW THINGS WORK

CAN AUTISM BE CHARACTERISED BY POOR 'EMPATHISING' AND GOOD 'SYSTEMISING'?

BAYESIAN ACCOUNTS

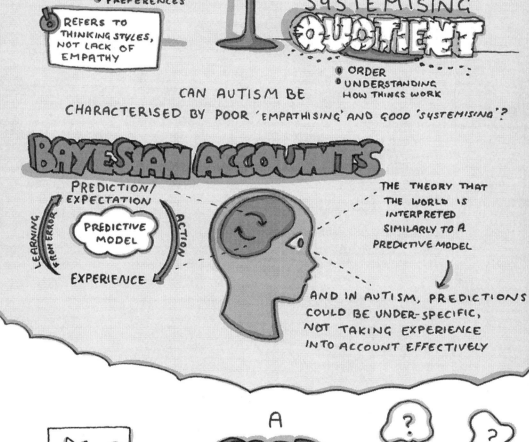

PREDICTION/ EXPECTATION
PREDICTIVE MODEL
LEARNING FROM ERROR
ACTION
EXPERIENCE

THE THEORY THAT THE WORLD IS INTERPRETED SIMILARLY TO A PREDICTIVE MODEL

AND IN AUTISM, PREDICTIONS COULD BE UNDER-SPECIFIC, NOT TAKING EXPERIENCE INTO ACCOUNT EFFECTIVELY

A GOOD MODEL

INFORMS BEST PRACTICES

LESS CLEAR HOW TO ADAPT THESE MODELS TO SUPPORT PERHAPS FOCUSED EMPLOYMENT

EXPLAINS

CAN INFORMATION PROCESSING MODELS EXPLAIN SOCIAL TRAITS IN AUTISM?

PERHAPS, IF THE NECESSARY PROCESSING IS IMPACTED

8 Autism at the cognitive level
Domain-general information processing models

S O FAR, THE cognitive models reviewed in this book, whether taking a developmental perspective or not, have largely focused on explaining the social features of autism. While attempts have been made to extend the explanatory power of these models to encompass non-social aspects of the condition, as we have seen, these are rarely adequate. In addition, there are open questions about the position of what we call "social cognition" within development – are our social interactions with others a test-bed in which we hone our domain-general skills, such as attention and executive functions? Or do these domain-general skills come first and our social interactions draw on these underlying processes?

In response to the incompleteness of social-focused theoretical accounts, and in recognition of the prevalence and importance of non-social components of autism, a number of theorists have proposed domain-general cognitive interpretations. We group these under the umbrella term 'information processing' because they all emphasise the different ways in which autistic people seem to take in, organise and respond to input from the world. Crucially, these models focus on aspects of input that are common to both social and non-social contexts, often at the level of perceptual features of the environment.

1. Perceptual process accounts: weak central coherence theory

The 'weak central coherence' account was the first domain-general theory to attempt to explain strengths, as well as difficulties, in autism. Uta Frith coined the term 'central coherence' to refer to the tendency neurotypical people have to draw information together, integrating details in context to form a gestalt (i.e. an organised whole that is more than the sum of its parts), see the bigger picture and get the overall meaning (Frith & Happé, 1994). Her early and pioneering studies of autistic strengths in block design (see Figure 8.1) and embedded figures tests, with her then-PhD student Amitta Shah, formed the bedrock for this theory, which proposed that in autism, the neurotypical drive for 'central coherence' is reduced, resulting in better attention to and memory for local details, but lessened global processing (Shah & Frith, 1983, 1993).

FIGURE 8.1   The block design test

In fact, Kanner also noticed the eye for detail in autism, writing in 1943 of the children's

> *inability to experience wholes without full attention to the constituent parts. . . . A situation, a performance, a sentence is not regarded as complete if it is not made up of exactly the same elements that were present at the time the child was first confronted with it. If the slightest ingredient is altered or removed, the total situation is no longer the same and therefore is not accepted as such.*

(Kanner, 1943, p. 246)

Fragmented perception and thinking is also described in autobiographies: Donna Williams has described her senses as "*chaotic, fragmented and constantly shifting and fluctuating*" (Williams, 2009),[1] and Gunilla Gerland writes,

> *Every little bit of fact seemed to land in its own compartment in my head and refused to be linked with any other. I tried poking into details. I dissected them and hoped a unified whole would appear, but it rarely did.*

(Gerland, 2003)

---

1   https://www.donnawilliams.net/

In the original version of this book, an anecdote (shown in Figure 8.2) was given to illustrate the notion of weak central coherence, something that the great Lorna Wing had told Francesca when she was still a PhD student. This is perhaps still the easiest way in which to convey the idea of weak central coherence:

Lorna Wing, when assessing a bright autistic boy, presented him with a toy bed, and asked the child to name the parts. The child correctly labelled the bed, mattress and quilt. Lorna then pointed to the pillow and asked, 'And what is this?' The boy replied, 'It's a piece of ravioli'.

The child in the anecdote was not joking, nor was his sight impaired – indeed Lorna commented that the pillow did indeed look just like a piece of ravioli, if taken out of context. However, she would never have seen it that way, because, like most neurotypical people, her interpretation of information was constrained by the context. The central coherence theory suggests that autistic perception, attention and memory are free from such contextual constraints.

Context affects not only visual, but also verbal and auditory processing; when we read homographs (words with two meanings and pronunciations but one spelling; see Figure 8.3), we rarely notice the potential ambiguity, because

FIGURE 8.2   An example of de-contextualised perception

Reproduced by kind permission of the artist, Axel Scheffler.

we automatically use the sentence context to identify the meaning; e.g. 'In her eye there was a big *tear*' versus 'In her dress there was a big *tear*'. Not using the sentence context to determine the correct pronunciation of homographs has been shown in autism, but importantly, this is a default only; if asked to read for meaning or alerted to the ambiguous words, autistic people have no difficulty integrating the sentence. This, and other evidence (reviewed in Happé & Frith, 2006), suggests weak coherence is a cognitive style and represents a bias not a deficit. Just as neurotypical people can, if necessary, memorise unconnected information without meaning (e.g. cramming for an exam, remembering a pin number), so autistic people can, if necessary, integrate local details into global meaning, but it seems neither comes naturally or without some effort.

Might an apparent local focus in autism just reflect difficulties with executive functions? For example, when drawing, autistic people may begin with details, which is unusual in neurotypical people; is this because of problems planning ahead? In line with the 'fractionated triad' account described in Chapter 3, there is some evidence that detail focus and executive difficulties are distinct (Brunsdon & Happé, 2014); for example, boys with ADHD who have

FIGURE 8.3   The homograph task, 'lead and tears'

problems planning and inhibiting their actions don't show detail focus, and detailed drawing style doesn't correlate with poor planning during drawing (Booth et al., 2003).

A recent meta-analysis, albeit drawing on tasks that tend to conflate global and local processing styles, demonstrated that slower global processing was the only robust effect found across studies (van der Hallen et al., 2015). More recently, Francesca and her colleague Rhonda Booth have suggested that superior local processing on one hand and reduced global/integrative processing on the other may be distinct and somewhat independent in autism, even though most tasks used to date have conflated the two (Booth & Happé, 2018). They report tasks designed to tap global and local processing independently, and suggest that measuring these dimensions separately may help untangle heterogeneity of cognitive style within autism.

2. Other perceptual process models

Weak central coherence theory is accompanied by other models which draw on overlapping evidence, with subtle differences in interpretation. Laurent Mottron's enhanced perceptual functioning model proposes that the perceptual systems of autistic people may out-perform their neurotypical peers, resulting in skills that can be interpreted as biases (Mottron et al., 2006). The theory predicts superiority in local processing, without a parallel difficulty at the global processing level. Evidence includes studies using drawing tasks in which people with autism are more capable of drawing an impossible figure compared with adults without autism. More recently, this account has inspired an investigation of whether estimates of the intellectual ability of autistic children may be more accurate when drawing on measures that capitalise on perceptual strengths. The authors found that using a battery of measures selected in this way (e.g. Raven's progressive matrices) resulted in much higher estimates of ability than a traditional IQ test (Courchesne et al., 2015).

Kate Plaisted-Grant and colleagues have proposed another variant, which suggests that the specific features affected in autism are discrimination and generalisation. These are framed as an opposing pair of skills, the former enhanced and the latter reduced in autism. This model is particularly based on data from visual search tasks which reveal that autistic people show particular strengths for the most difficult, conjunctive search tasks, requiring excellent discriminatory abilities (Plaisted et al., 1998a, 1998b; O'Riordan et al., 2001). A recent analysis of the locus for superior visual search in autism concluded that autistic adults "*excel in non-search processes, especially in the simultaneous discrimination of multiple visual stimuli*" (Shirama et al., 2017).

How are we to make sense of these multiple, subtly different explanations of the perceptual profile in autism? While they may make different predictions regarding performance on carefully designed experimental tasks, it is not clear to what extent distinguishing between these accounts would impact on, for example, classroom practice or home life. A sensitive psychological battery might provide a personalised profile of an autistic individual's perceptual processing – perhaps distinguishing between people who struggle with global processing and those with especially powerful local perceptual skills. But in the meantime, what we can draw from this literature is twofold. First, the emphasis on describing and explaining autistic strengths provides a welcome relief from the majority deficit-focused psychological literature on autism. Second, the research offers clues about how we might enhance teaching of children with autism and provide suitable employment opportunities for adults on the spectrum. Of course, such recommendations should not be allowed to drown out what autistic people themselves tell us directly about their needs, or the very real existence of individual differences. Nevertheless, these findings can provide a useful starting place, especially when working with those who may appear at first glance to have a significant learning disability. For this reason, it is essential that this work is shared with practitioners and translated into relevant guidelines.

Returning to the purely scientific perspective, we note that these explanatory models do not propose a specific mechanistic account. In each case, differences in the way that autistic people take in and respond to sensory input are evident, but the underlying process that governs these differences has not been elucidated. In Section 5, we review one new model of brain function which may have relevance here.

3. Integration and complexity

Another attempt to characterise autism from an information processing perspective comes from investigations of differences in processing and integrating multiple sources of information (Minshew et al., 1997; Minshew & Goldstein, 1998). These models do not focus on the perceptual level – approaching and responding to input – but instead explore the ways in which information is integrated in the brain, between the input and response phases. For example, Neumann and colleagues (2006) used a computational modelling approach to propose that the looking patterns to faces shown by many autistic people (looking more at mouths and less at eyes, compared with non-autistic people) result from differences in the top-down modulation of attention, rather than from bottom-up perceptual processes. Much evidence for this theory comes from fMRI studies which reveal differences in functional brain responses to multi-modal input and structural differences in circuits considered necessary for information integration (e.g. Castelli et al., 2002; Bird et al., 2006). One meta-analysis concluded that, while sample sizes are often small and thus results may not be robust, findings to date suggest differences in integration of different brain regions, rather than on any localised 'deficit' (Philip et al., 2012).

At the behavioural level, specific differences have been found in the tendency to integrate multiple sensory inputs – such as visual, auditory and tactile information (Iarocci & McDonald, 2006). Relatedly, some studies have found that autistic people need a larger quantity of motion cues to detect movement (Milne et al., 2005) – though this finding is not consistent (Foss-Feig et al., 2013). One interpretation of these data is that insensitivity to motion cues reflects a difficulty combining the multiple sources of information – such as relative position of foreground figure to background – required to detect movement. This work has been used to interpret the finding, discussed in Chapter 7, that infants who later receive an autism diagnosis attend more to areas of a stimulus that display audio-visual synchrony (Klin et al., 2009). Applying an information processing account here suggests that this attention to multi-modal synchrony is a reflection of effortful processing of multi-sensory input, rather than a simple attentional preference. The same interpretation can be used to frame findings from the eye-tracking literature, which consistently show the greatest group differences between participants with and without autism when stimuli are multi-modal (i.e. audio and visual input) and moving (Chevallier et al., 2015).

Another theoretical account which might fall under the broad heading of integration and complexity is the interest-based theory, monotropism (Murray et al., 2005). This theory, developed by autistic academics, posits that the defining feature of autism is atypical allocation of attention. The difference between autistic and non-autistic people is characterised as follows: "*It is the difference between having few interests highly aroused, the monotropic tendency, and having many interests less highly aroused, the polytropic tendency*" (ibid., p. 140). Consequently, this model places causal primacy on the intense focus apparent in the diagnostic domain of RRBIs, with other diagnostic features following from this underlying difference. To the extent that social interaction requires diffuse and distributed attention, autistic people are not well suited to that activity. Monotropic theory, which awaits empirical testing, provides a vivid description of the autistic experience of novelty and change, giving a valuable insight into the autistic experience of a crisis, or "meltdown":

> To a person in an attention tunnel every unanticipated change is abrupt and is truly, if briefly, catastrophic: a complete disconnection from a previous safe state, a plunge into a meaningless blizzard of sensations, a frightening experience which may occur many times in a single day.
>
> (Ibid., p. 147)

All of the theoretical approaches listed in this section share a high level of relevance to aspects of the lived experience of autistic people, not always well captured by cognitive models. For example, difficulties integrating sensory information could explain sensitivity to sensory input. Failure to integrate could make separate sensory signals overwhelming (hyper-sensitivity) or might cause some sensory input to be ignored because it is processed in isolation, instead of being boosted by concurrent input signals (hypo-sensitivity). Differences in how movement is processed and perceived could lead to atypical gross motor patterns and to dyspraxia, which is common among autistic people. Monotropic attention would lead to the development of specialised skills but also difficultly dealing with change. All of these features would impact on social cognitive abilities, by inhibiting the online, rapid processing of social information which often incorporates multiple inputs – e.g. speech, gesture, facial expression. However, this theory family is severely limited by a lack of data directly testing the predictions of the model. Rather, the model has largely been derived from post-hoc interpretations of patterns of neurological and behavioural data, and is currently lacking robust experimental support.

4. Systemising and empathising

An influential account, growing out of Simon Baron-Cohen's notion of a 'male brain' type in autism (though see Fine, 2010, for a robust critique of apparent gender differences in neuroscience research) suggests that autism can be understood as a combination of poor 'empathising' and good 'systemising'. Both constructs are measured as trait dimensions using self-report checklists; the Empathising Quotient asks about social skills and preferences, while the systemising quotient asks how much one likes to impose or discover order, or work out how things work. The extent to which these constructs are orthogonal dimensions or trade-off against one another remains uncertain (Wheelwright et al., 2006).

The systemising quotient attempts to capture the tendency to engage in systematic activities and thinking styles, apparent in rule-based, predictable and logical contexts – for example, common degree subject choices for someone with a high systemising quotient might be engineering, mathematics or computer sciences (Manson & Winterbottom, 2012). In the context of autism, systemising does not contradict previously described perceptual accounts. In fact, systemising presupposes low-level characteristics such as an eye for detail, though it remains an open question whether a detail-focused perceptual style leads to a preference for systemising, or whether systemising activities hone relevant perceptual skills. There are consistently high systemising quotient scores among the autistic population and also in their close relatives, though the field is weakened by reliance on self-report. Lawson et al. (2004) created a Physical Prediction Questionnaire, using items taken from the Vincent Mechanical Diagrams Test, to assess understanding of physical systems – but an ideal test of systemising would present individuals with a wholly novel system to 'crack' (and hence avoid confounds with prior experience/interests/teaching). Harvey and colleagues (2016) found a correlation between self-reported systemising and performance on a code-breaking task in a small group of hackers and a larger unselected group, but to our knowledge this ability hasn't been tested in autistic people. One study that tested 'foraging' found no evidence of a more systematic approach in children with autism compared to children with typical development (Pellicano et al., 2011). Further work, ideally presenting novel challenges that can be solved using either systematic or non-systematic solutions, would push forward the evidence base for this dimensional theory.

Turning to the Empathising Quotient, here the nomenclature of "empathising" is highly problematic. The dictionary definition of empathising is *"to understand and share the feelings of another"*, and in general discourse, empathy is often used to mean simply *caring about* or *resonantly responding to* other people's feelings. We have seen in Chapter 6 that many social cognitive models attempting to explain autism suggest that autistic people have a difficulty representing other people's mental states – but knowing what other people are thinking (ToM) is *not* the same as caring what they are feeling (emotional empathy). Whether emotional empathy is affected at all in autism is hotly debated both by scientists (Bird & Viding, 2014) and self-advocates – with the latter often remarking that their lived experience is of feeling too much, rather than too little, of others' emotions.

Many autistic advocates have pointed out the damage which has been done to their community by the spread of the idea that autistic people are incapable of empathy. In particular, this construct is offensive to a group of people who may be working harder than most to work out others' mental state and to respond as expected by social norms. To label any mismatch between the expected behaviour in a particular social context and what an autistic person actually does, as resulting from a lack of empathy, betrays a significant lack of empathy on the part of the non-autistic observer. In Chapter 9, we extend this discussion of empathy and autism with reference to the double empathy problem proposed by Milton (2012).

5. Bayesian accounts

A relatively new approach to understanding the brain, at the time of writing, is the Bayesian, or predictive coding model. This is fiendishly hard to understand in detail, but in essence the model suggests that our brains operate by (rapidly, constantly) making top-down predictions about the world and comparing these against incoming perceptual evidence. The goal is to minimise mismatch or 'prediction error' – so predictions (known as "priors") get more and more accurate at matching with incoming information, and this guides behaviour. A key component of the system is that experience contributes to the formulation of more precise priors.

In the context of autism, one account derived from the Bayesian brain framework, suggests that the autistic brain relies on under-specified predictions because it does not take experience into account effectively (Pellicano & Burr, 2012). In some cases, such a neurological underpinning would result in greater precision – as when autistic people show reduced susceptibility to visual illusions (Happé, 1996). A Bayesian interpretation could be that autistic people view the illusion on its own terms because they do not (mis)apply expectations based on experience. However, in the majority of situations, prior experience helps non-autistic people to 'smooth' their sensory input, classifying it according to their expectations so that they do not need to be distracted by variability at a detailed level. For example, prior knowledge allows neurotypical people to experience a familiar space as the same every time, even though in reality small details will have changed. Meanwhile, autistic people might experience that space as brand new, or at least full of distracting changes.

However, an alternative Bayesian account suggests autism is characterised by excessive precision in predictions (Lawson et al., 2004). According to this theory, autism is associated with predictions that are over-specified and detailed, resulting in a larger experience of error. In other words, by this account, autistic people do use prior experience, but these priors are very detailed and strong, resulting in 'overfitting' and a lack of generalisation (Van de Cruys et al., 2013, 2014). This opposite hypothesis can explain exactly the same phenomenon as noted earlier – autistic people might struggle with minor changes in a familiar space because their prior expectation of that space is over-specified and includes fine details. Meanwhile, neurotypical people benefit from a prior that corresponds to an approximate, generalisable representation of the space.

These interpretations of autism, based on a Bayesian model of the fundamental workings of the brain, require a great deal more investigation before their value can be estimated. The Bayesian theories of the brain in general are relatively untested, and most evidence so far has focused on basic perceptual processes and has limited relevance to higher functions. Moreover, experimental tasks, while they may be coherent with a predictive coding interpretation, rarely if ever provide a robust test of this theory. In the case of autism, it would be encouraging if a Bayesian account could make a completely novel prediction about task performance in autism, rather than delivering new interpretations of existing patterns in the literature.

6. Information processing and the social domain

Just as social cognitive models of autism can be critiqued for failing to account for features outside the social domain, it is an open question whether the theoretical models of autism reviewed in this chapter can also explain the presence of specific social differences. One basis on which we might link perceptual and social differences is to characterise social interactive experiences as requiring holistic processing, integrated across multiple input streams and without a systematic, rule-based structure. If this holds, we could argue that problems in the social domain are based on disruptions to the specific type of processing required to capture the social world. Some evidence which aligns with this interpretation comes from work arguing that atypical social attention is most apparent when stimuli are complex (Birmingham et al., 2012).

On the other hand, there is no agreed, evidence-based way to determine objectively the complexity of a stimulus. Additionally, human brains have evolved for certain types of task; we find easy and effortless what computer systems find hard (e.g. extracting objects in a 3-D scene), and vice versa (e.g. division of very large numbers). Therefore, it remains impossible to verify the statement that the social world is somehow uniquely or even particularly 'complex' in relation to other types of information, despite the appeal of this notion. Information-processing and perceptual theories are also hard to apply to findings of 'fine cuts', – autism-specific differences between social and closely matched non-social tasks. For example, can domain-general processing differences explain why so many children with autism can conjure a meta-representation in relation to an out-of-date photograph, but that the same task in relation to an out-of-date belief proves impossible?

7. Current debates

Summary

A number of theoretical models move beyond the social domain in an attempt to describe non-social diagnostic features and experimental findings, including autistic strengths. However, these efforts to capture the unique information processing styles of autistic people have not yet provided a coherent account that can encompass the wide variability in findings. A number of models have been proposed which are relatively similar in their predictions and interpretations (e.g. weak central coherence versus enhanced perceptual functioning). In other cases, separate theories are not mutually exclusive: e.g. differences in predictive coding might give rise to detail focus which is then manifest as a preference for systemising. The area still suffers from a reliance on small samples in individual experimental studies with too little replication and large-sample work, making it even harder to distinguish between competing accounts or derive practical lessons from them.

Big questions

What is the relation between the social features of autism and the basic information processing style which (presumably, theoretically) governs all incoming data? Have autistic people just been subject to a mysterious, coincidental combination of differences in both social interaction and information processing styles? Why should these two things have co-occurred in so many? Or are there cohorts of un-identified people who experience each of these broad symptom domains independently?

How can these accounts, or any accounts, explain the sensory hyper- and hypo-sensitivities apparent in autism? Bayesian models look promising in this regard, but as yet no robust experimental tests have been developed, and research pertaining to autism specifically is in its infancy.

Is it necessary to arrive at a single, accepted account of the information processing style of autistic people? Might we simply allow all of the theoretical accounts described earlier to co-exist, each providing a subtly different emphasis or level of interpretation in relation to the shared question of how autistic people (uniquely) take in and process information. This proposal relates to the practical significance of the work covered in this chapter – perhaps it is enough to have evidence-based models that legitimise the differing sensory experiences, perceptual skills and preferences of autistic people, by illustrating aspects of their fundamental underpinnings? Or is there benefit to autistic people to be gained by having a more fine-grained understanding of the precise ways in which autistic information processing differs from the mainstream norm?

COMMUNITY CONTRIBUTION, JON ADAMS – *ARTIST AND AUTISTIC ADVOCATE*

I've always asked questions; ever since I can remember, I've asked about the world around me. I picked up a stone aged five on a holiday in Wales and on seeing fossils asked what they were. This one act set me on a quest for all the rest of my life. I had to understand the world below me, around me and above. Now I can see that this didn't necessarily mean socially. I had a thirst for detail but was also equally compelled to see where this fitted on the global scale, be it in 'time' or positioning. I was always asking "Where did this fit?", I needed the bigger picture as the detail without this reference was useless.

For example, the fossils I'd found had a certain definable taxonomy and age. I needed to know what they were and their positioning in the geological and evolutionary timeline. I constructed this 3-D larger view quite naturally, made out of these fragments both by reading widely and practical experience. It's never linear, always a cloud not a spectrum. I seemed to have no problem with time as a concept, partly I think because being synaesthetic, I can reach out and touch it. It wasn't the same with people, as there seemed to be an unwritten rogue element within their patterning I had to factor in. I couldn't join them up in the way I could in sciences or history.

When I was seven, reaching deep within me, I said I'd be an artist. I coped at school for a few years until my ability to cover my differences failed. Schooling in the late 1960s was not fun, and I soon fell afoul of the differing demands and systems. I was rescued by my abilities with facts and drawing. Then one of my pictures was torn up by the teacher in front of the class, as I'd spelt my name wrong, and I decided to hide more of myself. I didn't go to art college but rather university to train to be a palaeontologist. I had the skills to find, describe and recognise fossils' positioning in the bigger picture of geological time. I could apply these skills to other subjects, including contemporary arts where I now create and direct socially engaged art projects.

I was apprehensive in the run up to my autism diagnosis as I didn't seem to fit criteria around detail/bigger picture as my lived experience seemed to contradict. Yes, I systemise well, but I feel what if maybe the current theories don't wholly fit 'our bigger picture' rather than autistic people fitting within them?

Recommended reading

Gerland, G. (2003). *A real person: Life on the outside*. London: Souvenir Press.

Happé, F., & Frith, U. (2006). The weak coherence account: Detail-focused cognitive style in autism spectrum disorders. *Journal of Autism and Developmental Disorders, 36*, 5–25.

Murray, D., Lesser, M., & Lawson, W. (2005). Attention, monotropism and the diagnostic criteria for autism. *Autism, 9*(2), 139–156.

Pellicano, E., & Burr, D. (2012). When the world becomes 'too real': A Bayesian explanation of autistic perception. *Trends in Cognitive Sciences, 16*(10), 504–510.

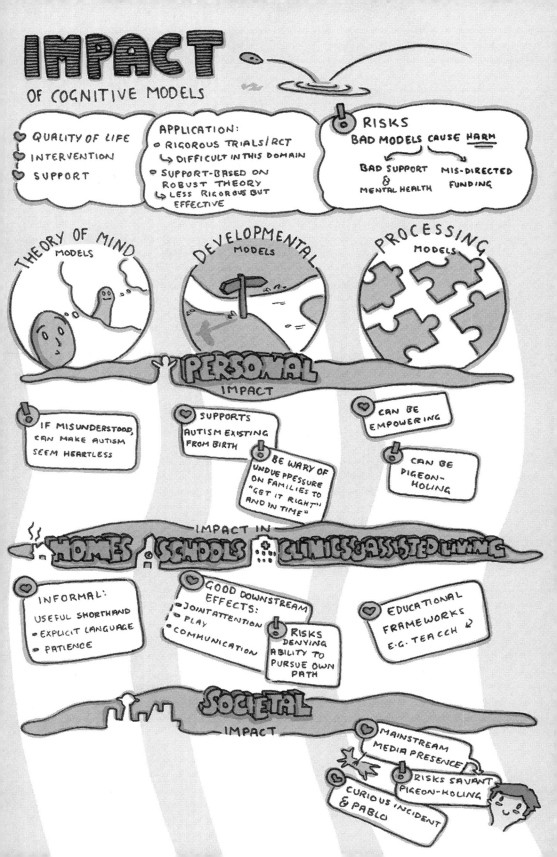

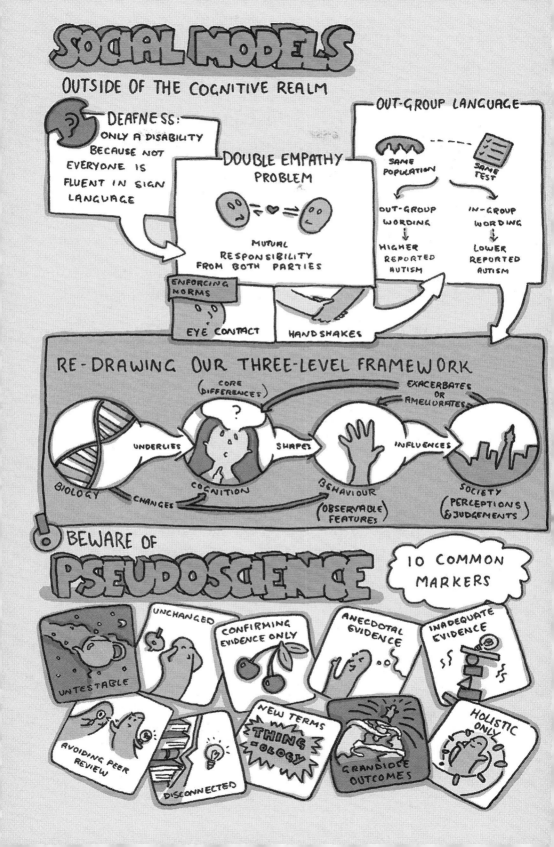

9 The impact of cognitive models on autism understanding and practice

IN THIS BOOK, we have focused on attempts to describe autism at the cognitive level. This is the largely hidden, conceptual layer between directly observable behaviour and biology. We have grouped psychological theories of autism into *primary deficit models, developmental accounts* and *cognitive difference models*. While each account has experimental evidence in its favour, none of them is universally accepted as an adequate way to describe how autism differs from the neurotypical cognitive experience.

There is another way to examine the validity of these psychological models, however, which is to consider to what extent they – individually or as a collection – have had an impact on society. Here we consider the prevalence and success of approaches to supporting autistic people, grounded in psychological theory. We also review how psychological theory has shifted attitudes to autism, including the important question of autistic people's perceptions of these theoretical models.

Before launching into this investigation, it is crucial to make a statement about the role that an evidence-based support might have in the life of an autistic person. There is no doubt that large swathes of the literature have described interventions with therapeutic goals that can be summed up as a drive to make autistic people less autistic. In some cases, this amounts to little more than rote training in behaving like a neurotypical person. This isn't to say, however, that evidence-based interventions (when used in psychological research, the word 'intervention' merely describes anything that a person doesn't already routinely do) cannot align with a progressive agenda. There are numerous ways in which psychological theory and robust scientific methods can be leveraged to deliver genuine benefits to the autistic community, without undermining an individual's identity and self-esteem. For example, an intervention might target specific aspects of common autistic profiles which are agreed to be disadvantageous, like supporting children with autism to develop their communication – whether this focuses on speaking or alternative and augmented communication aids. We might also create autism-enabling versions of generic mental health supports, like cognitive behavioural therapy. Or drugs might be developed to allow an autistic individual to dampen their sensory responses at will – in the same way someone with allergies might take medication before visiting a friend with a pet cat.

1. What does it mean to be evidence based?

There are two ways that a specific approach to supporting autistic people might have a basis in psychological evidence. First, they may have been evaluated using an appropriate scientific method. The 'gold standard' for building an evidence base is a double-blind randomised controlled trial (RCT) and, where multiple trials have been completed on the same or similar approaches, systematic reviews and meta-analyses of these. There are numerous excellent texts describing these methods properly (e.g. Petticrew & Roberts, 2008; Boutron et al., 2017), so we will limit ourselves to just one or two key observations.

It is essential to understand that trial and meta-analytic methods were developed with reference to investigations of drug efficacy. Drug trials nearly always have a specific, objectively measurable target (e.g. lowering blood pressure) which is known to have clinical relevance. It is straightforward to measure and compare things like dosage (how much you're meant to take) and adherence (how much you did take) across trials, you can easily have a placebo condition and no-one, including the patients, their family and the trial doctors, needs to know who is taking active drugs and who is getting placebo. For psychological and educational interventions, none of these things is straightforward, some are downright impossible, and all are expensive to achieve. This makes RCTs and meta-analyses of psycho-behavioural supports rare and, often when judged against standard criteria for quality of evidence, poorly rated.

Thus, for psychology-derived supports, these types of evidence may not always be the most appropriate options. It may well be more informative to do a high-quality observational or interview study than to do a low-quality RCT, even if the results are technically less robust. But even if you could design and deliver an excellent RCT, that might not be the right type of evidence for your question – perhaps you're just not interested in the type of outcome-focused data that this produces. Take the example of 'conversation clubs' for autistic people. While we might choose an objective, measurable outcome, such as scores on a self-report questionnaire of well-being, in some ways, what we want to capture is the process, not just the outcome. What is the experience of being in the club? Is everyone having a good time? If not, why not, and what could we change to fix this? In the USA a wide-ranging research project on transitions for youth with autism identified a need for greater focus on systems-level factors and population-based outcomes to develop and evaluate measures to improve transitions (Shattuck et al., 2018). Thus, when considering the evidence for or against a specific practical approach, we should not merely apply standard metrics for judging quality of evidence, but also consider whether the evidence is relevant to the claims being made and to the context in which the support is being used.

The second way in which evidence may be brought to bear on practical questions, is that approaches may be grounded in robust theory. In this case, there may be no direct test of the intervention itself, but if it is founded on a theory that in turn is strongly supported by empirical data, then we can say it is evidence-based. An example would be advising families to use explicit and literal language to describe their thoughts and feelings to avoid confusion resulting from difficulty tracking a speaker's intentions. Or using technology to motivate learning in a student who shows reduced response to social rewards. Or creating a low-impact sensory environment to avoid processing delays and prevent information overload. In these cases, the approach may not have been rigorously evaluated, but the underlying theory has and, to the extent that you endorse that theory, you might also endorse the practical approaches derived from it.

There is no doubt that, from a scientific standpoint, the second type of evidence base is inferior, but also more realistic, especially for things like every-day classroom practices or new technologies. We simply can't expect an RCT of everything, and we could wait a long time for such studies to get funded. Under these circumstances, an important aspect to consider when evaluating the evidence base for a particular guideline or approach is to reflect on the potential benefits but also harms of that approach. Harms come in many guises. The most obvious is when the novel aspect of the intervention is actively harmful – for example, when a drug has negative side-effects. But just as important to weigh in the balance are economic harms; how much money is being spent on this approach that could otherwise be invested elsewhere? Other resources will also be assigned: time for teacher training and family activities or communal

TABLE 9.1 Common markers of pseudoscience – reproduced from Finn et al., 2005

1	Untestable. *Is the treatment unable to be tested or disproved?*
2	Unchanged. *Does the treatment approach remain unchanged even in the face of contradictory evidence?*
3	Confirming evidence. *Is the rationale for the treatment approach based only on confirming evidence, with disconfirming evidence ignored or minimized?*
4	Anecdotal evidence. *Does the evidence in support of the treatment rely on personal experience and anecdotal accounts?*
5	Inadequate evidence. *Are the treatment claims incommensurate with the level of evidence needed to support these claims?*
6	Avoiding peer review. *Are treatment claims unsupported by evidence that has undergone critical scrutiny?*
7	Disconnected. *Is the treatment approach disconnected from well-established scientific models or paradigms?*
8	New terms. *Is the treatment described by terms that appear to be scientific but upon further inspection are found not to be scientific at all?*
9	Grandiose outcomes. *Is the treatment approach based on grandiose claims or poorly specified outcomes?*
10	Holistic. *Is the treatment claimed to make sense only within a vaguely described holistic framework?*

space may be given over to a therapeutic system. If it does not deliver benefit, or even *enough* benefit, this can be characterised as harmful. Parents can feel under enormous pressure to try any new intervention, at great personal and family cost, both economic and emotional. Another key factor, especially pertinent in the case of autism, is to consider how experiencing some kinds of specialist support might affect self-confidence and self-esteem. We must be sure that any attempts to develop skills or provide opportunities to autistic people are not at the expense of their self-belief and well-being.

Under the circumstances outlined earlier, decisions about the weight of evidence and appropriateness of any particular approach to supporting people with autism, must be made on a case by case basis. As well as considering the issues described, it is also essential to be on the lookout for pseudoscience. Key markers have been developed and published for this, and one example list is reproduced in Table 9.1 (Finn et al., 2005). Sadly, pseudoscience is rife in the autism intervention world and we advise readers to be alert to signs of pseudoscience and to exercise critical judgement when making decisions and recommendations. Parents, in particular, are often bombarded with interventions that have little by way of evidence base; even the most discerning and sceptical mum or dad may feel they have to try these, asking themselves 'what if' this is the thing that makes a real difference to their child's well-being.

2. Impact in homes, schools, clinics and assisted living

Many specific approaches to supporting autistic people are delivered in family, educational, clinical or community settings. Delivery can be led by a range of professionals including psychologists, speech and language therapists, teachers, doctors and care professionals in the third sector. The same groups of professionals may also deliver structured training or informal guidance to parents, who then try to implement autism support practices in the home. Crucially, within any of these groups, individuals will have very different levels of autism-specific knowledge and training.

If there is one cognitive theory that all autism training probably covers, it is Theory of Mind (ToM). Talk about ToM is often at the heart of any kind of introduction to autism. Regardless of what we might consider to be the evidence in favour of, or against, this theoretical model, learning that an autistic person may not automatically, accurately or confidently represent the mental states of other people is a very useful 'handle' for a novice. It reminds practitioners to make information more explicit and encourages them to be patient when an autistic person in their care doesn't behave quite as expected by neurotypical social norms. Despite this positive role for ToM models in guiding practice, the theory has not led to effective therapeutic approaches to date (Fletcher-Watson et al., 2014). In particular, specifically teaching ToM skills does not produce change in areas that extend beyond the taught skill. The clinical impact of ToM is also limited in terms of diagnostic tools or prognostic indicators. This exemplifies the gap that can exist between a theory's 'informal' impact on practice – shaping how people talk and think about autism – versus its 'formal' impact on things like diagnosis and post-diagnostic support.

Developmental theories have had some successful influence on the design and delivery of supports for very young autistic children. Interventions based on these models can sometimes lead to downstream effects – for example, by developing early joint attention, communication and play skills we can see better language outcomes a year later (e.g. Kasari et al., 2008). Some groups have tested training of parents of infants who are not diagnosed, but do have a higher likelihood of later getting an autism diagnosis, in their play and communication skills. These interventions have also shown downstream effects on later, broader social and communication abilities (Green et al., 2017).

However, this "developmental cascade" model – in which attention to an early pivotal skill is expected to deliver later, generalised, developmental change – is not always successful (e.g. Kaale et al., 2014). This kind of approach may require many hours of intensive intervention, which is a cost to the families involved. Although there is some evidence that earlier intervention relates to greater gains (Kasari et al., 2012), there is no research that directly compares how intervention at different ages yields benefit. Given the lack of a robust evidence base (Green & Garg, 2018), we must remember that the current drive for 'early intervention' at all costs can be very stressful for parents. For those whose child is diagnosed later, they may be led to believe they have 'missed the boat' in terms of providing meaningful help to their child. When the child receives a diagnosis early in life, parents' ability to adapt to, and accept, the diagnosis may be impeded by a desperate scramble to get some kind of intervention in place before it is too late. If intervention for 'high-likelihood' infants is rolled out, we need to consider the ethics of intervention prior to diagnosis. Finally, and crucially, we need to question whether by intervening in an attempt to enable autistic children to achieve normative developmental milestones we could be denying their right to follow their own, autistic, learning trajectory.

Developmental theories have also been applied to the quest for earlier diagnosis but, as for ToM, no markers have adequate diagnostic precision to support a change in clinical practice. In fact, as noted in Chapter 7, the most consistent early markers seem to come from non-social paradigms, which is at odds with socially focused theoretical accounts. Furthermore, the reliance on neurotypical comparison groups in these studies means that any application to differential diagnosis (i.e. distinguishing autism from other neurodevelopmental disorders, rather than just from typical development) is still far in the future.

There is relatively little to say on the role of information processing accounts in practice. A good educational or home setting will recognise the need, sometimes, to strip down information for an autistic person. There are some manualised educational frameworks which promote this concept – e.g. TEACCH (Virués-Ortega et al., 2017). Detail-focused cognitive style is a notion that teachers and parents find helpful in thinking about how autistic and neurotypical thinking styles may differ (Noens & Berckalaer-Onnes, 2005). However, few formal interventions have resulted from these theories as yet, and they have no role in diagnosis at present. Instead, information processing accounts may have had a greater impact on societal perceptions of autism, and these will be considered next.

3. Societal impact

One of the most marked distinctions between the academic literature and accounts of autism in the mainstream media is the prominence given to theories which we have grouped under the umbrella of "information processing" (see Chapter 8). One example is the so-called extreme male brain theory, characterised in psychological terms by the constructs of systemising and empathising. This account is frequently evoked when considering, for example, how to increase rates of employment among autistic people. Many employment programs aim to channel autistic people into industries characterised by a need for systemising – such as computer and data sciences, finance and risk analysis or engineering. This is all well and good provided that we do not make the mistake of treating autistic people as a homogenous group whose diverse career goals and personal preferences can be met by a one-size-fits-all employment scheme. Furthermore, quite apart from the fit of individual to industry, we also need to consider how autistic people are welcomed into, managed and supported in the workplace.

The influence of information processing models is also apparent in representations of autism in TV and film, where sensory sensitivities, learning disability and 'systemising' type skills are often apparent. For a long time, the film *Rain Man* was the bane of many families' lives, due to its compelling portrayal of an autistic man with minimal independent living skills but also a prodigious memory and mathematical ability. There was nothing inaccurate about the characterisation – in fact, the role was largely based on a real man with autism, Kim Peek, as well as many other talented autistic individuals – but of course, no single media representation can be accurate on its own. Nonetheless, in a recent analysis of representations of autism on screen, Nordahl-Hansen and colleagues (2018) identified that about 50% of autistic characters in popular films and TV shows had some kind of savant skill – much higher than estimates from the literature. They propose that this is probably driven by a creative need for characters with interesting features that can drive the plot of a movie or TV show. However, the same paper also reported that, savant skills aside, on-screen representations of autism are not, on the whole, inaccurate. Rather, they fit the diagnostic criteria almost too closely, resulting in a series of archetypal at best, stereotypic at worst, depictions of autism in the mainstream media. Thankfully, now there are increasing representations of autism and the diversity of the community is starting to be represented on screen (e.g. *The*

Bridge), on stage (*e.g. Curious Incident of the Dog in the Night-Time*) and in print (e.g. *Rubbernecker, The Rosie Project*). In addition, autistic characters are starting to be played by autistic actors, as in the new BBC show for children, *Pablo*. We look forward to this trend continuing, so that characterisations of autism in entertainment can become more authentic to the enormous variability of autistic experiences.

4. Personal impact

Developmental theories can have a positive influence on the experience of autistic people and especially their parents, because they emphasise that autism is present in the individual from infancy (or even before). This may contribute to the validity of the autistic identity and help to discount theories that falsely invoke a causal role for vaccines or other childhood experiences. But at the same time, emphasis on developmental factors prior to diagnosis may suggest a role for the parent in the 'onset' of autism. Recent UK headlines describing parents who had taken part in a parent-training intervention to help autistic children develop social and communication skills as "super parents" are dangerously close to inferring that autism (or disadvantageous accompaniments to autism, such as language disorders) results from inferior parenting. We should avoid undue pressure on families to 'get it right' and counter the false notion that autism can, or even should, be prevented with the right environmental influences.

The systematising/empathising account, with its suggestion of reduced empathy, can lead to inaccurate conceptualisations of autistic people as cruel or heartless. The media have hypothesised about the autism status of people who have committed horrific crimes and recently discussed whether autistic people might be more likely to be terrorists. By contrast, the ToM account makes it clear that only a circumscribed set of social representations is likely to be different in autism. We can break the steps required to display empathy down into four parts. First, one must notice someone else's emotional signals. Second, one must accurately interpret the internal mental state from the outward signals – is this person crying from sadness, happiness, pain or shock? Third, one must be motivated to respond by feeling empathy. And, finally, one must respond in the 'appropriate' way. A few autistic people might fall at the first hurdle, but many will only struggle with steps two and four. A difficulty extrapolating mental states from visible signs, and working out what is the normative way to respond, should never be confused with not caring. Attachment, empathy and affection are not reduced in autism – although they may not easily recognise another's thoughts, autistic people are no more likely to be callous than non-autistic people.

Information processing models that emphasise autistic strengths can be great, but these also risk pigeonholing autistic people. Increasingly, we are seeing a community of autistic artists and people in creative industries coming to the fore, though research on this aspect of autism remains lacking. Their talents contrast with the predictions and assumptions from many information processing models. For example, theoretical arguments about reduced generativity in autism are contradicted by the prolific and expansive nature of a lot of autistic art. These contrasts remind us that, even if autism were to be definitively characterised at a cognitive level, a wide variety of behavioural profiles may result.

5. Other ways to think about autism

In this book, we have referenced biological, cognitive and behavioural levels of explanation. These three levels are at the core of psychological studies in autism and beyond – in our efforts to comprehend and describe cognitive processes we must examine observations, derived from biological and behavioural data, which provide the input and output to the 'black box' of cognition. However, there are also ways to comprehend autism that operate outside this framework – namely social models (see Figure 9.1).

Social models of autism align with the wider social model of disability, which emphasises the disabling effect of the environment, including other people's negative attitudes. For example, deaf people might point out that hearing impairment is a disability primarily because not everyone is fluent in sign language. In the context of autism, one influential theory based on a social model, is the double empathy problem (Milton, 2012). This account makes the deceptively simple point that a successful social interaction requires the participation of two people. Where interactions between people with and without autism are unsatisfactory, both parties should take mutual responsibility for this situation. Specifically, in relation to empathy, Milton points out how little empathy neurotypical people routinely show for autistic people in their community. This is manifest in our failure to create autism-enabling environments or to adapt our behaviour – e.g. enforcing social norms like eye contact and

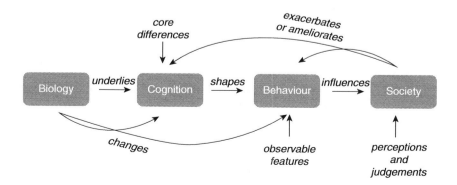

FIGURE 9.1   A four-level framework for understanding neurodevelopment

hand shaking – to the autistic person's interaction style. This observation, how-ever, should not be construed as suggesting that those who work and live with autistic people fail to accommodate their needs. There are myriad – formal and informal – ways in which parents, siblings and other family members, as well as many under-resourced professionals attempt to adjust their behaviour to accommodate the needs of the autistic people in their lives. The existence of a range of bespoke voice-output apps is just one case in point, where deep understanding of autism and of the essential role of communication for auton-omy has been enabling to many autistic people (Fletcher-Watson, 2016).

Although this model is not primarily a psychological theory, instead describing autism at the behavioural level, it can be tested experimentally. A number of pieces of evidence have recently emerged that support this model. Sasson and colleagues showed neurotypical raters "thin slices" of informa-tion – photographs and short video or audio clips – from autistic and non-au-tistic contributors (Sasson et al., 2017). They rated autistic people as more awkward and said they were less likely to become friends with them, despite judging both groups as equally trustworthy and intelligent. These judgements show how disadvantaged autistic people may be, as negative first impressions take hold incredibly quickly. Importantly, there was no difference when raters were given just a transcript of the original clips, showing that autistic peo-ple were saying all the right things, but just presenting themselves differently. More recently, Sasson has published follow-up work which reveals that disclos-ing the diagnostic status of the autistic people, and especially increasing the knowledge of autism in the rater, improves first impressions (Sasson & Mor-rison, 2017). This indicates that interventions in the neurotypical community could play a role in improving the social experiences of autistic people – and that disclosing diagnostic status may be an important part of that.

At the same time, Heasman (Heasman & Gillespie, 2017) showed that the self-ratings of people with autism for abilities like "handling criticism" and "making decisions" were higher than ratings provided by their family members. Autistic participants were well aware of these perceptions, correctly predicting low-ratings from their family. Conversely, neurotypical family members were less accurate at predicting how they would be rated by their autistic relatives. Objective measures of the rated skills were not included, but the patterns of disagreement between ratings of self, other and predicted-other reveal consid-erable complexity in the relationships of autistic and non-autistic people even within a family unit.

Further evidence comes from the finding (reported in Chapters 6 and 8) that neurotypical judges (and sometimes autistic judges; Brewer et al., 2016) struggle to identify the emotional expressions of autistic people, or interpret their expressions of mental states (Edey et al., 2016; Sheppard et al., 2016). Gernsbacher and colleagues modified a widely used measure of autism traits, the Autism Quotient (AQ), creating versions which emphasised in-group or out-group status (Gernsbacher et al., 2017). For example, items might say *I often understand what autistic people are thinking*, or *I often understand what non-autistic people are thinking* rather than the original: *I often understand what other people are thinking.* The authors found that for both autistic and non-autistic respondents, their self-reported autism quotient increased when given the version of the measure that emphasised their out-group and went down for the in-group version. All of these studies, in different ways, highlight that the neurotypical majority play a significant role in the interactive experiences of the autistic minority. Given this insight, it may be time to re-consider our three-level framework, which positioned environmental influences as a parallel 'stream' (Morton & Frith, 1995), and instead consider a four-level model for investigating neurodevelopment and neurodivergence.

6. The social model and learning disability

One common objection raised to the social model of disability, and to the neurodiversity movement that arose from that framework, is that they deny the very real challenges faced by some people with autism – especially those with a learning disability. Many feel that the focus on the rights of autistic people is at odds with a recognition of needs, including the needs of the families and supporters of autistic people. The previously substantial overlap between autism and learning disability is now diminishing (though they are still co-present for a significant minority) as diagnostic criteria change. One risk in this transition is that the difficulties faced by those with autism plus learning disability will be solely attributed to their learning disability, without any attempt to understand what part their autism may be contributing. Recognition that autism is partly disabling because of the 'baggage' that often accompanies it, should not be taken as a reason to disregard the need for autism understanding and accommodations. There is no doubt that a top priority for the field, and for society as a whole, is to develop more ways to allow people with autism and a learning disability to express themselves and achieve greater autonomy and influence (Long et al., 2017). However, while this goal remains elusive, effective and critical engagement with the neurodiversity movement ought to yield benefits for autistic people of all abilities.

There are three reasons to be optimistic about the potential for positive outcomes for learning disabled people as a part of the autistic rights agenda. First, vocal and effective advocates are drawing attention to autism, raising awareness and the level of public understanding and debate. Listening to their perspectives provides insights that may be relevant to other people in the constellation, even when they seem very different. For example, hearing why an autistic woman 'stims' and how she feels when she does so might help the brother of an autistic child be more accepting of his sister's flapping and spinning. Second, many autistic advocates have autistic siblings or children, choose to work in autism support settings, or simply meet other autistic people within their community. To presume that an autistic person only has experience of their own 'profile' denies the realities of a vibrant and engaged autistic community.

Moreover, many autistic adults who come across now as fluent and autonomous describe having a very different presentation in childhood – Temple Grandin is one famous case in point. Autistic people have been some of the most powerful advocates for increased understanding of, and attention to, the viewpoints of people with learning disabilities (e.g. Milton & Martin, 2016, 2017). Finally, it is hard to imagine how someone who does not display respect towards autistic people who are articulate self-advocates can claim to be respectful towards other people in the autism constellation. Ultimately, regardless of differences in presentation or lived experience, any attempt to understand and support autistic people cannot pick and choose whose viewpoint we want to hear.

7. Current debates

Summary

Psychologists have been concerned with attempts to describe autism at the cognitive level for more than 30 years. These attempts can be organised into three categories of psychological model: primary deficit models, developmental accounts, information processing models. In every case, there is, at best, fairly limited evidence of specifically designed and evaluated supports for autistic people derived from these accounts. However, each of these has had an impact on practice, public understanding and the autistic experience, sometimes via their integration into training and awareness-raising programmes or via their infiltration of public narratives about autism in the mainstream media. Some of the results of this influence may be positive but in other circumstances, a little knowledge of a psychological theory of autism can be applied in a damaging way. Social models of autism, and of disability more generally, offer a positive way to conceptualise autism, important for public awareness and understanding. Experimental evidence in support of these models is growing and should inform social change.

Big questions

What will be the role of psychological theory in the future, especially in relation to accounts grounded in a social model of disability? How can we leverage the power of experimental methods to yield meaningful benefits to people on the autism spectrum?

What should be the goals of psychology-derived supports for autism? How can we translate perspectives from the autistic adult community into the development of supports for young children? Can we develop measures that reflect autistic lived experiences while also having robust psychometric properties and theoretical relevance? Is there a risk that by stepping in to change something in early development we have a negative effect on a child's autistic strengths, identity, self-esteem or general well-being?

Is there a risk that growing up as an autistic child means every activity is branded as an intervention: trampolining becomes "rebound therapy", horse-riding becomes "equine therapy". Regardless of the quality and benefits of these individual approaches, a childhood crammed with therapeutic experiences could be stressful for both the individual and their family.

Do simplified versions of basic theories – such as the ToM model – have value in the context of providing a quick and easy handle on what autism is? Is it acceptable to boil the complexity and richness of autism down to a few sentences, and if not, how can we disseminate difficult ideas and debates to professionals, like teachers, with limited time and resources?

COMMUNITY CONTRIBUTION: FERGUS MURRAY – TEACHER AND CO-FOUNDER OF THE AUTISTIC MUTUAL AID SOCIETY, EDINBURGH (AMASE). THEY WRITE ON THE INTERNET UNDER THE NAME OOLONG

I have always found it odd how much about autistic experience is left untouched by most theories about autism. Executive dysfunction is a useful term to describe aspects of autistic thinking, but says nothing about perceptual differences and barely addresses social difficulties. Thinking in terms of ToM may provide a useful handle for novices, but it does nothing to help people to understand problems relating to inertia or, again, perceptual differences. The 'extreme male brain' theory leaves similar gaps. The enhanced perceptual functioning hypothesis, mentioned in Chapter 7, does deal with perceptual differences but is less convincing in providing an account of differences in social interactions and attentional control.

Scientific theories are useful to the extent they have explanatory and predictive power. From my perspective as an autistic adult and a science teacher, none of the theories presented in this chapter are altogether satisfactory on this front. Even within the domains of autistic experience that they do address, I have misgivings.

Theory of Mind deficit does little to explain communication difficulties resulting from literal-mindedness, or from neurotypicals having just as much difficulty understanding autistic minds as vice versa. As such, it is a weak explanation for observed social difficulties; worse, focusing on social manifestations of autism has evidently been a factor in the under-diagnosis of female autists, and others who blend in better (Lai et al., 2017). It also backfires when people wrongly assume autistics don't understand other people's perspectives (Heasman & Gillespie, 2018) and that problems in communication all stem from the autistic side.

The category of 'executive functions' includes several different cognitive abilities, and many other conditions also affect some of these in different ways, so distinguishing their role in autism requires considerable elaboration. The lack of parsimony here limits the usefulness of the idea in understanding autism; it needs breaking down into components before it really starts to explain anything.

In my experience, the biggest factor in autistic executive dysfunction is inertia; thinking in those terms provides a much tighter explanation than 'executive dysfunction' for most (but not all) of these difficulties.

The only theory I'm aware of that seems to make a decent stab at explaining the many seemingly disparate features of autistic psychology – from inertia to communication problems to hyperfocus and spiky profiles – is monotropism. However, this theory (formulated by autistics who aren't professional psychologists) has received relatively little attention from psychologists and awaits direct empirical verification.

Recommended reading

Boucher, J. (2008). *The autistic spectrum: Characteristics, causes and practical issues*. London, UK: SAGE Publications Ltd.

Gernsbacher, M. A., Stevenson, J. L., & Dern, S. (2017). Specificity, contexts, and reference groups matter when assessing autistic traits. *PloS One*, *12*(2), e0171931.

Milton, D. E. (2012). On the ontological status of autism: The 'double empathy problem'. *Disability & Society*, *27*(6), 883–887.

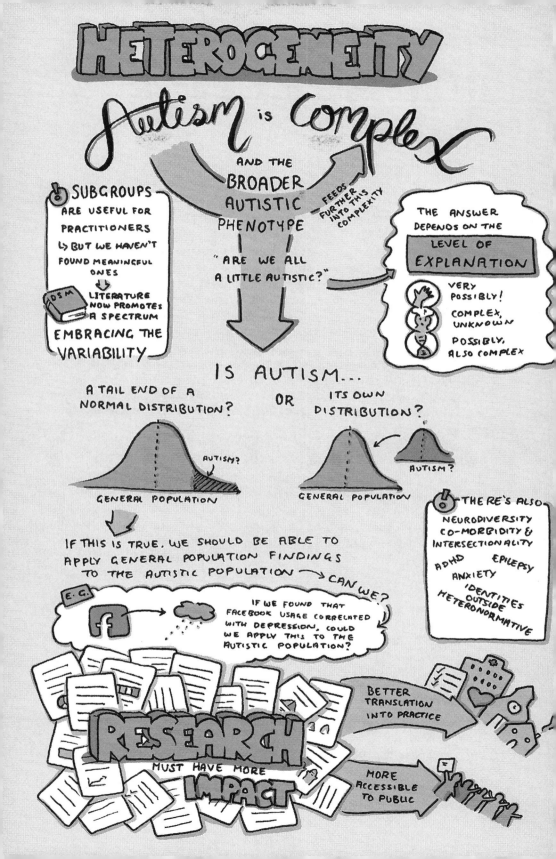

10 Looking to the future

THIS BOOK IS based on a volume written and published in the early 1990s. Writing this re-worked and updated account of psychological theory in autism research has highlighted the vast quantity of new information that has been accrued in that time. When Francesca began in autism research 30 years ago, it was possible to read every paper ever written about autism; in 1988, fewer than 200 papers on autism were published, and the total literature amounted to well under 3,000 specialist publications. Now, a search on PubMed for papers with "autism" in the title or abstract returns well over 4,000 results published in 2017 alone – a rate of more than 80 new papers *per week*. In total, the scientific literature on autism exceeds 60,000 papers as we write, and it would be impossible for any student to read more than a small fraction.

Over that time, we can see how things have changed for the better for autistic people and their allies, at least in the UK and other high income countries. Public awareness of autism has increased enormously, resulting in better understanding in the community. Identification of autism has likewise increased, reflected in higher diagnostic rates. Tailored educational provision is available, including training for teachers in mainstream schools, resulting in better further education and employment outcomes for autistic people. The growing grasp in the academic community of the breadth and complexity of the autistic spectrum has been beneficial in promoting a more sophisticated approach to study design and interpretation.

However, if we take as our goal a world in which an autistic person experiences no disadvantage as a result of their autism, we have a very long way still to go. Autistic people still experience high rates of mental health problems and have lower life expectancy, including high suicide rates. Quality of life is often low, with autistic people reporting limited autonomy and low rates of employment and independent living. Some groups remain very poorly understood – we know very little about autistic women and girls, including their experience of key life stages, such as puberty and the menopause. There is little information about the ageing process for autistic adults, including whether or not autism increases vulnerability to dementia, and how to care effectively for autistic adults in old age. When suitable knowledge and support are available, access to services is far from universal, even within the UK. Disseminating current findings and practices globally remains difficult, and there is a huge amount to learn about how autism is manifest in cultures beyond North American and European societies.

Autistic people also experience profound disadvantage as a result of commonly co-occurring conditions, including epilepsy, learning disability and language disorder. Treatments and supports for these continue to have limited effectiveness, as well as frequently being created and evaluated without autistic input. Moreover, many of the challenges experienced by autistic people reverberate through the family and beyond – parents and siblings experience stress and lower quality of life (Tint & Weiss, 2016), teachers of autistic children report high rates of burn-out (Boujut, et al., 2017). Community *awareness* of autism may be high, but Sue's recent UK survey showed that perceptions of *understanding* remain low (Macmillan et al., 2018). In this chapter, we explore some of the ways to move forward from this position.

1. Autistic rights and advocacy in research

The autism rights movement, founded on the work of pioneers, such as Larry Arnold, Martijn Dekker, Dinah Murray, Ari Ne'eman, Jim Sinclair and Donna Williams, has made enormous strides since the millennium. Autistic-led organisations have come to the fore, such as the *Autism Self-Advocacy Network* (ASAN) in the USA and *Autism Rights Group Highland* or the *Participatory Autism Research Collective* in the UK. While it would be false to say such organisations are thriving – funding sources remain scarce and many are sustained by the energy and goodwill of a handful of community leaders – they are becoming recognised by the academic and policy-making establishment as a key part of any autism-related initiative. The progress of autistic rights can be compared with other civil rights movements – the most common comparison is often with the LGBTQ+ community. Many parallels can be drawn between these groups: both experience disadvantages that are created, intensified and maintained by majority-group insistence on normative behaviour, for example. Homosexuality was once a diagnosable 'disorder' within the *DSM* (only removed in 1973), and associated 'cures' were promoted. As such, recent strides in gay rights give hope to the autistic community and provide a valuable reference point for non-autistic allies. It is instructive to ask oneself as an academic, if autism follows the same transformational pathway as homosexuality, will my work still be relevant to autistic people in five, ten or twenty years' time?

A key component of any endeavour to improve the lives of autistic people and their allies is to engage with those communities throughout the research process. Our position is that the incorporation of autistic perspectives into research is a matter of moral principle – neatly encapsulated by the disability rights slogan *Nothing About Us Without Us*. However, working with stakeholders also yields practical benefits, including facilitating recruitment to studies, and the fact that delivering research that matters to people will increase likelihood of translation into practice. Adopting an autistic rights framework is easiest when using participatory or collaborative methods to work alongside autistic people and their allies.

Engagement with autistic and autism communities (the former – people with a diagnosis and those who self-identify as autistic;[1] the latter – their friends, family and the professionals who work with them) is not straightforward, however. Finding ways to include autistic children, people with a learning disability and those who experience barriers to communication is a particular challenge which must be overcome. In cases like these, the role of the parent in advocating for their children is absolutely crucial. In fact, one key way in which the parallel between the LGBTQ+ community and the autistic community breaks down is in the role of parent advocates. Parents are often at the coal-face of autism support, providing year-round, sometimes 24/7, care to children and adults with complex and intense support needs.

Indeed, when reflecting on the history of autism support in the UK and beyond, it is clear how fundamental parents have been to the creation of infrastructure and knowledge about autism. Parents founded many of the leading autism organisations in the UK – the *National Autistic Society, Scottish Autism* and *Autism Initiatives* to name a few – and have been major donors to and fundraisers for autism provisions (e.g. schools, adult centres) and research. So we can see that understanding and recognising the parent perspective is also vital. But, when asked directly, parents and autistic adults frequently offer contrasting opinions on topics in autism research and practice, and this can make it hard for researchers to determine a clear, community-influenced direction for their work (e.g. Fletcher-Watson et al., 2017). One rarely acknowledged but growing group – as adult diagnosis rises, and those diagnosed under more recent, broad criteria grow up – is autistic parents. Since autism is highly heritable, they are more likely than most to have autistic children. Their perspectives and needs as a group are poorly characterised in the literature, despite the fact that autistic parents of autistic children provide a unique insight into both roles.

People often ask who is the 'right' group to work with in a research project – and the answer is that all stakeholder groups have something to offer. If working on a study pertaining to autistic adults who are cognitively able, you might still want to involve professionals, service providers and family members – though this might be partners or children rather than parents. For example, if the project hopes to produce information relevant to mental health services, it will be important to have the perspective of clinicians

---

1   We note that there is discomfort among both academic and non-academic stakeholders about the status of self-identification of autism. People mis-identifying themselves as autistic (perhaps when they in fact are experiencing a different form of neurodiversity) is a concern, as is the possibility that unscrupulous individuals might set themselves up as autistic advocates illegitimately. However, we also recognise the many reasons why an individual might want to identify as autistic without seeking independent medical endorsement.

represented, to maximise the chances of getting your findings translated into practice. What about non-speaking autistic people, or young children? Who speaks for them? Again, we would suggest that a range of voices should be present. Consider, as a parallel, a charity deciding what is the best way to help Muslim refugees in a faraway warzone. They can't talk to them directly, so instead, they might bring in representatives of the Muslim faith, people who have lived in that part of the world and people with professional experience of supporting refugees. Some might belong to multiple such categories. It is clear to see that a person who shares the same faith will have insights that are complementary to those of an international aid worker – neither's expertise trumps the other. The optimal solution needs to be found by all parties working together.

There are now some excellent guides for researchers who want to engage with the autistic and autism communities to help overcome this problem and others (see Fletcher-Watson et al., 2018). Next, we summarise a few examples of ways to engage at different stages of a typical research project in Table 10.1. These

TABLE 10.1   Ideas for participation in research for each stage of the project cycle

Research Stage	Actions
Formulating ideas	Spend time with some autistic people: as a befriender, volunteer, on twitter or socially
Writing a grant	Talk informally to the autistic people you know Do an online survey about your research questions Cost for autistic consultancy and advisers
Starting a project	Consider: do you need an autistic person on your interview panel? Agree clear terms of reference and communication modes for collaborators
Designing materials	Review with autistic people and other relevant stakeholders Consider aspects like contrast, font, layout and language, as well as content
Data collection	Check the space: do a sensory review, check for disrespectful posters Use the Standard Participant Question Response (SPQR) to invite feedback on the experience[2]
Analysis	Best scientific practice is best autism practice Pre-register your hypotheses and analyses
Dissemination	Tell the people who took part and thank them When talking about your research be respectful: don't assume there's no-one autistic in your audience Share as creatively, widely and openly as you can

2   https://blogs.exeter.ac.uk/exploringdiagnosis/resources/spqr/

presume that most autistic collaborators are outside academia, but of course, this doesn't have to be the case. A key goal for the future should be to improve access to research training, methods and resources for autistic people; encourage neurodivergent individuals into undergraduate and post-graduate study; and ensure that autistic-led research is a prominent part of the knowledge landscape.

2. Deriving meaning from the constellation

If there's one thing everyone can agree on, it is that autism is complicated. This complexity is especially striking in many of the areas of autism where our knowledge is most lacking: presentations that don't adhere to the 'classic' male type, multiple potential candidate genes and gene networks and their relation to behaviour, variety in developmental trajectories in childhood and adulthood and interactions between autism and cultural differences. All of these must be examined in relation to a shifting and subjective set of diagnostic criteria, further complicated by a rise in people self-identifying as autistic, without a formal diagnosis.

The role of the broader autism phenotype (BAP) also feeds in to this complexity. The connection, or division, between people with autism versus those who simply manifest many (subclinical) autism-linked traits remains unclear. Should we conceptualise autism as the tail end of a normal distribution? If so, then analysis of the relations between autism traits and other behaviours in the general population should have relevance for autism. For example, if we found that AQ scores mediate a positive correlation between Facebook use and depression, we could extrapolate that autistic people will be at higher risk of depression if they use Facebook and act accordingly. If, however, we believe that autism is qualitatively distinct from the general population's trait distribution, then studies of the BAP in people without autism may have limited relevance for autism itself.

This debate about the relation between autism and autistic traits has caused a great deal of consternation in the community. Understandably, autistic people are angered by statements, such as *"aren't we all a little bit autistic?"*, even when this is well meant. It would clearly be unacceptable to make the same statement about clinical depression, on the basis that everyone feels sad once in a while. On the other hand, ADHD is conceptualised as a dimensional, rather than a categorical, diagnosis. ADHD traits cause difficulties only for people who find themselves at the extreme end of the distribution, and even then, the degree of those difficulties depends on the environmental demands.

If we consider this question at each of our levels of explanation, the answer does appear more nuanced. At the behavioural level, it is certainly the case that there is a smooth continuum of scores on questionnaires, such as the autism quotient or social reciprocity scale: diagnosed people endorse more items but neurotypical people endorse some, and there is no clear water between. At the biological level, as discussed in Chapter 4, autism is in most cases a quantitative trait resulting, like height, from a combination of hundreds of common genetic variants, each of tiny effect. The same genetic influences therefore seem to operate on diagnosed autism and variation in autistic traits in the general population. However, some autistic people have pointed out that using this kind of information to suggest common ground between autistic and non-autistic people is a bit like saying someone is "a little bit pregnant" if they have a backache or swollen ankles.

At the psychological or cognitive level, the picture may be more complex and depend upon which theory one considers. For example, the ToM account suggests a possibly categorical difference; neurotypical people automatically and unconsciously track others' mental states, but autistic people do not (or do so only through conscious calculation). Meanwhile, weak central coherence is hypothesised to be a cognitive style characteristic of autism but also seen in neurotypicals – notably the close relatives of those with autism and perhaps in individuals with musical, artistic, memory or maths talents. So whether or not it makes sense to see autism as on a continuum with neurotypicality depends on the level of description and the psychological theory considered.

Setting aside for a moment the continuum from autistic to autistic traits, heterogeneity within the constellation remains a profound challenge. As scientists, how might we respond? Option one is to try to parse autism into meaningful sub-groups, at the biological, psychological and/or behavioural level. Sub-grouping on the basis of behaviour can be useful for a practitioner in a specific setting (e.g. seating children with a similar reading level at the same table in class), but this is unlikely to be functional for research, because behaviour varies widely depending on the physical environment, current activity, age and so on. To date, studies looking for behavioural sub-types have rarely provided evidence for much other than a split between autism with, versus autism without, intellectual impairment and/or language disorder. Attempts to use biological information to define sub-groups have also foundered. A combination of the sample sizes and expensive and intrusive data types required to derive biologically defined clusters has been prohibitive to date, though efforts are underway (Charman et al., 2017; Loth et al., 2017). These approaches also suffer from the fact that they inevitably rely on models from personalised medicine. This system aims to identify sub-types of a particular disease in order to relate them to a specific treatment – as in Type I versus Type II diabetes, or when prescribing specific cancer drugs according to a patient's genetic markers. This framework has limited applicability to autism, where we aim to improve self-defined quality of life, rather than offer a 'cure', though it might have relevance for unwanted co-occurring conditions, such as epilepsy.

Setting aside behaviour and biology, then, can psychology do any better at identifying meaningful underlying sub-groups? So far, our review of the theoretical literature suggests we are still a long way from understanding autism in these terms. However, psychology may have a valuable role to define, measure and provide supports for the additional needs of autistic people. *DSM-5* calls for characterisation of the individual, not according to a diagnostic sub-group (e.g. Asperger's syndrome, PDD-NOS, as in *DSM-IV*), but instead using a detailed picture of their strengths and challenges – sleep problems, high IQ, supportive family, depression. To do this, we need three things: precise measurement, understanding of autism-specific manifestations (e.g. is depression in autism the same as depression in neurotypical people?) and matched autism-enabling interventions. Psychology offers methods and frameworks to achieve all of these.

Plan B for tackling the challenge of heterogeneity in autism is simply to embrace it. Rather than attempting to break down the concept into internally consistent sub-groups, can we endorse a model of autism as a common thread which unites diverse people? In much the same way that our nationality both defines us and simultaneously offers almost infinite variety. In this scenario, the role of psychology might be to identify what are the common threads that unite autistic people, and what are the boundaries of this form of neurodiversity?

3. Neurodiversity, co-morbidity and intersectionality

The future of autism research is further complicated, not just by variability in presentation of autism itself, but also variability in presence and manifestation of accompanying diagnoses – clinical anxiety, epilepsy, ADHD, etc. – and the intersectional influence of facets, such as race, gender or sexuality. It is well known that autism frequently presents alongside other medical diagnoses, but new data are showing that a large proportion of the autistic community also identify outside hetero-normative categories in terms of gender and sexual orientation (George & Stokes, 2018; Gilmour et al., 2012).

There's no doubt that psychology has an important role to play in probing the experience and impact of co-occurring conditions and intersectional experiences. However, there is a risk that this complexity is erased by strict inclusion and exclusion criteria for studies attempting to achieve a statistically significant result – which is easier when the sample is relatively homogeneous. One possible solution is to focus less on diagnostic categories and more on trans-diagnostic domains of functioning, as in the Research Domain Criteria proposed as a new research framework by the National Institute of Mental Health in the USA (Insel et al., 2010). For example, one could design a study enrolling anyone with anxiety, regardless of their original diagnosis. A major challenge here would be identifying a funder and recruiting families – both of these often align under a specific diagnostic banner which may drive their decision-making. Either way, there is a push for larger and larger samples to be able to understand multiple influences on experience and outcome, and to derive recommendations that can be tailored to specific individuals. Of course, the opposite is also a valuable approach: small groups recruited to qualitative studies that take a 'deep dive', to provide rich and detailed pictures of the multiple influences on lives and outcomes.

Regarding the influence of intersectionality in autism, psychology may play a role to characterise lived experiences and make informative comparisons between groups. However, this work must take place as part of an interdisciplinary approach. Psychologists who wish to address or take account of intersectionality in their research or practice need to stay on top of the latest philosophical, sociological, legal and political debates to ensure that their work is current and relevant to the broader issues experienced by autistic people of all stripes. More than that, ideally autism research would be at the forefront of developing these debates, with results feeding back into a socio-political agenda for change.

4. Delivering results that matter

It is our hope that the future of autism research will include not just a maintenance of the staggering productivity which has characterised recent years, but also a consistent and pervasive focus on delivering findings that matter to autistic people. As one example, ten research priorities, published in 2016 by *Autistica* and the *James Lind Alliance*, provide an excellent starting point for UK researchers from which to look to the future (Table 10.2). The list was developed in partnership with a range of stakeholders, with careful attention

TABLE 10.2 Community research priorities, Autistica and the James Lind Alliance

1	*Which interventions improve mental health or reduce mental health problems in autistic people? How should mental health interventions be adapted for the needs of autistic people?*
2	*Which interventions are effective in the development of communication/ language skills in autism?*
3	*What are the most effective ways to support/provide social care for autistic adults?*
4	*Which interventions reduce anxiety in autistic people?*
5	*Which environments/supports are most appropriate in terms of achieving the best education/life/ social skills outcomes in autistic people?*
6	*How can parents and family members be supported/educated to care for and better understand an autistic relative?*
7	*How can autism diagnostic criteria be made more relevant for the adult population? And how do we ensure that autistic adults are appropriately diagnosed?*
8	*How can we encourage employers to apply person-centred interventions and support to help autistic people maximise their potential and performance in the workplace?*
9	*How can sensory processing in autism be better understood?*
10	*How should service delivery for autistic people be improved and adapted in order to meet their needs?*

paid to representation and diversity in the sample. The topics proposed can be addressed from a broad range of disciplinary perspectives and have relevance to autistic people of all ages, abilities and background.

Identifying the goals of research is only half of the solution, however. We also need to consider how research is carried out. In this chapter, we have highlighted the importance of adopting an autistic rights framework, embracing heterogeneity and recognising diversity in the autistic community. These things are easier said than done, especially when resources are scarce and professional environments are competitive. So what needs to change?

First, the research establishment. The current emphasis on research impact – the extent to which new findings can be shown to make a difference – must continue and expand. Training researchers to value impact and to understand how to achieve it should be a core part of their professional development. Funders also need to recognise that impact may take many years to unfold and find a way to follow-up with researchers, holding them to their impact plans while accommodating this slow process. Achieving impact includes collaboration and outreach, but it is also linked to scientific quality. Reproducible results, consistent measurement across studies and collaborations to share data and develop large samples are all essential to build a strong evidence-based case for change.

Second, public understanding of science. A common concern within the scientific community over partnership with stakeholder groups is that doing so compromises the scientific integrity of the work; will ideas be 'dumbed down' and findings simplified for public consumption? One solution is to nurture a scientifically expert community of practitioners, parents and autistic people. Of course, it still behoves academics to share jargon-free summaries of their work and present it to general audiences – it is unrealistic to expect community members without specialist training to read the latest issue of *Nature Neuroscience* or even *Autism Research*. But a degree of scientific understanding can facilitate partnerships and, crucially, give members of the public the confidence to question the headlines.

For practitioners, including clinicians and teachers, understanding the limits of research is essential to permit translation of findings into practice. Published studies in psychology are often very good at making generalised statements about averages across groups, but the practitioner must translate such generalisations into specific actions for their client or pupil. This is somewhere that the much-maligned medical approach should act as a beacon for practitioners in fields such as education and social work. Medical undergraduate training emphasises the changing nature of knowledge and the importance of keeping in touch with the latest research findings in order to apply them in practice. Medics are trained to understand basic science and to conduct evaluations in their services. In contrast, practitioners in social care and education are given little or no support and resources to do this, both during their training and once qualified, with negative consequences for the quality of support provided to autistic people and their families.

5. Current debates

Summary

Psychology research in autism has delivered thousands of papers based on millions of pounds of research funding, but a huge amount remains to be done before we can state that being autistic entails no systematic disadvantage in life. In part, this is because of the gap between research and practice. Research is often focused on long-term gains, benefit to future generations and generalised statements derived from group averages. In contrast, practice settings are focused on immediate needs for current service users, and tailored person-centred supports which take into account contextual and individual detail.

Psychology in the future needs to work harder to ask questions and employ methods that can increase translation of research into practical impacts on autistic people and their allies. Making these impacts meaningful and positive means partnering with autistic people in research and supporting autistic academics to achieve and lead new research programmes.

In doing so, we must not abandon what sets our discipline apart. Psychology builds strong theoretical frameworks that can distinguish between surface consequence and causal root. Psychologists have expertise in robust methods that merge scientific rigour with ecological validity, from RCTs to diaries and interviews, often in the same study. Psychology is a hub discipline, at the interface of biology, medicine, education and social sciences. For all of these reasons, psychologists are well placed to provide the raw material the autistic community needs to build the best possible future.

Big questions

Applying psychological theory to questions that matter is easier said than done. How can we strike the right balance between 'pure' psychological enquiry to develop theoretical models and delivering practice-relevant and community-endorsed projects?

How can we – scientists and communities together – change standards in the academic establishment to reward science that is rigorous *and* makes a difference in people's lives? Is there a way to develop science reporting in the mainstream media to be more accurate and responsible?

How can we partner effectively with autistic people, including those with learning disabilities, language disorder, or other barriers to communication? How can we balance input from autistic adults, parents of autistic children and those who fall into both categories? When there are disagreements within and between these groups, how should we respond?

6. COMMUNITY CONTRIBUTION: JAMES CUSACK – *DIRECTOR OF SCIENCE AT AUTISTICA*

Post-diagnosis most people go through a period of information seeking. I was no different when I was finally diagnosed in 1997 at 12 years old. I was desperate to understand what autism was and why this made me different. When I met other people on the spectrum, it was clear we all had things in common with each other, but we were also markedly different from each other. Why was that?

I remember thinking 'I don't understand this, but there'll be some experts somewhere who have got this nailed'. Around this time, psychological theories for autism were becoming increasingly common and the first text of this book had just been published. When I read about those theories, I remember thinking how illogical it was as someone growing up alongside other autistic people to try and use psychological theories to qualitatively describe autism in a homogenous way. I kept wondering if there was something I didn't get – surely academics get that it's not this simple?! It's welcome to see the authors embrace heterogeneity in this text.

After a PhD and post-doc in autism science, I am now the director of science at Autistica – the UK's autism research charity. Autism research has hugely matured during that time. One of the main things I spend a lot of time thinking about at Autistica is outcomes – how do we deliver a long, healthy, happy life for all autistic people? Psychological theories are central to that hope and can underpin the change we need. But to be the driver of that change they must:

1   Embrace complexity. It is increasingly becoming clear that autism is a useful construct, but that we are moving towards an era where we need to think more broadly about neurodevelopment or neurodiversity. It's evident both from research and the experiences of myself and others that the difficulties that autistic people face are neither simply a matter of the disabled person or society but an interaction between both. We also know that co-occurring conditions are enormously common and that this area is under-researched and offers opportunities to look at more specific populations.
2   Embrace the community and partners. Researchers who operate in isolation often fail to ask themselves "why?" They can get lost in the theory, failing to focus on delivering a better life for autistic people. Researchers need to work with autistic people and allies and listen to their priorities. They should also work with experts in involvement, policy and communications to ensure their big ideas, enormous expertise and unique skillsets are utilised to harness transformative change.

We have come a long way since the first edition of this book, and I am incredibly hopeful for the future of autism research. I know by working together and embracing the challenges we face, we can truly change lives. If we do that, when the time comes for the next edition of this book, I'm sure we will be able to look back on autism research and reflect on an era where autism research delivered positive change.

Recommended reading

Cusack, J., & Sterry, R. (2016). *Your questions: Shaping future autism research.* London, UK: Autistica.

Fletcher-Watson, S., Adams, J., Brook, K., Charman, T., Crane, L., Cusack, J., Leekam, S. R., Milton, D. E. M., Parr, J., & Pellicano, L. (2018). Making the future together: Shaping autism research through meaningful participation. *Autism.* doi: 10.1177/1362361318786721

Sinclair, J. (1993). Don't mourn for us. *Our Voice: The Autism Network International, 1*(3).

Bibliography

Abell, F., Happe, F., & Frith, U. (2000). Do triangles play tricks? Attribution of mental states to animated shapes in normal and abnormal development. *Cognitive Development, 15*(1), 1–16.

Amaral, D. G., Schumann, C. M., & Nordahl, C. W. (2008). Neuroanatomy of autism. *Trends in Neurosciences, 31*(3), 137–145.

Ameis, S. H., & Catani, M. (2015). Altered white matter connectivity as a neural substrate for social impairment in Autism Spectrum Disorder. *Cortex, 62*, 158–181.

American Psychiatric Association. (1994). *Diagnostic and statistical manual of mental disorders: DSM-IV*. American Psychiatric Publications.

American Psychiatric Association. (2013). *Diagnostic and statistical manual of mental disorders (DSM-5®)*. American Psychiatric Publications.

Ames, C., & Fletcher-Watson, S. (2010). A review of methods in the study of attention in autism. *Developmental Review, 30*(1), 52–73.

Anzulewicz, A., Sobota, K., & Delafield-Butt, J. T. (2016). Toward the autism motor signature: Gesture patterns during smart tablet gameplay identify children with autism. *Scientific Reports, 6*, 31107.

Arnold, L. (2013). Autonomy: Introduction to the second edition. Editorial. *Autonomy, 1*(2), www.larry-arnold.net/Autonomy/index.php/autonomy/article/view/ED2/html

Asperger, H. (1944). Die "Autistischen psychopathen" im kindesalter. *European Archives of Psychiatry and Clinical Neuroscience, 117*(1), 76–136.

Asperger, H. (1991). 'Autistic psychopathy' in childhood (U. Frith, Trans.). In U. Frith (Ed.), *Autism and Asperger Syndrome* (pp. 37–92). Cambridge: CUP.

Attwood, A., Frith, U., & Hermelin, B. (1988). The understanding and use of interpersonal gestures by autistic and Down's syndrome children. *Journal of Autism and Developmental Disorders, 18*(2), 241–257.

Bailey, A., Le Couteur, A., Gottesman, I., Bolton, P., Simonoff, E., Yuzda, E., & Rutter, M. (1995). Autism as a strongly genetic disorder: Evidence from a British twin study. *Psychological Medicine, 25*(1), 63–77.

Baron-Cohen, S. (1989). Perceptual role taking and protodeclarative pointing in autism. *British Journal of Developmental Psychology, 7*(2), 113–127.

Baron-Cohen, S. (1997). *Mindblindness: An essay on autism and theory of mind*. London, UK: MIT Press.

Baron-Cohen, S. (2000). Theory of mind and autism: A fifteen year review. *Understanding Other Minds: Perspectives from Developmental Cognitive Neuroscience, 2*, 3–20.

Baron-Cohen, S., & Goodhart, F. (1994). The 'seeing-leads-to-knowing' deficit in autism: The Pratt and Bryant probe. *British Journal of Developmental Psychology, 12*(3), 397–401.

Baron-Cohen, S., Allen, J., & Gillberg, C. (1992). Can autism be detected at 18 months? The needle, the haystack, and the CHAT. *The British Journal of Psychiatry, 161*(6), 839–843.

Baron-Cohen, S., Leslie, A. M., & Frith, U. (1985). Does the autistic child have a "Theory of mind"? *Cognition, 21*(1), 37–46.

Baron-Cohen, S., Spitz, A., & Cross, P. (1993). Do children with autism recognise surprise? A research note. *Cognition & Emotion, 7*(6), 507–516.

Baron-Cohen, S., Wheelwright, S., Skinner, R., Martin, J., & Clubley, E. (2001). The autism-spectrum quotient (AQ): Evidence from Asperger syndrome/high-functioning autism, malesand females, scientists and mathematicians. *Journal of Autism and Developmental Disorders, 31*(1), 5–17.

Bascom, J. (2012). *Loud hands: Autistic people, speaking.* Washington: Autistic Self-Advocacy Network.

Baxter, A. J., Brugha, T. S., Erskine, H. E., Scheurer, R. W., Vos, T., & Scott, J. G. (2015). The epidemiology and global burden of autism spectrum disorders. *Psychological Medicine, 45*(3), 601–613.

Bedford, R., Gliga, T., Shephard, E., Elsabbagh, M., Pickles, A., Charman, T., & Johnson, M. H. (2017). Neurocognitive and observational markers: Prediction of autism spectrum disorder from infancy to mid-childhood. *Molecular Autism, 8*(1), 49.

Ben-Sasson, A., Hen, L., Fluss, R., Cermak, S. A., Engel-Yeger, B., & Gal, E. (2009). A meta-analysis of sensory modulation symptoms in individuals with autism spectrum disorders. *Journal of Autism and Developmental Disorders, 39*(1), 1–11.

Bertone, A., Mottron, L., Jelenic, P., & Faubert, J. (2003). Motion perception in autism: A "complex" issue. *Journal of Cognitive Neuroscience, 15*(2), 218–225.

Bieleninik, Ł., Posserud, M. B., Geretsegger, M., Thompson, G., Elefant, C., & Gold, C. (2017). Tracing the temporal stability of autism spectrum diagnosis and severity as measured by the autism diagnostic observation schedule: A systematic review and meta-analysis. *PloS One, 12*(9), e0183160.

Bird, G., & Cook, R. (2013). Mixed emotions: The contribution of alexithymia to the emotional symptoms of autism. *Translational Psychiatry, 3*(7), e285.

Bird, G., & Viding, E. (2014). The self to other model of empathy: Providing a new framework for understanding empathy impairments in psychopathy, autism, and alexithymia. *Neuroscience & Biobehavioral Reviews, 47*, 520–532.

Bird, G., Catmur, C., Silani, G., Frith, C., & Frith, U. (2006). Attention does not modulate neural responses to social stimuli in autism spectrum disorders. *Neuroimage, 31*(4), 1614–1624.

Birmingham, E., Ristic, J., & Kingstone, A. (2012). Investigating social attention: A case for increasing stimulus complexity in the laboratory. *Cognitive Neuroscience, Development, and Psychopathology: Typical and Atypical Developmental Trajectories of Attention*, 251–276.

Bishop, D. V., Maybery, M., Maley, A., Wong, D., Hill, W., & Hallmayer, J. (2004). Using self-report to identify the broad phenotype in parents of children with autistic spectrum disorders: A study using the autism-spectrum quotient. *Journal of Child Psychology and Psychiatry, 45*(8), 1431–1436.

Blakemore, S. J., & Choudhury, S. (2006). Brain development during puberty: State of the science. *Developmental Science, 9*(1), 11–14.

Bleuler, E. (1908). The prognosis of dementia praecox. The group of schizophrenias. In Cutting, J. and Shepherd, M. eds., 1987. *The Clinical roots of the schizophrenia concept: translations of seminal European contributions on schizophrenia*. Cambridge: CUP Archive.

Booth, R. D., & Happé, F. G. (2018). Evidence of reduced global processing in autism spectrum disorder. *Journal of Autism and Developmental Disorders, 48*, 1397–1408.

Booth, R., Charlton, R., Hughes, C., & Happé, F. (2003). Disentangling weak coherence and executive dysfunction: Planning drawing in autism and attention – deficit/hyperactivity disorder. *Philosophical Transactions of the Royal Society B: Biological Sciences, 358*(1430), 387–392.

Boujut, E., Popa-Roch, M., Palomares, E. A., Dean, A., & Cappe, E. (2017). Self-efficacy and burnout in teachers of students with autism spectrum disorder. *Research in Autism Spectrum Disorders, 36*, 8–20.

Boutron, I., Altman, D. G., Moher, D., Schulz, K. F., & Ravaud, P. (2017). CONSORT statement for randomized trials of nonpharmacologic treatments: A 2017 update and a CONSORT extension for nonpharmacologic trial abstracts. *Annals of Internal Medicine, 167*(1), 40–47.

Brewer, N., Young, R. L., & Barnett, E. (2017). Measuring theory of mind in adults with autism spectrum disorder. *Journal of Autism and Developmental Disorders, 47*(7), 1927–1941.

Brewer, R., Biotti, F., Catmur, C., Press, C., Happé, F., Cook, R., & Bird, G. (2016). Can neurotypical individuals read autistic facial expressions? Atypical production of emotional facial expressions in autism spectrum disorders. *Autism Research, 9*, 262–271.

Brock, J. (2012). Alternative Bayesian accounts of autistic perception: Comment on Pellicano and Burr. *Trends in Cognitive Sciences, 16*(12), 573–574.

Brunsdon, V. E., & Happé, F. (2014). Exploring the 'fractionation' of autism at the cognitive level. *Autism, 18*(1), 17–30.

Buescher, A. V., Cidav, Z., Knapp, M., & Mandell, D. S. (2014). Costs of autism spectrum disorders in the United Kingdom and the United States. *JAMA Pediatrics, 168*(8), 721–728.

Buttelmann, D., Zmyj, N., Daum, M., & Carpenter, M. (2013). Selective imitation of in-group over out-group members in 14-month-old infants. *Child Development*, *84*(2), 422–428.

Carruthers, P., & Smith, P. K. (Eds.). (1996). *Theories of theories of mind*. Cambridge: Cambridge University Press.

Cassidy, S., & Rodgers, J. (2017). Understanding and prevention of suicide in autism. *The Lancet Psychiatry*, *4*(6), e11.

Castelli, F., Frith, C., Happé, F., & Frith, U. (2002). Autism, Asperger syndrome and brain mechanisms for the attribution of mental states to animated shapes. *Brain*, *125*(8), 1839–1849.

Castelloe, P., & Dawson, G. (1993). Subclassification of children with autism and pervasive developmental disorder: A questionnaire based on Wing's subgrouping scheme. *Journal of Autism and Developmental Disorders*, *23*(2), 229–241.

Chandler, M., Fritz, A. S., & Hala, S. (1989). Small-scale deceit: Deception as a marker of two-, three-, and four-year-olds' early theories of mind. *Child Development*, 1263–1277.

Charman, T. (2003). Why is joint attention a pivotal skill in autism? *Philosophical Transactions of the Royal Society B: Biological Sciences*, *358*(1430), 315–324.

Charman, T., Loth, E., Tillmann, J., Crawley, D., Wooldridge, C., Goyard, D., . . . Baron-Cohen, S. (2017). The EU-AIMS Longitudinal European Autism Project (LEAP): Clinical characterisation. *Molecular Autism*, *8*(1), 27.

Chawarska, K., Volkmar, F., & Klin, A. (2010). Limited attentional bias for faces in toddlers with autism spectrum disorders. *Archives of General Psychiatry*, *67*(2), 178–185.

Chevallier, C., Parish-Morris, J., McVey, A., Rump, K. M., Sasson, N. J., Herrington, J. D., & Schultz, R. T. (2015). Measuring social attention and motivation in autism spectrum disorder using eye-tracking: Stimulus type matters. *Autism Research*, *8*(5), 620–628.

Chevallier, C., Parish-Morris, J., Tonge, N., Le, L., Miller, J., & Schultz, R. T. (2014). Susceptibility to the audience effect explains performance gap between children with and without autism in a theory of mind task. *Journal of Experimental Psychology: General*, *143*(3), 972.

Christensen, J., Grønborg, T. K., Sørensen, M. J., Schendel, D., Parner, E. T., Pedersen, L. H., & Vestergaard, M. (2013). Prenatal valproate exposure and risk of autism spectrum disorders and childhood autism. *Jama*, *309*(16), 1696–1703.

Claiborne Park, Clara. (1968). *The siege*. Gerrards Cross: Colin Smythe.

Constantino, J. N., & Todd, R. D. (2003). Autistic traits in the general population: A twin study. *Archives of General Psychiatry*, *60*(5), 524–530.

Constantino, J. N., Kennon-McGill, S., Weichselbaum, C., Marrus, N., Haider, A., Glowinski, A. L., . . . Jones, W. (2017). Infant viewing of social scenes is under genetic control and is atypical in autism. *Nature*, *547*(7663), 340.

Cooper, K., Smith, L. G. E., & Russel, A. J. (2018). Gender identity in autism: Sex differences in social affiliation with gender groups. *Journal of Autism and Developmental Disorders*. doi: 10.1007/s10803-018-3590-1.

Courchesne, V., Meilleur, A. A. S., Poulin-Lord, M. P., Dawson, M., & Soulières, I. (2015). Autistic children at risk of being underestimated: School-based pilot study of a strength-informed assessment. *Molecular Autism*, 6(1), 12.

Croen, L. A., Zerbo, O., Qian, Y., Massolo, M. L., Rich, S., Sidney, S., & Kripke, C. (2015). The health status of adults on the autism spectrum. *Autism*, 19(7), 814–823.

Czech, H. (2018). Hans Asperger, national socialism, and "race hygiene" in Nazi-era Vienna. *Molecular Autism*, 9(1), 29.

Daniels, A. M., & Mandell, D. S. (2014). Explaining differences in age at autism spectrum disorder diagnosis: A critical review. *Autism*, 18(5), 583–597.

Dawson, G., Meltzoff, A. N., Osterling, J., Rinaldi, J., & Brown, E. (1998). Children with autism fail to orient to naturally occurring social stimuli. *Journal of Autism and Developmental Disorders*, 28(6), 479–485.

Dawson, M., Mottron, L., & Gernsbacher, M. A. (2008). Learning in autism. *Learning and Memory: A Comprehensive Reference*, 2, 759–772.

Dawson, M., Soulières, I., Gernsbacher, M. A., & Mottron, L. (2007). The level and nature of autistic intelligence. *Psychological Science*, 18(8), 657–662.

de Guzman, M., Bird, G., Banissy, M. J., & Catmur, C. (2016). Self – other control processes in social cognition: From imitation to empathy. *Philosophical Transactions of the Royal Society B*, 371(1686), 20150079.

Dean, M., Harwood, R., & Kasari, C. (2017). The art of camouflage: Gender differences in the social behaviors of girls and boys with autism spectrum disorder. *Autism*, 21(6), 678–689.

Dekker, M. (1999). *On our own terms: Emerging autistic culture*. Autism99 online conference. Republished in 2015 at www.autscape.org/2015/programme/handouts/Autistic-Culture-07-Oct-1999.pdf

Dennett, D. (1978). Beliefs about beliefs. *Behavioral and Brain Sciences*, 4, 568–570.

Dennett, D. C. (1989). *The intentional stance*. Cambridge, MA: MIT Press.

Devine, R. T., & Hughes, C. (2014). Relations between false belief understanding and executive function in early childhood: A meta-analysis. *Child Development*, 85(5), 1777–1794.

Dewinter, J., Van Parys, H., Vermeiren, R., & van Nieuwenhuizen, C. (2017). Adolescent boys with an autism spectrum disorder and their experience of sexuality: An interpretative phenomenological analysis. *Autism*, 21(1), 75–82.

Dickerson, P., Stribling, P., & Rae, J. (2007). Tapping into interaction: How children with autistic spectrum disorders design and place tapping in relation to activities in progress. *Gesture*, 7(3), 271–303.

Diener, M. L., Wright, C. A., Smith, K. N., & Wright, S. D. (2014). Assessing visual-spatial creativity in youth on the autism spectrum. *Creativity Research Journal, 26*(3), 328–337.

Dingfelder, H. E., & Mandell, D. S. (2011). Bridging the research-to-practice gap in autism intervention: An application of diffusion of innovation theory. *Journal of Autism and Developmental Disorders, 41*(5), 597–609.

Donvan, J. J., & Zucker, C. B. (2017). *In a different key: The story of autism.* New York, NY: Broadway Books.

DuBois, D., Ameis, S. H., Lai, M. C., Casanova, M. F., & Desarkar, P. (2016). Interoception in autism spectrum disorder: A review. *International Journal of Developmental Neuroscience, 52,* 104–111.

Duvekot, J., van der Ende, J., Verhulst, F. C., Slappendel, G., van Daalen, E., Maras, A., & Greaves-Lord, K. (2017). Factors influencing the probability of a diagnosis of autism spectrum disorder in girls versus boys. *Autism, 21*(6), 646–658.

Ecker, C. (2017). The neuroanatomy of autism spectrum disorder: An overview of structural neuroimaging findings and their translatability to the clinical setting. *Autism, 21*(1), 18–28.

Ecker, C., Bookheimer, S. Y., & Murphy, D. G. (2015). Neuroimaging in autism spectrum disorder: Brain structure and function across the lifespan. *The Lancet Neurology, 14*(11), 1121–1134.

Edey, R., Cook, J., Brewer, R., Johnson, M. H., Bird, G., & Press, C. (2016). Interaction takes two: Typical adults exhibit mind-blindness towards those with autism spectrum disorder. *Journal of Abnormal Psychology, 125*(7), 879.

Eisenmajer, R., Prior, M., Leekam, S., Wing, L., Gould, J., Welham, M., & Ong, B. (1996). Comparison of clinical symptoms in autism and Asperger's disorder. *Journal of the American Academy of Child & Adolescent Psychiatry, 35*(11), 1523–1531.

Elsabbagh, M., Divan, G., Koh, Y. J., Kim, Y. S., Kauchali, S., Marcín, C., . . . Yasamy, M. T. (2012). Global prevalence of autism and other pervasive developmental disorders. *Autism Research, 5*(3), 160–179.

Elsabbagh, M., Gliga, T., Pickles, A., Hudry, K., Charman, T., Johnson, M. H., & BASIS Team. (2013). The development of face orienting mechanisms in infants at-risk for autism. *Behavioural Brain Research, 251,* 147–154.

Elsabbagh, M., Mercure, E., Hudry, K., Chandler, S., Pasco, G., Charman, T., . . . BASIS Team. (2012). Infant neural sensitivity to dynamic eye gaze is associated with later emerging autism. *Current Biology, 22*(4), 338–342.

Falck-Ytter, T., Rehnberg, E., & Bölte, S. (2013). Lack of visual orienting to biological motion and audiovisual synchrony in 3-year-olds with autism. *PloS One, 8*(7), e68816.

Fein, D., Barton, M., Eigsti, I. M., Kelley, E., Naigles, L., Schultz, R. T., . . . Troyb, E. (2013). Optimal outcome in individuals with a history of autism. *Journal of Child Psychology and Psychiatry, 54*(2), 195–205.

Feinstein, A. (2011). *A history of autism: Conversations with the pioneers.* Hoboken, NJ: John Wiley & Sons.

Fine, C. (2010). From scanner to sound bite: Issues in interpreting and reporting sex differences in the brain. *Current Directions in Psychological Science, 19*(5), 280–283.

Finn, P., Bothe, A. K., & Bramlett, R. E. (2005). Science and pseudoscience in communication disorders: Criteria and applications. *American Journal of Speech-Language Pathology, 14*(3), 172–186.

Fletcher-Watson, B., & May, S. (2018). Enhancing relaxed performance: Evaluating the autism arts festival. *Research in Drama Education: The Journal of Applied Theatre and Performance,* 1–15.

Fletcher-Watson, S. (2016). Supporting communication in non-speaking autistic adults. In D. Milton & N. Martin (Eds.), *Autism and intellectual disability.* Hove: Pavilion Publishing.

Fletcher-Watson, S., Adams, J., Brook, K., Charman, T., Crane, L., Cusack, J., . . . Pellicano, E. (2018). Making the future together: Shaping autism research through meaningful participation. *Autism,* 1362361318786721.

Fletcher-Watson, S., Adams, J., Brook, K., Charman, T., Crane, L., Cusack, J., . . . Pellicano, E. (2018). Making the future together: Shaping autism research through meaningful participation. *Autism,* 1362361318786721.

Fletcher-Watson, S., Apicella, F., Auyeung, B., Beranova, S., Bonnet-Brilhault, F., Canal-Bedia, R., . . . Farroni, T. (2017a). Attitudes of the autism community to early autism research. *Autism, 21*(1), 61–74.

Fletcher-Watson, S., Larsen, K., Salomone, E., & COST ESSEA Working Groups. (2017b). What do parents of children with autism expect from participation in research? A community survey about early autism studies. *Autism.* doi: 10.1177/1362361317728436.

Fletcher-Watson, S., Leekam, S. R., Benson, V., Frank, M. C., & Findlay, J. M. (2009). Eye-movements reveal attention to social information in autism spectrum disorder. *Neuropsychologia, 47*(1), 248–257.

Fletcher-Watson, S., McConnell, F., Manola, E., & McConachie, H. (2014). Interventions based on the theory of mind cognitive model for autism spectrum disorder (ASD). *Cochrane Database of Systematic Reviews, 3,* CD008785.

Folstein, S., & Rutter, M. (1977). Infantile autism: A genetic study of 21 twin pairs. *Journal of Child Psychology and Psychiatry, 18*(4), 297–321.

Fombonne, E. (2005). The changing epidemiology of autism. *Journal of Applied Research in Intellectual Disabilities, 18*(4), 281–294.

Foss-Feig, J. H., Tadin, D., Schauder, K. B., & Cascio, C. J. (2013). A substantial and unexpected enhancement of motion perception in autism. *Journal of Neuroscience, 33*(19), 8243–8249.

Frazier, T. W., Strauss, M., Klingemier, E. W., Zetzer, E. E., Hardan, A. Y., Eng, C., & Youngstrom, E. A. (2017). A meta-analysis of gaze differences to social and nonsocial information between individuals with and without autism. *Journal of the American Academy of Child & Adolescent Psychiatry*, 56(7), 546–555.

Frith, U. (1989). *Autism: Explaining the enigma*. Blackwell Publishing, Oxford UK.

Frith, U. (1991). Asperger and his syndrome. In U. Frith (Ed.), *Autism and asperger syndrome*, Cambridge: Cambridge University Press, pp. 1–36.

Frith, U., & Happé, F. (1994). Autism: Beyond "Theory of mind". *Cognition*, 50(1–3), 115–132.

Frith, U., Morton, J., & Leslie, A. M. (1991). The cognitive basis of a biological disorder: Autism. *Trends in Neurosciences*, 14(10), 433–438.

George, R., & Stokes, M. A. (2018). Sexual orientation in autism spectrum disorder. *Autism Research*, 11(1), 133–141.

Gerland, G. (2003). *A real person: Life on the outside*. London, UK: Souvenir Press.

Gernsbacher, M. A., Stevenson, J. L., & Dern, S. (2017). Specificity, contexts, and reference groups matter when assessing autistic traits. *PloS One*, 12(2), e0171931.

Geschwind, D. H. (2008). Autism: Many genes, common pathways? *Cell*, 135(3), 391–395.

Geschwind, D. H., & Staite, M. W. (2015). Gene hunting in autism spectrum disorder: On the path to precision medicine. *The Lancet Neurology*, 14(11), 1109–1120.

Gilmour, L., Schalomon, P. M., & Smith, V. (2012). Sexuality in a community based sample of adults with autism spectrum disorder. *Research in Autism Spectrum Disorders*, 6(1), 313–318.

Grandin, T. (1986). *Emergence, labeled autistic*. Novato, CA: Academic Therapy Publications.

Green, J., & Garg, S. (2018). Annual research review: The state of autism interventions science: Progress, target psychological and biological mechanisms and future prospects. *Journal of Child Psychology and Psychiatry*, 59(4), 424–443.

Green, J., Charman, T., Pickles, A., Wan, M. W., Elsabbagh, M., Slonims, V., . . . Jones, E. J. (2015). Parent-mediated intervention versus no intervention for infants at high risk of autism: A parallel, single-blind, randomised trial. *The Lancet Psychiatry*, 2(2), 133–140.

Green, J., Pickles, A., Pasco, G., Bedford, R., Wan, M. W., Elsabbagh, M., . . . Charman, T. (2017). Randomised trial of a parent-mediated intervention for infants at high risk for autism: Longitudinal outcomes to age 3 years. *Journal of Child Psychology and Psychiatry*, 58(12), 1330–1340.

Grelotti, D. J., Klin, A. J., Gauthier, I., Skudlarski, P., Cohen, D. J., Gore, J. C., . . . Schultz, R. T. (2005). fMRI activation of the fusiform gyrus and amygdala to cartoon characters but not to faces in a boy with autism. *Neuropsychologia*, 43(3), 373–385.

Griffith, G. M., Totsika, V., Nash, S., Jones, R. S., & Hastings, R. P. (2012). "We are all there silently coping". The hidden experiences of parents of adults with Asperger syndrome. *Journal of Intellectual and Developmental Disability, 37*(3), 237–247.

Grossman, R. B. (2015). Judgments of social awkwardness from brief exposure to children with and without high-functioning autism. *Autism, 19*, 580–587.

Grzadzinski, R., Huerta, M., & Lord, C. (2013). DSM-5 and autism spectrum disorders (ASDs): An opportunity for identifying ASD subtypes. *Molecular Aautism, 4*(1), 12.

Guénolé, F., Godbout, R., Nicolas, A., Franco, P., Claustrat, B., & Baleyte, J. M. (2011). Melatonin for disordered sleep in individuals with autism spectrum disorders: Systematic review and discussion. *Sleep Medicine Reviews, 15*(6), 379–387.

Guillon, Q., Hadjikhani, N., Baduel, S., & Rogé, B. (2014). Visual social attention in autism spectrum disorder: Insights from eye tracking studies. *Neuroscience & Biobehavioral Reviews, 42*, 279–297.

Hamilton, A. F. D. C. (2013). Reflecting on the mirror neuron system in autism: A systematic review of current theories. *Developmental Cognitive Neuroscience, 3*, 91–105.

Happé, F. (2015). Autism as a neurodevelopmental disorder of mind-reading. *Journal of the British Academy, 3*, 197–209.

Happé, F. G. (1994). An advanced test of theory of mind: Understanding of story characters' thoughts and feelings by able autistic, mentally handicapped, and normal children and adults. *Journal of Autism and Developmental Disorders, 24*(2), 129–154.

Happé, F. G. (1996). Studying weak central coherence at low levels: Children with autism do not succumb to visual illusions. A research note. *Journal of Child Psychology and Psychiatry, 37*(7), 873–877.

Happé, F. G., Mansour, H., Barrett, P., Brown, T., Abbott, P., & Charlton, R. A. (2016). Demographic and cognitive profile of individuals seeking a diagnosis of autism spectrum disorder in adulthood. *Journal of Autism and Developmental Disorders, 46*(11), 3469–3480.

Happé, F., & Charlton, R. A. (2012). Aging in autism spectrum disorders: A mini-review. *Gerontology, 58*(1), 70–78.

Happé, F., & Frith, U. (2006). The weak coherence account: Detail-focused cognitive style in autism spectrum disorders. *Journal of Autism and Developmental Disorders, 36*(1), 5–25.

Happé, F., & Ronald, A. (2008). The 'fractionable autism triad': A review of evidence from behavioural, genetic, cognitive and neural research. *Neuropsychology Review, 18*(4), 287–304.

Happé, F., Ronald, A., & Plomin, R. (2006). Time to give up on a single explanation for autism. *Nature Neuroscience, 9*(10), 1218.

Harms, M. B., Martin, A., & Wallace, G. L. (2010). Facial emotion recognition in autism spectrum disorders: A review of behavioral and neuroimaging studies. *Neuropsychology Review, 20*(3), 290–322.

Hartley, C., & Fisher, S. (2018). Mine is better than yours: Investigating the ownership effect in children with autism spectrum disorder and typically developing children. *Cognition, 172*, 26–36.

Harvey, I., Bolgan, S., Mosca, D., McLean, C., & Rusconi, E. (2016). Systemizers are better code-breakers: Self-reported systemizing predicts code-breaking performance in expert hackers and naïve participants. *Frontiers in Human Neuroscience, 10*.

Hazlett, H. C., Gu, H., Munsell, B. C., Kim, S. H., Styner, M., Wolff, J. J., . . . Collins, D. L. (2017). Early brain development in infants at high risk for autism spectrum disorder. *Nature, 542*(7641), 348.

Hearst, C. (2015). *Does language affect our attitudes to autism?* www.autismmatters.org.uk/blog/category/language

Heasman, B., & Gillespie, A. (2018). Perspective-taking is two-sided: Misunderstandings between people with Asperger's syndrome and their family members. *Autism, 22*(6), 740–750. doi: 10.1177/1362361317708287.

Hedden, T., & Gabrieli, J. D. (2004). Insights into the ageing mind: A view from cognitive neuroscience. *Nature Reviews Neuroscience, 5*(2), 87.

Heyes, C. (2014). False belief in infancy: A fresh look. *Developmental Science, 17*(5), 647–659.

Hill, E. L. (2004). Executive dysfunction in autism. *Trends in Cognitive Sciences, 8*(1), 26–32.

Hirschfeld, L., Bartmess, E., White, S., & Frith, U. (2007). Can autistic children predict behavior by social stereotypes? *Current Biology, 17*(12), R451–R452.

Hirvikoski, T., Mittendorfer-Rutz, E., Boman, M., Larsson, H., Lichtenstein, P., & Bölte, S. (2016). Premature mortality in autism spectrum disorder. *The British Journal of Psychiatry, 208*(3), 232–238.

Hobson, R. P., & Lee, A. (1998). Hello and goodbye: A study of social engagement in autism. *Journal of Autism and Developmental Disorders, 28*(2), 117–127.

Hobson, R. P., & Lee, A. (1999). Imitation and identification in autism. *The Journal of Child Psychology and Psychiatry and Allied Disciplines, 40*(4), 649–659.

Hobson, R. P., & Meyer, J. A. (2005). Foundations for self and other: A study in autism. *Developmental Science, 8*(6), 481–491.

Howlin, P., & Magiati, I. (2017). Autism spectrum disorder: Outcomes in adulthood. *Current Opinion in Psychiatry, 30*(2), 69–76.

Howlin, P., Goode, S., Hutton, J., & Rutter, M. (2009). Savant skills in autism: Psychometric approaches and parental reports. *Philosophical Transactions of the Royal Society B: Biological Sciences, 364*(1522), 1359–1367.

Howlin, P., Savage, S., Moss, P., Tempier, A., & Rutter, M. (2014). Cognitive and language skills in adults with autism: A 40-year follow-up. *Journal of Child Psychology and Psychiatry, 55*(1), 49–58.

Hughes, C., & Russell, J. (1993). Autistic children's difficulty with mental disengagement from an object: Its implications for theories of autism. *Developmental Psychology, 29*(3), 498.

Hughes, C., Russell, J., & Robbins, T. W. (1994). Evidence for executive dysfunction in autism. *Neuropsychologia, 32*(4), 477–492.

Hull, L., Petrides, K. V., Allison, C., Smith, P., Baron-Cohen, S., Lai, M. C., & Mandy, W. (2017). "Putting on my best normal": Social camouflaging in adults with autism spectrum conditions. *Journal of Autism and Developmental Disorders, 47*(8), 2519–2534.

Hulme, C., & Snowling, M. J. (2016). Reading disorders and dyslexia. *Current Opinion in Pediatrics, 28*(6), 731–735.

Hundley, R. J., Shui, A., & Malow, B. A. (2016). Relationship between subtypes of restricted and repetitive behaviors and sleep disturbance in autism spectrum disorder. *Journal of Autism and Developmental Disorders, 46*(11), 3448–3457.

Iao, L. S., & Leekam, S. R. (2014). Nonspecificity and theory of mind: New evidence from a nonverbal false-sign task and children with autism spectrum disorders. *Journal of Experimental Child Psychology, 122,* 1–20.

Iao, L. S., Leekam, S., Perner, J., & McConachie, H. (2011). Further evidence for nonspecificity of theory of mind in preschoolers: Training and transferability in the understanding of false beliefs and false signs. *Journal of Cognition and Development, 12*(1), 56–79.

Iarocci, G., & McDonald, J. (2006). Sensory integration and the perceptual experience of persons with autism. *Journal of Autism and Developmental Disorders, 36*(1), 77–90.

Ingersoll, B. (2010). Broader autism phenotype and nonverbal sensitivity: Evidence for an association in the general population. *Journal of Autism and Developmental Disorders, 40*(5), 590–598.

Insel, T., Cuthbert, B., Garvey, M., Heinssen, R., Pine, D. S., Quinn, K., Sanislow, C., & Wang, P. (2010). Research domain criteria (RDoC): Toward a new classification framework for research on mental disorders. *American Journal of Psychiatry, 167*(7), 748–751.

Jain, A., Marshall, J., Buikema, A., Bancroft, T., Kelly, J. P., & Newschaffer, C. J. (2015). Autism occurrence by MMR vaccine status among US children with older siblings with and without autism. *Jama, 313*(15), 1534–1540.

Johnson, M. H. (2012). Executive function and developmental disorders: The flip side of the coin. *Trends in Cognitive Sciences, 16*(9), 454–457.

Johnson, M. H. (2014). Autism: Demise of the innate social orienting hypothesis. *Current Biology, 24*(1), R30–R31.

Johnson, M. H., Siddons, F., Frith, U., & Morton, J. (1992). Can autism be predicted on the basis of infant screening tests? *Developmental Medicine & Child Neurology, 34*(4), 316–320.

Jones, C. R., Simonoff, E., Baird, G., Pickles, A., Marsden, A. J., Tregay, J., Happé, F., & Charman, T. (2018). The association between theory of mind, executive function, and the symptoms of autism spectrum disorder. *Autism Research, 11*, 95–109.

Jones, E. J., Gliga, T., Bedford, R., Charman, T., & Johnson, M. H. (2014). Developmental pathways to autism: A review of prospective studies of infants at risk. *Neuroscience & Biobehavioral Reviews, 39*, 1–33.

Jones, W., & Klin, A. (2013). Attention to eyes is present but in decline in 2–6-month-old infants later diagnosed with autism. *Nature, 504*(7480), 427.

Jones, W., Carr, K., & Klin, A. (2008). Absence of preferential looking to the eyes of approaching adults predicts level of social disability in 2-year-old toddlers with autism spectrum disorder. *Archives of General Psychiatry, 65*(8), 946–954.

Jonsson, U., Choque Olsson, N., & Bölte, S. (2016). Can findings from randomized controlled trials of social skills training in autism spectrum disorder be generalized? The neglected dimension of external validity. *Autism, 20*(3), 295–305.

Kaale, A., Fagerland, M. W., Martinsen, E. W., & Smith, L. (2014). Preschool-based social communication treatment for children with autism: 12-month follow-up of a randomized trial. *Journal of the American Academy of Child & Adolescent Psychiatry, 53*(2), 188–198.

Kang, K. S., & Kang, D. K. (Eds.). (1988). *151 Folk tales of India.* Columbia, MO: South Asia Books.

Kanner, L. (1943). Autistic disturbances of affective contact. *Nervous Child, 2*(3), 217–250.

Kanner, L. (1973). The birth of early infantile autism. *Journal of Autism and Developmental Disorders, 3*(2), 93–95.

Kanner, L., & Eisenberg, L. (1957). Early infantile autism, 1943–1955. *Psychiatric Research Reports* (7), 55.

Kapp, S. K., Gillespie-Lynch, K., Sherman, L. E., & Hutman, T. (2013). Deficit, difference, or both? Autism and neurodiversity. *Developmental Psychology, 49*(1), 59.

Kasari, C., Gulsrud, A., Freeman, S., Paparella, T., & Hellemann, G. (2012). Longitudinal follow-up of children with autism receiving targeted interventions on joint attention and play. *Journal of the American Academy of Child & Adolescent Psychiatry, 51*(5), 487–495.

Kasari, C., Paparella, T., Freeman, S., & Jahromi, L. B. (2008). Language outcome in autism: Randomized comparison of joint attention and play interventions. *Journal of Consulting and Clinical Psychology, 76*(1), 125.

Klin, A., Jones, W., Schultz, R., Volkmar, F., & Cohen, D. (2002). Visual fixation patterns during viewing of naturalistic social situations as predictors of social competence in individuals with autism. *Archives of General Psychiatry, 59*(9), 809–816.

Klin, A., Lin, D. J., Gorrindo, P., Ramsay, G., & Jones, W. (2009). Two-year-olds with autism orient to non-social contingencies rather than biological motion. *Nature, 459*(7244), 257.

Knapp, M., Romeo, R., & Beecham, J. (2009). Economic cost of autism in the UK. *Autism, 13*(3), 317–336.

Komeda, H., Kosaka, H., Saito, D. N., Mano, Y., Jung, M., Fujii, T., . . . Okazawa, H. (2014). Autistic empathy toward autistic others. *Social Cognitive and Affective Neuroscience, 10*(2), 145–152.

Lai, M. C., Lombardo, M. V., Ruigrok, A. N., Chakrabarti, B., Auyeung, B., Szatmari, P., Happé, F., Baron-Cohen, S. & MRC AIMS Consortium. (2017). Quantifying and exploring camouflaging in men and women with autism. *Autism, 21*(6), 690–702.

Lai, M. C., Lombardo, M. V., Ruigrok, A. N., Chakrabarti, B., Auyeung, B., Szatmari, P., . . . MRC AIMS Consortium. (2017). Quantifying and exploring camouflaging in men and women with autism. *Autism, 21*(6), 690–702.

Lasgaard, M., Nielsen, A., Eriksen, M. E., & Goossens, L. (2010). Loneliness and social support in adolescent boys with autism spectrum disorders. *Journal of Autism and Developmental Disorders, 40*(2), 218–226.

Lavelle, T. A., Weinstein, M. C., Newhouse, J. P., Munir, K., Kuhlthau, K. A., & Prosser, L. A. (2014). Economic burden of childhood autism spectrum disorders. *Pediatrics, 133*(3), e520–e529.

Lawson, J., Baron-Cohen, S., & Wheelwright, S. (2004). Empathising and systemising in adults with and without Asperger syndrome. *Journal of Autism and Developmental Disorders, 34*(3), 301–310.

Lawson, R. P., Rees, G., & Friston, K. J. (2014). An aberrant precision account of autism. *Frontiers in Human Neuroscience, 8.*

LeCouteur, A., Lord, C., & Rutter, M. (2003). *The Autism Diagnostic Interview-Revised (ADI-R).* Los Angeles, CA: Western Psychological Services.

Leekam, S. R., Nieto, C., Libby, S. J., Wing, L., & Gould, J. (2007b). Describing the sensory abnormalities of children and adults with autism. *Journal of Autism and Developmental Disorders, 37*(5), 894–910.

Leekam, S., Tandos, J., McConachie, H., Meins, E., Parkinson, K., Wright, C., . . . Couteur, A. L. (2007). Repetitive behaviours in typically developing 2-year-olds. *Journal of Child Psychology and Psychiatry, 48*(11), 1131–1138.

Leslie, A. M. (1987). Pretense and representation: The origins of "Theory of mind". *Psychological Review, 94*(4), 412.

Lever, A. G., & Geurts, H. M. (2016). Age-related differences in cognition across the adult lifespan in autism spectrum disorder. *Autism Research, 9*(6), 666–676.

Lin, A., Adolphs, R., & Rangel, A. (2011). Social and monetary reward learning engage overlapping neural substrates. *Social Cognitive and Affective Neuroscience, 7*(3), 274–281.

Livingston, L. A., & Happé, F. (2017). Conceptualising compensation in neurodevelopmental disorders: Reflections from autism spectrum disorder. *Neuroscience & Biobehavioral Reviews, 80,* 729–742.

Long, J., Panese, J., Ferguson, J., Hamill, M. A., & Miller, J. (2017). Enabling voice and participation in autism services: Using practitioner research to develop inclusive practice. *Good Autism Practice (GAP), 18*(2), 6–14.

Loomes, R., Hull, L., & Mandy, W. P. L. (2017). What is the male-to-female ratio in autism spectrum disorder? A systematic review and meta-analysis. *Journal of the American Academy of Child & Adolescent Psychiatry, 56*(6), 466–474.

López, B. (2015). Beyond modularisation: The need of a socio-neuro-constructionist model of autism. *Journal of Autism and Developmental Disorders, 45*(1), 31–41.

Lord, C., & Schopler, E. (1987). Neurobiological implications of sex differences in autism. In *Neurobiological issues in autism* (pp. 191–211). Boston, MA: Springer.

Lord, C., Petkova, E., Hus, V., Gan, W., Lu, F., Martin, D. M., Ousley, O., Guy, L., Bernier, R., Gerdts, J., & Algermissen, M. (2012a). A multisite study of the clinical diagnosis of different autism spectrum disorders. *Archives of General Psychiatry, 69*(3), 306–313.

Lord, C., Rutter, M., DiLavore, P. C., Risi, S., Gotham, K., & Bishop, S. (2012b). *Autism diagnostic observation schedule: ADOS-2.* Los Angeles, CA: Western Psychological Services.

Losh, M., & Capps, L. (2006). Understanding of emotional experience in autism: Insights from the personal accounts of high-functioning children with autism. *Developmental Psychology, 42*(5), 809.

Loth, E., Charman, T., Mason, L., Tillmann, J., Jones, E. J., Wooldridge, C., . . . Banaschewski, T. (2017). The EU-AIMS Longitudinal European Autism Project (LEAP): Design and methodologies to identify and validate stratification biomarkers for autism spectrum disorders. *Molecular Autism, 8*(1), 24.

Loth, E., Spooren, W., Ham, L. M., Isaac, M. B., Auriche-Benichou, C., Banaschewski, T., . . . Charman, T. (2016). Identification and validation of biomarkers for autism spectrum disorders. *Nature Reviews Drug Discovery, 15*(1), 70–73.

Lovaas, O. I., Schreibman, L., & Koegel, R. L. (1974). A behavior modification approach to the treatment of autistic children. *Journal of Autism and Childhood Schizophrenia, 4*(2), 111–129.

Luyster, R., Gotham, K., Guthrie, W., Coffing, M., Petrak, R., Pierce, K., . . . Richler, J. (2009). The autism diagnostic observation schedule – toddler module: A new module of a standardized diagnostic measure for autism spectrum disorders. *Journal of Autism and Developmental Disorders, 39*(9), 1305–1320.

Macintosh, K. E., & Dissanayake, C. (2004). Annotation: The similarities and differences between autistic disorder and Asperger's disorder: A review of the empirical evidence. *Journal of Child Psychology and Psychiatry*, *45*(3), 421–434.

Macmillan, K., Goodall, K., & Fletcher-Watson, S. (2018, November 12). Do autistic individuals experience understanding in school? OSF preprint, https://doi.org/10.17605/OSF.IO/E9KFA

Maguire, E. A., Woollett, K., & Spiers, H. J. (2000). London taxi drivers nad bus drivers: A structural MRI and neuropsychological analysis. *Hippocampus*, *16*(12), 1091–1101.

Mandell, D. S., & Novak, M. (2005). The role of culture in families' treatment decisions for children with autism spectrum disorders. *Developmental Disabilities Research Reviews*, *11*(2), 110–115.

Mandy, W., & Tchanturia, K. (2015). Do women with eating disorders who have social and flexibility difficulties really have autism? A case series. *Molecular Autism*, *6*(1), 6.

Manson, C., & Winterbottom, M. (2012). Examining the association between empathising, systemising, degree subject and gender. *Educational Studies*, *38*(1), 73–88.

McConachie, H., Mason, D., Parr, J. R., Garland, D., Wilson, C., & Rodgers, J. (2017). Enhancing the validity of a quality of life measure for autistic people. *Journal of Autism and Developmental Disorders*, 1–16.

McKechanie, A. G., Moffat, V. J., Johnstone, E. C., & Fletcher-Watson, S. (2017). Links between autism spectrum disorder diagnostic status and family quality of life. *Children*, *4*(4), 23.

Meltzoff, A. N. (1990). Foundations for developing a concept of self: The role of imitation in relating self to other and the value of social mirroring, social modeling, and self practice in infancy. In D. Cicchetti & M. Beeghly (Eds.), *The John D. and Catherine T. MacArthur foundation series on mental health and development. The self in transition: Infancy to childhood* (pp. 139–164). Chicago, IL: University of Chicago Press.

Milne, E., Swettenham, J., & Campbell, R. (2005). Motion perception and autistic spectrum disorder: A review. *Current Psychology of Cognition*, *23*(1/2), 3.

Milton, D. E. (2012). On the ontological status of autism: The 'double empathy problem'. *Disability & Society*, *27*(6), 883–887.

Milton, D. E. (2014). Autistic expertise: A critical reflection on the production of knowledge in autism studies. *Autism*, *18*(7), 794–802.

Milton, D., & Martin, N. (2016). *Autism and Intellectual disability in adults* (Vol. 1). Hove, UK: Pavilion Publishing and Media.

Milton, D., & Martin, N. (2017). *Autism and intellectual disability in adults*, (Vol. 2). Hove, UK: Pavilion Publishing and Media.

Minshew, N. J., & Goldstein, G. (1998). Autism as a disorder of complex information processing. *Mental Retardation and Developmental Disabilities Research Reviews*, *4*(2), 129–136.

Minshew, N. J., Goldstein, G., & Siegel, D. J. (1997). Neuropsychologic functioning in autism: Profile of a complex information processing disorder. *Journal of the International Neuropsychological Society, 3*(4), 303–316.

Modabbernia, A., Velthorst, E., & Reichenberg, A. (2017). Environmental risk factors for autism: An evidence-based review of systematic reviews and meta-analyses. *Molecular Autism, 8*(1), 13.

Moore, C. (2004). *George and Sam.* London, UK: Penguin.

Moore, D. J. (2015). Acute pain experience in individuals with autism spectrum disorders: A review. *Autism, 19*(4), 387–399.

Morton, J., & Frith, U. (1995). Causal modelling: A structural approach to developmental psychopathology. *Manual of Developmental Psychopathology, 1,* 357–390.

Mottron, L., Dawson, M., Soulieres, I., Hubert, B., & Burack, J. (2006). Enhanced perceptual functioning in autism: An update, and eight principles of autistic perception. *Journal of Autism and Developmental Disorders, 36*(1), 27–43.

Muhle, R. A., Reed, H. E., Stratigos, K. A., & Veenstra-VanderWeele, J. (2018). The emerging clinical neuroscience of autism spectrum disorder: A review. *JAMA Psychiatry, 75*(5), 514–523.

Murphy, J., Catmur, C., & Bird, G. (2018). Alexithymia is associated with a multidomain, multidimensional failure of interoception: Evidence from novel tests. *Journal of Experimental Psychology: General, 147*(3), 398.

Murray, D., Lesser, M., & Lawson, W. (2005). Attention, monotropism and the diagnostic criteria for autism. *Autism, 9*(2), 139–156.

Murray, K., Johnston, K., Cunane, H., Kerr, C., Spain, D., Gillan, N., . . . Happé, F. (2017). A new test of advanced theory of mind: The "Strange Stories Film Task" captures social processing differences in adults with autism spectrum disorders. *Autism Research, 10,* 1120–1132.

Ne'eman, A. (2010). The future (and the past) of autism advocacy, or why the ASA's magazine, the advocate, wouldn't publish this piece. *Disability Studies Quarterly, 30*(1).

Neumann, D., Spezio, M. L., Piven, J., & Adolphs, R. (2006). Looking you in the mouth: Abnormal gaze in autism resulting from impaired top-down modulation of visual attention. *Social Cognitive and Affective Neuroscience, 1*(3), 194–202.

Noens, I. L., & van Berckelaer-Onnes, I. A. (2005). Captured by details: Sense-making, language and communication in autism. *Journal of Communication Disorders, 38*(2), 123–141.

Nordahl-Hansen, A., Tøndevold, M., & Fletcher-Watson, S. (2018). Mental health on screen: A DSM-5 dissection of portrayals of autism spectrum disorders in film and TV. *Psychiatry Research, 262,* 351–353.

O'Leary, F. (2018). *The aspergers/autistic divide,* https://fionaolearyblog. wordpress.com/2018/02/19/the-aspergers-autistic-divide/

O'Reilly, C., Lewis, J. D., & Elsabbagh, M. (2017). Is functional brain connectivity atypical in autism? A systematic review of EEG and MEG studies. *PloS One, 12*(5), e0175870.

O'Reilly, M., Lester, J. N., & Muskett, T. (2017). *A practical guide to social interaction research in autism spectrum disorders*. London, UK: Palgrave Macmillan.

O'Riordan, M. A., Plaisted, K. C., Driver, J., & Baron-Cohen, S. (2001). Superior visual search in autism. *Journal of Experimental Psychology: Human Perception and Performance, 27*(3), 719.

Padmanabhan, A., Lynch, C. J., Schaer, M., & Menon, V. (2017). The default mode network in autism. *Biological Psychiatry: Cognitive Neuroscience and Neuroimaging, 2*(6), 476–486.

Palomo, R., Belinchón, M., & Ozonoff, S. (2006). Autism and family home movies: A comprehensive review. *Journal of Developmental & Behavioral Pediatrics, 27*(2), S59–S68.

Pellicano, E. (2007). Links between theory of mind and executive function in young children with autism: Clues to developmental primacy. *Developmental Psychology, 43*(4), 974.

Pellicano, E., & Burr, D. (2012). When the world becomes 'too real': A Bayesian explanation of autistic perception. *Trends in Cognitive Sciences, 16*(10), 504–510.

Pellicano, E., Smith, A. D., Cristino, F., Hood, B. M., Briscoe, J., & Gilchrist, I. D. (2011). Children with autism are neither systematic nor optimal foragers. *Proceedings of the National Academy of Sciences, 108*(1), 421–426.

Pellicano, L., Dinsmore, A., & Charman, T. (2013). *A future made together: Shaping autism research in the UK*. London: Centre for Research in Autism and Education, University College London.

Pelton, M. K., & Cassidy, S. A. (2017). Are autistic traits associated with suicidality? A test of the interpersonal-psychological theory of suicide in a non-clinical young adult sample. *Autism Research, 10*(11), 1891–1904.

Perner, J., Frith, U., Leslie, A. M., & Leekam, S. R. (1989). Exploration of the autistic child's theory of mind: Knowledge, belief, and communication. *Child Development*, 689–700.

Petticrew, M., & Roberts, H. (2008). *Systematic reviews in the social sciences: A practical guide*. London, UK: John Wiley & Sons.

Philip, R. C., Dauvermann, M. R., Whalley, H. C., Baynham, K., Lawrie, S. M., & Stanfield, A. C. (2012). A systematic review and meta-analysis of the fMRI investigation of autism spectrum disorders. *Neuroscience & Biobehavioral Reviews, 36*(2), 901–942.

Plaisted, K., O'Riordan, M., & Baron-Cohen, S. (1998a). Enhanced discrimination of novel, highly similar stimuli by adults with autism during a perceptual learning task. *The Journal of Child Psychology and Psychiatry and Allied Disciplines, 39*(5), 765–775.

Plaisted, K., O'Riordan, M., & Baron-Cohen, S. (1998b). Enhanced visual search for a conjunctive target in autism: A research note. *The Journal of Child Psychology and Psychiatry and Allied Disciplines, 39*(5), 777–783.

Premack, D., & Woodruff, G. (1978). Does the chimpanzee have a theory of mind? *Behavioral and Brain Sciences, 1*(4), 515–526.

Pring, L., Ryder, N., Crane, L., & Hermelin, B. (2012). Creativity in savant artists with autism. *Autism, 16*(1), 45–57.

Prior, M., Eisenmajer, R., Leekam, S., Wing, L., Gould, J., Ong, B., & Dowe, D. (1998). Are there subgroups within the autistic spectrum? A cluster analysis of a group of children with autistic spectrum disorders. *The Journal of Child Psychology and Psychiatry and Allied Disciplines, 39*(6), 893–902.

Reddy, V. (1991). Playing with others' expectations: Teasing and mucking about in the first year. In A. Whiten (Ed.), *Natural theories of mind: Evolution, development and simulation of everyday mindreading* (pp. 143–158). Cambridge, MA: Basil Blackwell.

Reid, V. M., Dunn, K., Young, R. J., Amu, J., Donovan, T., & Reissland, N. (2017). The human fetus preferentially engages with face-like visual stimuli. *Current Biology, 27*(12), 1825–1828.

Remington, A., Swettenham, J., Campbell, R., & Coleman, M. (2009). Selective attention and perceptual load in autism spectrum disorder. *Psychological Science, 20*(11), 1388–1393.

Repacholi, B. M., & Gopnik, A. (1997). Early reasoning about desires: Evidence from 14-and 18-month-olds. *Developmental Psychology, 33*(1), 12.

Robertson, A. E., & Simmons, D. R. (2013). The relationship between sensory sensitivity and autistic traits in the general population. *Journal of Autism and Developmental Disorders, 43*(4), 775–784.

Robinson, E. B., Koenen, K. C., McCormick, M. C., Munir, K., Hallett, V., Happé, F., Plomin, R., & Ronald, A. (2011). Evidence that autistic traits show the same etiology in the general population and at the quantitative extremes (5%, 2.5%, and 1%). *Archives of General Psychiatry, 68*(11), 1113–1121.

Robinson, E. B., Koenen, K. C., McCormick, M. C., Munir, K., Hallett, V., Happé, F., Plomin, R., & Ronald, A. (2012). A multivariate twin study of autistic traits in 12-year-olds: Testing the fractionable autism triad hypothesis. *Behavior Genetics, 42*(2), 245–255.

Rogers, S. J., Vismara, L., Wagner, A. L., McCormick, C., Young, G., & Ozonoff, S. (2014). Autism treatment in the first year of life: A pilot study of infant start, a parent-implemented intervention for symptomatic infants. *Journal of Autism and Developmental Disorders, 44*(12), 2981–2995.

Russell, G., Starr, S., Elphick, C., Rodogno, R., & Singh, I. (2018). Selective patient and public involvement: The promise and perils of pharmaceutical intervention for autism. *Health Expectations, 21*(2), 466–473.

Salomone, E., Beranová, Š., Bonnet-Brilhault, F., Briciet Lauritsen, M., Budisteanu, M., Buitelaar, J., . . . Fuentes, J. (2016). Use of early intervention for young children with autism spectrum disorder across Europe. *Autism, 20*(2), 233–249.

Salomone, E., Charman, T., McConachie, H., & Warreyn, P. (2015). Prevalence and correlates of use of complementary and alternative medicine in children with autism spectrum disorder in Europe. *European Journal of Pediatrics, 174*(10), 1277–1285.

Salomone, E., Charman, T., McConachie, H., & Warreyn, P. (2016). Child's verbal ability and gender are associated with age at diagnosis in a sample of young children with ASD in Europe. *Child: Care, Health and Development, 42*(1), 141–145.

San José Cáceres, A., Keren, N., Booth, R., & Happé, F. (2014). Assessing theory of mind nonverbally in those with intellectual disability and ASD: The penny hiding game. *Autism Research, 7*(5), 608–616.

Sasson, N. J., & Morrison, K. E. (2017). First impressions of adults with autism improve with diagnostic disclosure and increased autism knowledge of peers. *Autism.* doi: 10.1177/1362361317729526.

Sasson, N. J., Faso, D. J., Nugent, J., Lovell, S., Kennedy, D. P., & Grossman, R. B. (2017). Neurotypical peers are less willing to interact with those with autism based on thin slice judgments. *Scientific Reports, 7*, 40700.

Schauder, K. B., Mash, L. E., Bryant, L. K., & Cascio, C. J. (2015). Interoceptive ability and body awareness in autism spectrum disorder. *Journal of Experimental Child Psychology, 131*, 193–200.

Schneider, D., Bayliss, A. P., Becker, S. I., & Dux, P. E. (2012). Eye movements reveal sustained implicit processing of others' mental states. *Journal of Experimental Psychology: General, 141*(3), 433.

Schuwerk, T., Vuori, M., & Sodian, B. (2015). Implicit and explicit theory of mind reasoning in autism spectrum disorders: The impact of experience. *Autism, 19*(4), 459–468.

Scott, R. M., & Baillargeon, R. (2017). Early false-belief understanding. *Trends in Cognitive Sciences, 21*(4), 237–249.

Scott-Barrett, J., Cebula, K., & Florian, L. (2018). Listening to young people with autism: Learning from researcher experiences. *International Journal of Research & Method in Education*, 1–22.

Senju, A., Southgate, V., Snape, C., Leonard, M., & Csibra, G. (2011). Do 18-month-olds really attribute mental states to others? A critical test. *Psychological Science, 22*(7), 878–880.

Setoh, P., Scott, R. M., & Baillargeon, R. (2016). Two-and-a-half-year-olds succeed at a traditional false-belief task with reduced processing demands. *Proceedings of the National Academy of Sciences*, 201609203.

Shah, A., & Frith, U. (1983). An islet of ability in autistic children: A research note. *Journal of Child Psychology and Psychiatry, 24*(4), 613–620.

Shah, A., & Frith, U. (1993). Why do autistic individuals show superior performance on the block design task? *Journal of Child Psychology and Psychiatry, 34*(8), 1351–1364.

Shah, A., Holmes, N., & Wing, L. (1982). Prevalence of autism and related conditions in adults in a mental handicap hospital. *Applied Research in Mental Retardation, 3*(3), 303–317.

Shah, P., Hall, R., Catmur, C., & Bird, G. (2016). Alexithymia, not autism, is associated with impaired interoception. *Cortex, 81*, 215–220.

Shapiro, J. P. (1994). *No pity: People with disabilities forging a new civil rights movement.* New York, NY: Three Rivers Press.

Shattuck, P. T., Lau, L., Anderson, K. A., & Kuo, A. A. (2018). A national research agenda for the transition of youth with autism. *Pediatrics, 141*(Supplement 4), S355–S361.

Sheppard, E., Pillai, D., Wong, G. T. L., Ropar, D., & Mitchell, P. (2016). How easy is it to read the minds of people with autism spectrum disorder? *Journal of Autism and Developmental Disorders, 46*(4), 1247–1254.

Shirama, A., Kato, N., & Kashino, M. (2017). When do individuals with autism spectrum disorder show superiority in visual search? *Autism, 21*(8), 942–951.

Silberman, S. (2016). *Neurotribes: The legacy of autism and the future of neurodiversity.* New York, NY: Avery.

Simonoff, E., Pickles, A., Charman, T., Chandler, S., Loucas, T., & Baird, G. (2008). Psychiatric disorders in children with autism spectrum disorders: Prevalence, comorbidity, and associated factors in a population-derived sample. *Journal of the American Academy of Child & Adolescent Psychiatry, 47*(8), 921–929.

Sinclair, J. (1993). Don't mourn for us. *Our Voice: The Autism Network International Newsletter, 1*(3).

Sinclair, J. (2005). *Autism network international: The development of a community and its culture*, www.autreat.com/History_of_ANI.html

Sinclair, J. (2010). Being autistic together. *Disability Studies Quarterly, 30*(1).

Sinclair, J. (2012). Don't mourn for us. *Autonomy, the Critical Journal of Interdisciplinary Autism Studies, 1*(1). Later republished.

Singer, J. (1998). *Odd people in: The birth of community amongst people on the autistic spectrum: A personal exploration of a new social movement based on neurological diversity.* Thesis, Faculty of Humanities and Social Science, University of Technology, Sydney. Republished in *Neurodiversity: The Birth of an Idea* (2016).

Sinha, P., Kjelgaard, M. M., Gandhi, T. K., Tsourides, K., Cardinaux, A. L., Pantazis, D., Diamond, S. P., & Held, R. M. (2014). Autism as a disorder of prediction. *Proceedings of the National Academy of Sciences, 111*(42), 15220–15225.

Smith, U. (Ed.). (1979). *Folktales from Australia's children of the world.* Sydney: Paul Hamlyn.

Solomon, A. (2008). The autism rights movement. *New York Magazine, 25*, 2008.

Sowden, S., & Shah, P. (2014). Self-other control: A candidate mechanism for social cognitive function. *Frontiers in Human Neuroscience, 8*, 789.

Spain, D., Sin, J., Chalder, T., Murphy, D., & Happe, F. (2015). Cognitive behaviour therapy for adults with autism spectrum disorders and psychiatric co-morbidity: A review. *Research in Autism Spectrum Disorders, 9*, 151–162.

Stevens, M. C., Fein, D. A., Dunn, M., Allen, D., Waterhouse, L. H., Feinstein, C., & Rapin, I. (2000). Subgroups of children with autism by cluster analysis: A longitudinal examination. *Journal of the American Academy of Child & Adolescent Psychiatry, 39*(3), 346–352.

Stewart, M. E., & Austin, E. J. (2009). The structure of the Autism-Spectrum Quotient (AQ): Evidence from a student sample in Scotland. *Personality and Individual Differences, 47*(3), 224–228.

Sutherland, R., Hodge, A., Bruck, S., Costley, D., & Klieve, H. (2017). Parent-reported differences between school-aged girls and boys on the autism spectrum. *Autism, 21*(6), 785–794.

Tager-Flusberg, H., Paul, R., & Lord, C. (2005). Language and communication in autism. *Handbook of Autism and Pervasive Developmental Disorders, Volume 1, Third Edition*, 335–364.

Tammet, D. (2007). *Born on a blue day: Inside the extraordinary mind of an autistic savant.* New York, NY: Simon & Schuster.

Taylor, B., Jick H., & MacLaughlin D. (2013). Prevalence and incidence rates of autism in the UK: Time trend from 2004–2010 in children aged 8 years. *British Medical Journal Open, 3*(10):e003219. doi: 10.1136/bmjopen-2013-003219

Taylor, B., Miller, E., Farrington, C., Petropoulos, M. C., Favot-Mayaud, I., Li, J., & Waight, P. A. (1999). Autism and measles, mumps, and rubella vaccine: No epidemiological evidence for a causal association. *The Lancet, 353*(9169), 2026–2029.

Taylor, L. E., Swerdfeger, A. L., & Eslick, G. D. (2014). Vaccines are not associated with autism: An evidence-based meta-analysis of case-control and cohort studies. *Vaccine, 32*(29), 3623–3629.

Teague, S. J., Gray, K. M., Tonge, B. J., & Newman, L. K. (2017). Attachment in children with autism spectrum disorder: A systematic review. *Research in Autism Spectrum Disorders, 35*, 35–50.

Tick, B., Bolton, P., Happé, F., Rutter, M., & Rijsdijk, F. (2016). Heritability of autism spectrum disorders: A meta-analysis of twin studies. *Journal of Child Psychology and Psychiatry, 57*(5), 585–595.

Tillotson, R., Selfridge, J., Koerner, M. V., Gadalla, K. K., Guy, J., De Sousa, D., . . . Bird, A. (2017). Radically truncated MeCP2 rescues Rett syndrome-like neurological defects. *Nature, 550*(7676), 398.

Tint, A., & Weiss, J. A. (2016). Family wellbeing of individuals with autism spectrum disorder: A scoping review. *Autism, 20*(3), 262–275.

Torres, E. B., & Denisova, K. (2016). Motor noise is rich signal in autism research and pharmacological treatments. *Scientific Reports, 6*, 37422.

Tsai, H. W. J., Cebula, K., & Fletcher-Watson, S. (2017). The role of the broader autism phenotype and environmental stressors in the adjustment of

siblings of children with autism spectrum disorders in Taiwan and the
United Kingdom. *Journal of Autism and Developmental Disorders, 47*(8),
2363–2377.

Uljarevic, M., & Hamilton, A. (2013). Recognition of emotions in autism:
A formal meta-analysis. *Journal of Autism and Developmental Disorders,
43*(7), 1517–1526.

Van de Cruys, S., de-Wit, L., Evers, K., Boets, B., & Wagemans, J. (2013). Weak
priors versus overfitting of predictions in autism: Reply to Pellicano and
Burr (TICS, 2012). *I-Perception, 4*(2), 95–97.

Van de Cruys, S., Evers, K., Van der Hallen, R., Van Eylen, L., Boets, B., de-Wit,
L., & Wagemans, J. (2014). Precise minds in uncertain worlds: Predictive
coding in autism. *Psychological Review, 121*(4), 649.

Van der Hallen, R., Evers, K., Brewaeys, K., Van den Noortgate, W., &
Wagemans, J. (2015). Global processing takes time: A meta-analysis
on local – global visual processing in ASD. *Psychological Bulletin,
141*(3), 549.

Van Heijst, B. F., & Geurts, H. M. (2015). Quality of life in autism across the
lifespan: A meta-analysis. *Autism, 19*(2), 158–167.

Van Steensel, F. J. A., & Bogels, S. M. (2011). Anxiety disorders in children and
adolescents with autistic spectrum disorders: A meta-analysis. *Clinical
Child and Family Psychology Review, 14*, 302–317.

Vanvuchelen, M., Roeyers, H., & De Weerdt, W. (2011). Do imitation
problems reflect a core characteristic in autism? Evidence from a
literature review. *Research in Autism Spectrum Disorders, 5*(1), 89–95.

Vernetti, A., Smith, T. J., & Senju, A. (2017). Gaze-contingent reinforcement
learning reveals incentive value of social signals in young children and
adults. *Proceedings of the Royal Society B, 284*(1850), 20162747.

Virués-Ortega, J., Arnold-Saritepe, A., Hird, C., & Phillips, K. (2017). The
TEACCH program for people with autism: Elements, outcomes, and
comparison with competing models. In *Handbook of treatments for
autism spectrum disorder* (pp. 427–436). Cham: Springer.

Vital, P. M., Ronald, A., Wallace, G. L., & Happé, F. (2009). Relationship
between special abilities and autistic-like traits in a large population-
based sample of 8-year-olds. *Journal of Child Psychology and Psychiatry,
50*(9), 1093–1101.

Wade, M., Prime, H., Jenkins, J. M., Yeates, K. O., Williams, T., & Lee, K. (2018).
On the relation between theory of mind and executive functioning:
A developmental cognitive neuroscience perspective. *Psychonomic
Bulletin & Review*, 1–22.

Wass, S. V., Jones, E. J., Gliga, T., Smith, T. J., Charman, T., Johnson, M. H., . . .
Davies, K. (2015). Shorter spontaneous fixation durations in infants with
later emerging autism. *Scientific Reports, 5*, 8284.

Wellman, H. M., Cross, D., & Watson, J. (2001). Meta-analysis of
theory-of-mind development: The truth about false belief. *Child
Development, 72*(3), 655–684.

Wheelwright, S., Baron-Cohen, S., Goldenfeld, N., Delaney, J., Fine, D., Smith, R., . . . Wakabayashi, A. (2006). Predicting autism spectrum quotient (AQ) from the systemizing quotient-revised (SQ-R) and empathy quotient (EQ). *Brain Research, 1079*(1), 47–56.

Wigham, S., Rodgers, J., South, M., McConachie, H., & Freeston, M. (2015). The interplay between sensory processing abnormalities, intolerance of uncertainty, anxiety and restricted and repetitive behaviours in autism spectrum disorder. *Journal of Autism and Developmental Disorders, 45*(4), 943–952.

Williams, D. (2009). *Nobody nowhere: The remarkable autobiography of an autistic girl.* London, UK: Jessica Kingsley Publishers.

Williams, J. H., Whiten, A., & Singh, T. (2004). A systematic review of action imitation in autistic spectrum disorder. *Journal of Autism and Developmental Disorders, 34*(3), 285–299.

Williams, J. H., Whiten, A., Suddendorf, T., & Perrett, D. I. (2001). Imitation, mirror neurons and autism. *Neuroscience & Biobehavioral Reviews, 25*(4), 287–295.

Wing, L. (1996). *The autistic spectrum: A guide for parents and professionals.* London: Constable & Co.

Wing, L., & Gould, J. (1979). Severe impairments of social interaction and associated abnormalities in children: Epidemiology and classification. *Journal of Autism and Developmental Disorders, 9*(1), 11–29.

Wolff, J. J., Gu, H., Gerig, G., Elison, J. T., Styner, M., Gouttard, S., . . . Evans, A. C. (2012). Differences in white matter fiber tract development present from 6 to 24 months in infants with autism. *American Journal of Psychiatry, 169*(6), 589–600.

World Health Organization. (2018). *The ICD-11 classification of mental and behavioural disorders: Clinical descriptions and diagnostic guidelines* (Vol. 1). World Health Organization. http://www.who.int/classifications/icd/en/

Zwaigenbaum, L., Bryson, S., Rogers, T., Roberts, W., Brian, J., & Szatmari, P. (2005). Behavioral manifestations of autism in the first year of life. *International Journal of Developmental Neuroscience, 23*(2–3), 143–152.

Zwaigenbaum, L., Young, G. S., Stone, W. L., et al. (2014). Early head growth in infants at risk of autism: A baby siblings research consortium study. *Journal of the American Academy of Child and Adolescent Psychiatry, 53*(10), 1053–1062.

Index

Note: Page numbers in *italic* indicate a figure and page numbers in **bold** indicate a table on the corresponding page.

Plaisted-Grant, K. 126
play 18–19, **31**, 142; and the biological level 70; and the cognitive level 74; developmental trajectory models and 113–114; primary deficit models and 85–86
polygenic scores 53
post-social model 22
predictive coding 130–132
Premack, D. 85
pretending 18, 69–70, 85–97
prevalence 36–38, 46, 105–106, 114
primacy 91–94, 128
primary deficit models 5, 84–85, 138, 148; current debates related to 97–98; questioning assumptions related to 96–97; the role of 96; *see also* Theory of Mind (ToM)
propositional attitudes 69–70
pseudoscience **140**, 141
psychogenic models 20, 52, 59
public awareness 2, 21, 143, 148, 154–155
public perception *see* public awareness

quality of life 36, 44, 97, 115, 154–155, 159

racism 23
Reddy, V. 93
refrigerator parenting 7, 20, 52
relationships **31**, 34–35, 110, 114–115, 146; *see also* friendships
resilience 40–41, 46
restricted and repetitive behaviours and interests (RRBIs) 6; and the behavioural level **31**, 32–33, 36, 38, 46; and the biological level 58; and the cognitive level 74–77, 79; and developmental trajectory models 112, 115; and domain-general information processing models 128; and primary deficit models 84, 92, 95
rights *see* autistic rights
Russell, J. *see* Hughes, C.
Rutter, M. 18

Sally-Anne task 70, *71*, 85, 88
Salomone, E. 102
sameness *see* insistence on sameness
Sasson, N. J. 146
savant 8, 143
schools 5, 21, 78, 98, 141–143, 154
Schopler, E. 18
Scottish Autism 21, 156

Scottish Intercollegiate Guidelines Network (SIGN) 35
Scottish Society for Autism, The 21
self-diagnosis 36, 156
sensory features 38–39, 76; and overload 117, 140; *see also* hyper-sensitivity; hypo-sensitivity
sexism 23
Shah, A. 122
shared attention 86–87, 93; Shared Attention Mechanism 86–87
Sheppard, E. 111
siblings 114, 155
sibling studies 105–110, 116
Sinclair, J. 21–23, 155
Singer, J. 23
sleep 9, 23, 46, 76–77, 160
Smith, U. 15
social attention accounts 108, 112, 116, 132
social cognition 59, 70–71, 85, 122
social domain 69, 72, 90, 105, 108; early development outside the 112–113; information processing and the 131–132
social interaction 18–19; and the behavioural level **31**, 36; and the biological level 54; and the cognitive level 68–69, 84, 110, 128, 132, 145; *see also* communication
socialisation 9, 46
social model 22, 145, 147–148
social motivation accounts 109–110, 116–117
social orienting accounts 106–110, 117
socio-political theory 2, 161
special interest 17
specificity 30, 84, 105–106, 109, 112; Theory of Mind model and 91–94
spontaneousness 16–17, 70, 88, 91, 95, 110
stimming 21, 112
stimuli 16, 75–76, 126, 128, 132; developmental trajectory models and 107–109, 111
Strange Stories 71, 88, *89*
suicide 39, 154; and suicidality 115
systemising 129–130, 132, 134, 143

text-to-speech device 33
Theory of Mind (ToM) i, 18, 68–70, 85–86, 97–99, 159; alternatives to 94–95; and the biological level 56; challenges to 87–94; and developmental trajectory models 102; and domain-general information